THE
SEVENTEENTH-CENTURY
TRADITION

STUDIES IN THE HISTORY OF CHRISTIAN THOUGHT

EDITED BY

HEIKO A. OBERMAN, Tübingen

IN COOPERATION WITH

HENRY CHADWICK, Oxford
EDWARD A. DOWEY, Princeton, N.J.
JAROSLAV PELIKAN, New Haven, Conn.
BRIAN TIERNEY, Ithaca, N.Y.
E. DAVID WILLIS, San Anselmo, California

VOLUME XVI

GEORGE H. TAVARD

THE SEVENTEENTH-CENTURY TRADITION

LEIDEN
E. J. BRILL
1978

THE
SEVENTEENTH-CENTURY
TRADITION

A Study in Recusant Thought

BY

GEORGE H. TAVARD

LEIDEN
E. J. BRILL
1978

ISBN 90 04 05456 1

CONTENTS

BIBLIOGRAPHICAL NOTE

English Recusant theology is a field that has remained practically unmined by historians or theologians. Nothing for the 17th century can be compared to the excellent introduction to 16th century Recusant literature provided by A. C. Southern: *Elizabethan Recusant Prose*, London 1950. The few relevant studies have been mentioned in the footnotes of the present volume. To facilitate further investigation by interested scholars, I will simple note that, besides the volumes of Recusant literature available in the Library of the British Museum, there is an extensive collection in the Library of St Mary's Seminary, New Oscott (Warwickshire, England), with a convenient printed catalogue: *Recusant Books at St Mary's, Oscott*, Part I (1518-1687), 1964; Part II (1641-1830), 1966. I am also acquainted with a Recusant collection at Downside Abbey, and I have found that the Library of the Venerable English College in Rome has a small, but very useful collection. A number of reprints of Recusant works, chiefly relating to spiritual life, have been made by the Catholic Record Society. Unstudied manuscripts touching the Recusants will be found in the Municipal Library of the city of Douai, in France; these come, presumably, from the English College which trained priests for "the English mission" during penal times, and was located at Douai after being at Reims for some years.

INTRODUCTION

In 1959 I published a study of the problem of Scripture and Tradition in the 16th century. *Holy Writ or Holy Church: The Crisis of the Protestant Reformation* was focused on the Catholic theologians and polemicists who, from the rise of the Lutheran movement to the Council of Trent, examined the value of the Tradition and the traditions, in the light of the objections which the Reformers drew from their conception of *Scriptura sola* as the source of faith and the *norma non normata* of the Church's life. A short summary and revision of the main ideas of this volume will help to understand the perspective of the present book.

The 16th century Catholic theologians did not create a new doctrine. The patristic era and the Middle Ages had developed a general conception of Scripture and Tradition which I called classical. The Fathers, followed by the monastic theology of the earlier Middle Ages and by the first age of scholasticism, assumed that there must reign a fundamental harmony between the Scriptures taken as a norm of faith and doctrine, and the Church taken also as a norm of faith and doctrine. The Reformers' distinction between *norma normans non normata* and *norma normata* was not made, presumably because there was no experience yet of a discrepancy between what the Scriptures witnessed to and what the Church taught. Scripture and the Church were not taken as parallel sources, still less as partial sources, of Christian doctrine. Rather, each was inconceivable without the other, on the assumption and with the consequence— assumption and consequence being correlative poles of the theological circle which was then operative—that what the Church taught was what the Scriptures contained and that what the Scriptures contained was what the Church taught. Each of these two foci necessarily threw light on the other.[1]

Certain shortcomings of this approach may be recognized immediately. The Scriptures were not read with a sharply critical eye, whether from the point of view of history or from that of literary composition. The hermeneutics which saw the Scriptures as being always in harmony with the Church's teaching and practice was more spiritual

---

[1] On patristic and medieval hermeneutics, see Henri de Lubac, *Exégèse Médiévale. Les Quatre Sens de l'Ecriture*, Paris, 4 vol., 1959-1964.

than literal. By and large, the Middle Ages followed the example of St. Gregory the Great whose *Moralia in Job* expounded the Scripture along the three senses provided by analogy, tropology, anagogy, through which faith, love and hope could discover the deeper meaning of the letter. When Thomas Aquinas, at the beginning of the *Summa theologica*, I, q. 1, a. 8, adopted the principle that only the literal sense of Scripture is acceptable for theological argumentation, he stated a new principle which was heavy with consequences. For he relegated the traditional exposition of the senses of Scripture to a non theological level, the level, let us say, of religious imagination. By the same token, he placed the historical investigation of the literal sense at the basis of theological argumentation. Although Thomas Aquinas did not draw all the logical implications of this step, he established a premise from which the Reformers, had they been familiar with his works, could have argued cogently in favor of the *Scriptura sola* principle. For if the literal sense alone is acceptable in theological argumentation, then no amount of traditional ecclesiastical interpretation over and above this sense, not to say contrary to it, can be recognized to have any binding force.

Furthermore, the limits of Scripture were not clearly recognized. While the *lectio divina* of the monastic tradition started from the *sacra pagina*, that is, the text itself of the Scriptures, the scholastics, and Thomas Aquinas himself, made no sharp distinction between *sacra pagina, sacra scriptura, sacra doctrina*. The canon of the Old Testament, in the editions of the Latin Vulgate which were copied in the *scriptoria* of the monasteries, remained somewhat variable. It included some or all of what later Catholic authors entitle the deutero-canonical books and Protestants usually call the apocrypha of the Old Testament. It often added a few more books, such as III and IV Esdras, that were not retained by the Decree *pro Jacobitis* of the Council of Florence (February 4, 1442) or by the fourth session of the Council of Trent (April 8, 1546). The artists and craftsmen who found inspiration in the apocryphal New Testament for the decoration of romanesque and gothic churches were not fundamentally at variance with the theology of the monasteries and the schools. Yet, here again, the principle of Thomas Aquinas on the value of the literal sense of the Bible for probative theological argumentation contained the seed of further evolution: only if the limits of the text are certain can the investigation of the literal sense proceed properly. Here also, the Reformation will force the issue of clarification.

The later Middle Ages experienced a progressive breakdown of the principle that Church and Scripture are always in full harmony. Already before the end of the 13th century Henri of Ghent asked if there could be a contradiction between the authority of Scripture and the authority of the Church. My treatment of this evolution was focused on two 14th century authors, Gerald of Bologna and William of Ockham, with rapid looks at Wycliffe and a few others. These authors witness to the waning of the classical conception of *sacra doctrina* as so closely related to *sacra scriptura* that, in a sense, they are one. There emerges the view that there are (in Ockham's vocabulary) "Catholic truths", even (in William of Waterford's language) "an infinity of truly Catholic doctrines", which are not to be found in Scripture.[2]

As described in *Holy Writ or Holy Church*, the stage for the Reformation, concerning the question of Scripture and the traditions, was set by the fifteenth century. By and large, theology faced a dilemma: one must admit that many Catholic truths do not derive from Scripture, yet one dare not abandon the principle that Scripture and Church are somehow co-extensive. The picture which I drew of this century may have to be completed with the help of Heiko Oberman's study of Gabriel Biel.[3] But it was the basic problematic of this dilemma which confronted the Humanists' desire to return to the sources and to discover a more biblical method for theology, and the Reformers' concern to reach beyond the scholastic apparatus for the authentic doctrine contained in the Word of God. A study of the Humanists, of Luther and of Calvin, introduced the heart of my study, namely the theology of the Catholic polemicists, who defended the older synthesis of Scripture and Church and yet faced the problems raised by the later scholasticism, by the Humanists, and by the Reformers.

Admittedly, the programme of the defenders of the traditions was largely polemical. This did not place them in a favorable position to understand the real thrust of the Reformers' doctrine, though the Reformers' frontal attacks on institutions and teachings which the Catholic polemicists considered to be intangible were not themselves calculated to win their opponents over. The discussions of the sixteenth century may have been a debate, but they were not a dialogue. Furthermore, the Catholics themselves were far from agreed on how to respond to the multiple challenges which they faced. Four

---

[2] *Holy Writ or Holy Church*, London, 1959, pp. 35 and 43.
[3] *The Harvest of Medieval Theology*, Cambridge, Massachusetts, 1963.

orientations converged materially, if not formally, in the discussions of the fourth session of the Council of Trent. Briefly, these four orientations were as follows.[4]

First, several authors, the most important of whom are Johann Eck and Johann Cochläus, were forced by the Reformers' problematic to revise their own conceptions, passing, roughly, from the classical medieval stance to what will later be called a two-source theory of the sources of faith. Eck's trajectory is the more remarkable in that his last writings on the question were quite at variance with his original positions.

Second, the outlines of a new synthesis emerged in the works of some major theologians, such as Johannes Driedo and Albert Pigge at the University of Louvain. Synthesis may not be a fully adequate word, since these authors favored a sort of two-source theory, which found acceptance in the majority of the Council of Trent and among most theologians of the Counter-Reformation.

Third, in another direction several authors tried to chart new territory by suggesting that the Revelation somehow still continues in the Church, the Councils being inspired equally with the Scriptures. Thus the Dominican Johann Mensing, the Franciscan Kaspar Schatzgayer in his early works, the Benedictine Nikolaus Ellenbog.[5]

Fourth, there were still, in the twenty-five years preceding the opening of the Council of Trent, partisans of the older, classical, conception. In various ways, the Franciscan Kaspar Schatzgeyer in his later works, the Dominicans Johann Dietenberger and Ambrose Catarinus defended the identity of Scripture and the Church in the teaching of faith and doctrine, the tradition of the Church being already fully contained in the Scriptures. Incorporated in the *Regensburg Book* of 1541 under the auspices of Cardinal Contarini, this theology was expressed at the fourth session of the Council of Trent by some members of the minority.

The convergence of these lines of thought at the fourth session of the Council of Trent is ultimately responsible for the ambiguity of the decree adopted by the Council on the 8th of April, 1546. In my interpretation of the conciliar debates, I was particularly influenced by the weight of the classical position as found in patristic and medieval thought before the fourteenth-fifteenth centuries, and by the

---

[4] For what follows, see *Holy Writ or Holy Chuch*, ch. 8-11.

[5] *A Forgotten Theology of Inspiration*: *Nikolaus Ellenbog's Refutation of 'Scriptura Sola'* (*Franciscan Studies*, vol. 15, n. 5, 1955, pp. 106-122).

evidence that this view, still prevailing in some theological quarters, was voiced at the Council itself by some spokesmen for the minority which opposed the two-source theory included in the draft originally presented to the Council. The modifications of this draft at key points in the course of the debates may of course be interpreted in different ways, depending on the interpreter's hermeneutical principles and on his own theological positions. I took the position that the final text of the Council, from which the dualistic expression "partly... partly..." (*partim... partim...*) had been excised, *de facto* excluded the theory of two sources of faith. But other scholars have concluded differently.[6]

The last two chapters of *Holy Writ or Holy Church* round up the picture of the 16th century by studying the Anglican literature. Much of this, being written under Elizabeth, followed the Council of Trent. Precisely at this time, when a great theologian like Richard Hooker and lesser theological figures like William Whitaker and John Jewel drew the outlines of the Elizabethan settlement in theology, English Recusant literature also began. There were major theologians, like Nicholas Sanders, Thomas Harding, the Jesuit Robert Persons, Thomas Stapleton, among the Catholics who rejected the Established Church. While these were not in agreement on all points, they presented a theological defense of "the old religion" against both the Anglican moderates and the churchmen, more influenced by Calvinism, whose successors will be called Puritan. On the whole, however, the Anglicans remained closer to the medieval position on Scripture and the traditions than the Recusants, who leaned, with the exception of Harding, toward a two-source of faith conception.[7]

The present volume arose out of the interest which I took in Recusant literature after publishing *Holy Writ or Holy Church*. But I have also been more broadly interested in pushing further my study of Tradition. In particular I have wished to check what interpretation of the Council of Trent prevailed in the Counter-Reformation. The

---

[6] *Holy Writ or Holy Church*, ch. 12. For a survey of the different positions, see Gabriel Moran, *Scripture and Tradition. A Survey of the Controversy*, New York, 1963. More recent studies have not significantly altered the horizon of the problem: J. Ermel, *Les Sources de la Foi. Concile de Trente et Oecuménisme contemporain*, Tournai, 1963; Mario Midali, *Rivelazione, Chiesa, Scrittura e Tradizione alla IV Sessione del Concilio di Trento*, Rome, 1973.

[7] *Holy Writ or Holy Church*, ch. 13.

two-source theory came to be so taken for granted that practically all textbooks of Catholic theology in the first half of the twentieth century identified it as the normative conception. In an article I paid special attention to Melchior Cano and Perez de Ayala.[8] In planning an investigation of the seventeenty century, I left aside the major Counter-Reformation scholastics, who have already been well studied.[9] Instead of mining this rich vein, I have concentrated on two areas: the debates on Tradition in France during the seventeenth century, and the English Recusant literature of the same period. As a result of this investigation, *La Tradition au XVIIe siècle en France et en Angleterre*, was published in Paris in 1969.

The French authors of the time are not among the major theologians of the Counter-Reformation. Indeed, their lasting contribution lies in the area of historical theology, with the works of the Jesuit Denys Petau and the Oratorian Louis Thomassin, and of biblical studies with Richard Simon. By and large, however, French theological thought grapples with controversies. Some of these are made against Protestants, as with St Francis of Sales or Cardinal du Perron at the beginning of the century or with Bossuet toward the end. But the chief controversies are internal polemics among Catholics. Jansenism, Gallicanism, and Quietism channel theological thought in directions that are not, in the long run, very fruitful, although they seemed to be of major importance at the time. *La Tradition au XVIIe siècle* shows that these debates raised the problem of Tradition in several different ways. It shows also that these discussions raised more explicitly than ever before the question of the development of Christian doctrine. The views of Tradition which come to light in the course of these debates are far from uniform. Bossuet, in particular, appears much more progressive in his outlook on the possibility of new understanding of the Scriptures than he seems to be in Owen Chadwick's volume, *From Bossuet to Newman*.[10] Urgent questions are raised, yet seldom receive an adequate solution. For instance, by arguing for a distinction between *le fait et le droit* in the matter of the five propositions of Jansenius, the Jansenists, and especially Antoine

---

[8] *Tradition in Early Post-Tridentine Theology* (*Theological Studies*, 23, n. 3, September 1962, pp. 377-405).

[9] See Candido Pozo, *La Teoría del Progreso Dogmático en los Teólogos de la Escuela de Salamanca*, Madrid, 1959; Yves Congar, *La Tradition et les Traditions*, vol. I; *Essai Historique*, Paris, 1960; Johannes Beumer, *Die Mündliche Überlieferung als Glaubensquelle*, Freiburg, 1962.

[10] *From Bossuet to Newman. The Idea of Doctrinal Development*, London, 1957.

Arnauld, place the problem of authority in a new light, and the scope of infallibility is shown to be ambiguous. Or also, by denouncing the inconsistencies of Bossuet's attacks on his own studies of the Old and the New Testament, Richard Simon raises major questions concerning the authority to interpret Scripture and the hermeneutical principles to be applied. Thus also, during the controversy on Quietism, Fénelon showed evidently that the self-appointed defender of the Tradition, Bossuet, was insufficiently acquainted with the Tradition to speak about it competently. In this case, Bossuet's appeal to Tradition, which also formed the backbone of his polemics with Protestants, was *de facto*, if not *de jure*, very weak. But what constitutes a valid argument from Tradition never emerged clearly from these controversies.

It is, on the whole, surprising how little impact these violent discussions have had on Catholic theology in general. The movement which led to the definition of papal infallibility at Vatican Council I did not clarify the points raised by the Jansenist polemics. Furthermore, although Bossuet was the loser in his fight with Richard Simon, Catholic theology sided with Bossuet's rejection of a scientific reading of the Bible until well into the twentieth century. It also continued to polemicize against the variations of Protestantism without acknowledging its own variations.

All in all, the decree of the fourth session of the Council of Trent had little influence on the polemics of the seventeenth century. The text is seldom quoted. And when it is, as in the argument between Bossuet and Antoine Charlas on Gallicanism, attention is not drawn to the question of the source or sources of faith but to the unanimous consensus of the Fathers as a hermeneutical rule for the interpretation of Scripture.

It is at this point of my researches that the present study fits in. *Holy Writ or Holy Church* ended on an investigation of the Elizabethan settlement and of the theology of the English Recusants in the matter of Scripture and Tradition. This study of Anglican theology was pursued in a later volume entitled, *The Quest for Catholicity* (London, 1963). This book examined what concept of catholicity has been entertained by High Church Anglicanism from the sixteenth to the twentieth century. Tradition and Scripture were featured at several key points of this volume. While *The Quest for Catholicity* also dealt with some topics that need not retain our attention at this time, its treatment of the seventeenth century is directly relevant to the concern of the present study. For, whether they lived in exile abroad or in hiding in England, the Recusants thought and worked within the orbit of the events that shook the Church of England during this period.

The century begins with the reign of James I (1604-1625). As under Elizabeth, the Church of England theologians are spiritually divided by their attitude to Geneva and the influence of Calvinism. The Puritans, whose feelings and principles in regard to worship and doctrine were predominantly inspired by Geneva and the Calvinism of John Knox in neighboring Scotland, remain in the Establishment until the Restoration, when the Act of Uniformity of 1662 pushes them into dissent. Recusant literature does not distinguish between Anglican and Puritan. There are several reasons for this. Both are yet members of the same Church. And a polemist writing, figuratively speaking, from Rome, can feel at an advantage if he can claim to see no difference between Canterbury and Geneva: this makes his attitude more aggressive and his pen sharper. Admittedly, it does not help the dialogue between Anglicans and Recusants; but, with the exception of Christopher Davenport and a few others, dialogue is not the aim of the Recusants. Here one sees the basic weakness of the polemical stance of most Recusants. Because they are engaged in what seems to them a life and death struggle with the Church of England, they are unable to distinguish among their adversaries. As a result, they are blind to the similarities between the Catholicity of the Caroline divines and the Catholicism which they defend. Be that as it may, the present study of Recusant literature follows the Recusant practice of treating Anglicans and Puritans together. This would not do in a study of the seventeenth century in general; but it is appropriate to a study of Recusancy.

The great age of the Caroline divines, under Charles I (1625-1649) and Charles II (1660-1685), is itself cut in two by what is called, depending on one's political and religious sympathies, the Interregnum or the Commonwealth (1649-1660). Following the conflict between the King and his Puritan-oriented Parliament, civil war breaks out in 1642. The archbishop of Canterbury, William Laud, is executed in 1645. In 1648, the Cavaliers, supporters of the King, are defeated by the Roundheads of Oliver Cromwell's Puritan army. Charles I is beheaded in 1649. For the next ten years, Cromwell, as "Lord Protector", reorganizes the Church in a Protestant direction, through a compromise between the most important Protestant parties, the Presbyterians and the Independents. The doctrinal and liturgical bases of the reform are established in 1643 by the Westminster Assembly of divines. Here again, however, apart from some writings of Christopher Davenport and the conversion of a few Anglicans to Catholicism, notably that of Serenus Cressy, these events have little impact on the Recusants.

Both Charles I and Charles II had Catholic wives. As a result, the only Catholics who officially had some degree of freedom in England belonged to the entourage of the Queen. Christopher Davenport was chaplain to Henrietta-Maria, the wife of Charles I. With James II (1685-1688), things changed, for the king had himself been converted to Rome. While his protection of Catholics raised the hopes of the Recusants, these were dashed by the Revolution of 1688, when James II was replaced by his Dutch brother-in-law, William of Orange, and his Protestant sister, Mary. The necessity for the Anglican clergy to take an oath of allegiance to the new King and Queen, when they had already pledged allegiance to James, provoked the schism of the Non-Jurors.

These political events throw some light on the situation of the Recusants. These form a small group. The energies of those who live abroad are channelled toward keeping a flow of priests going into England to look after the scattered groups that have remained in the home country. The seminary at Douai for diocesan priests, and various scholasticates of the Jesuits or the Franciscans are the chief organs of this activity. In England the priests tend to live in London where they can hide in the crowd, or in the country estates of the remnants of the Catholic nobility. Their only legal places of worship are the private chapels of the Catholic Queens and of several foreign embassies. The writers among them publish most of their works in France or the Netherlands. They often mask their identity under innumerable pennames.

But the Recusants are not themselves united. They are involved in internal conflicts of Church politics, chiefly about the presence of religious Orders in England, and of theology, notably around questions raised by the theology of Thomas White. This is reflected in their writings. But they also react to the writings of Anglicans. The Anglican-Puritan struggle does not retain their attention, no doubt because the issues do not touch directly the points on which Protestants and Catholics disagree. But the Recusants react abundantly to the writings of Chillingworth and of Stillingfleet against the Catholic conception of the Church. For they remain sensitive to the Anglican theological opinions that touch on their own convictions.

The present study of Recusant theology on the matter of Scripture and Tradition follows roughly the chronological order. Chapters 1 and 2 examine the two major questions posited in the first decades of the century, that is, the sufficiency of Scripture (ch. 1), and the proper judge of controversies in the Church (ch. 2). Chapter 3 studies several authors who write on these topics in the 1630's, just before the Chillingworth controversy; Chillingworth's *The Religion of Protestants* was published in 1638 against one of them. Chapter 4 is focused on the question of Scripture alone, as discussed in the writings of Richard Smith, bishop of Chalcedon and Ordinary for England, in opposition to the Anglican distinction between fundamentals and non-fundamentals. Chapters 5 to 7 examine specific authors of the middle of the century, first several converts (ch. 5), then the great and still little known Christopher Davenport (ch. 6), and a first class theologian, who is still less known, Thomas White (ch. 7). Chapters 8 and 9 examine specific points of theology. The question of infallibility is treated by Henry Holden, who lives and works in Paris. His book on the analysis of faith was published in 1552 in Latin and in 1558 in English (ch. 8). The development of doctrine, as envisaged by several authors, especially during the Stillingfleet controversy in the 1660's, is the topic of chapter 9. Chapter 10 brings the investigation of the Recusants to a climax with a major theological figure of the last part of the century, John Sergeant, in whom all the previous trends converge. In chapter 11 I have tried to see the Recusants in relation to the more recent history of theology, focusing on the growth of the idea of doctrinal development which reached its acme with Newman.

I have made use of material which appeared in two articles of *Theological Studies* (*Christopher Davenport and the Problem of Tradition*, vol. 24, n. 2, June 1963, p. 278-290; *Scripture and Tradition among Seventeenth-century Recusants*, vol. 25, n. 3, Sept. 1964, p. 343-385). A French rendering of most of my text was included in the second part of *La Tradition au XVIIe siècle*. But a modern French translation of seventeenth-century English is an impoverishment of a very vivid language and is misleading for any student of English theology.

The Recusants deserve to be read and evaluated in the context of English history, literature and religion before being contrasted with the authors caught in the controversies over Jansenism, Gallicanism and Quietism. The present publication is the original version of my study of the Recusants; delays in publication have been due to the current difficulties of scholarly publishing.

I wish to thank those who have made this publication possible, especially the Methodist Theological School in Ohio for a sabbatical which enabled me to revise my manuscript, to Professor Heiko A. Oberman for his constructive advice, and to my publisher, E. J. Brill.

CHAPTER ONE

SUFFICIENCY AND INSUFFICIENCY

The most relevant years for our study are the middle decades of the century. One may wonder to what extent the Recusant writing activity of this second third of the seventeenty century was due to the combativity of the Anglicans of the same period. William Laud (1573-1645), who was as anxious to avoid Romanism as to fight Puritanism, engaged one of the ablest debaters of his time, the Jesuit John Fisher.[1] William Chillingworth (1602-1644), a former convert who had returned to the Church of England, challenged Catholics in 1638 with his long book, *The Religion of Protestants a Safe Way to Salvation*, directly aimed at the Jesuit Edward Knott, but attacking Catholicism as a whole. Later, under Charles II, Edward Stillingfleet (1635-1699) published his *Rational Account of the Grounds of the Protestant Religion* (1664), which defended Laud against Fisher, and left lasting echoes in English theology.[2]

Thus the Anglicanism of the seventeenth century, both in Laudian theology and in nascent Latitudinarianism, inspired first class apologists. And these provoked remarkable Catholic efforts in defense of the Roman tradition.[3] That a dialectical relationship should exist between these worthy antagonists would seem to be a reasonable hypothesis. I am not referring only to what occasioned the Catholic works, often written to answer previous Anglican publications. A dialectical relationship would imply more, namely that the Anglicans contributed, by their doubts, their questions, and their criticisms, to the formation and formulation of Catholic thought on the subject under discussion. This, however, would prove to be arduous to document; and we may be content, at this point, with raising the question.

Even before 1630 the problem of Tradition figured prominently

---

[1] On Laud, see E. C. E. Bourne, *The Anglicanism of William Laud*, London, 1947.

[2] On Chillingworth and Stillingfleet, see the classical studies of Anglican theology in the seventeenth century, such as H. R. McAdoo, *The Spirit of Anglicanism. A survey of Anglican Theological Method in the Seventeenth Century*, New York, 1965; Robert S. Bosher, *The Making of the Restoration Settlement. The Influence of the Laudians, 1649-1662*, London, 1951; George Every, *The High Church Party, 1688-1719*, London, 1956.

[3] *Aspects of English Church History, 1660-1768*, Cambridge, 1959.

in the preoccupations of Catholic polemicists, although it was often touched upon as a side issue or by implication, and, on the whole, rather briefly. Yet as later authors were acquainted with the works of the first decades of the century, our survey should start with these. A number of secondary theologians briefly allude to the question of Tradition and traditions; and, although their testimony, taken by itself, may not be of very great weight, the convergence of their thoughts and expressions helps to perceive the intellectual atmosphere in which the greater writers worked. Several of these productions were very worthwhile attempts to encompass our problem as a whole and to focus discussion on the essential questions.

In the first years of the century, a Scottish convert to the Catholic Church, John Colville (1542?-1605), briefly and colorfully explained the relationship of the Church to Scripture: "Again to discern in questions of religion controverted we can admit no judge but the dumb letter, which is a paradox so absurd and without example preceding as to this hour by antiquity it cannot be verified where the actor and defender pleading at any bar or court have been judged by written laws. . . .".[4]

The analogy of civil courts does not favor taking Scripture alone as the judge of controversy in religious matters. This in itself is not a very strong argument. But a series of comparisons clearly shows the positive aspect of Colville's understanding of Scripture in relation to the Church:

> It cannot be denied that the Church is to the Scripture as the pilot to the rudder, the mason to the line, the magistrate to the laws. . . . Even so, the rudder and compass, the line and square of the Holy Scripture and laws contained therein, except they have the Church to be their steerman, mason and judge, they of themselves shall never pacify parties contending in faith and religion, more nor the compass alone can guide the ship, or the line alone build the house.

Colville's point comes out well: Scripture cannot be a judge, because it is only a book. A book needs someone to read it and be aware of its meaning. In the courts this is the task of the judge, who speaks in the name of the laws, at the same time interpreting their use and determining their application. In disputed religious questions

---

[4] *The Paroenese or Admonition of John Colville (lately returned to the Catholic Roman Religion, in which he was baptized and brought up till he had full 14 years of age) unto his countrymen*, Paris, 1602, pp. 7-8.

the Church is such a judge; the book with the help of which she knows the law is Scripture, but Scripture without the Church as judge could not pronounce sentence and pass judgment: "Even so, albeit by the most equal line and level of the Scripture the Church does judge betwixt orthodox and heretical opinions, yet she, not the Scripture only, are [sic] to be esteemed lawful judge".[5] This is not enough to conclude that, for John Colville, the Church knows nothing apart from the Scriptures. This would seem to lie in the logical direction he has taken. Yet his main interest lies in the Church's function in deciding controversies: whatever the Scriptures may be (rudder, line, square, etc.), the Church is the judge. For the Scriptures are too obscure to be open to individual opinions. Colville knows better than those who believe the Scriptures to be understandable even to "children, women and idiots".[6] He would agree with the Jesuit Richard Walpole (1564-1607) that interpretations of Scripture are "phantastical expositions" and "supersophistical" if they are not guided by the Church: "As for Catholics, I find such a rule prescribed unto them, as I cannot see how this charge may be laid against them. For that by a General Council they are straitly commanded to expound the Scriptures, not according to their own private phantasy, as you profess to do, *sed secundum unanimem consensum Patrum*, but according to the uniform consent of the Fathers".[7]

Around the same time, John Radford (1561-1630) asks the hypothetical question: "But what if we had never had Scriptures left us?" which ushers in the answer that we would then have believed "the mouth and tradition of the Church, who was believed, and taught her children to believe and follow her, before any Scriptures were written...".[8] The Church keeps in her custody traditions, which Radford vaguely describes as "nothing but godly precepts, orders, uses, rites, ceremonies and infallible truths of Christ, God, his Saints and sacraments, and due administration of the same, which we receive by word of mouth without writing of our forefathers, as they did of theirs from one generation to another, from Christ and his Apostles' time".[9] This list includes all sorts of things which, as Radford is well

---

[5] l.c., p. 8.

[6] l.c., p. 14.

[7] W. R., *A brief and clear confutation of a new, vain and vaunting challenge*, 1603, fol. 155 r.

[8] *A directory teaching the way to the truth, in a brief and plain discourse against the heresies of this time*, 1605, p. 453.

[9] l.c., p. 454.

aware, do not belong together even though the word "tradition", then as now, covers them all. Some of these the Church may alter, "especially some external rites and ceremonies"; others "she never does nor will alter, as Christ's words therein and the traditions of the Apostles".[10] In any case, the Church is equally to be believed "when she says of Tradition, 'this is the word or deed of Christ or the Apostles', as when she tells me of the Scripture, 'This is God's word'. . .".

As to Scripture, Protestants should not boast so much of their fidelity to it, for "we reverence (it) more than any people in the world". Catholic objections are not aimed at the Scriptures but at "the false understanding". Radford concludes with this balanced statement: "Though the Scripture be profitable to instruct, teach and the like, yet many other things that be not written be expedient and necessary to be known." As an example he mentions "the word of the Trinity, (which) is not written in Scripture, yet necessary to be known and believed".

Another author, who treats each question with brevity,[11] yet elaborately supports his theses with "proofs out of Scripture, out of the Fathers, by reason" and, as often as possible, with "assertions of Protestants", is the Scottish Jesuit James Gordon Huntley (1541-1620). He published three Latin volumes of controversy from 1612 to 1620, which were partially translated and published in English by "J.L.", who was his colleague the English Jesuit William Wright (1563-1639). The first two questions treated in Wright's translation, *A Summary of Controversies* (1616), hold the key to the rest of the book: "Of the Holy Scriptures", and "Of Traditions". Each "controversy" follows a number of "points" (seven for Scripture, one only for Traditions) which are formulated briefly and followed by a series of proofs. The discussion of Scripture hinges around the following points:

---

[10] l.c., p. 455.

[11] Still more concisely, John Pickford formulates his views in these few lines: "Concerning the word of God, part of it is written and part is not written: the written is called the Holy Scripture or commonly the Bible. The not written is called apostolical or ecclesiastical tradition, because it contains Scripture in itself and does deliver it by voice, also because the Church, the pillar and foundation of truth, does deliver it to posterity from hand to hand". (*The Safegarde from Shipwracke, or Heaven's Haven*, Douai, 1618, Article 28, p. 140). John J. Pickford (d. 1657) is Edward Daniel, who studied at Douai and Lisbon, worked at the English mission, was President of the College in Lisbon and Professor at Douai before spending his last years in England. His brother, John Daniel, alias Jerome

Fourth point: That the Scripture is not of itself so plain and easy as that it may suffice without any other explication, to determine controversies in religion.

Fifth point: That the judge of controversies is not the Scripture interpreted according to each particular man's private spirit, but the Church, or the chief pastor with a council of other bishops.

Sixth point: That the Scriptures are not absolutely necessary.

Seventh point: That in the Holy Scripture all that doctrine which is necessary to faith and manners is not expressly contained.[12]

With Gordon, attention begins to bear on what will become the focal point of English Recusant theology: who is "judge of controversies"? It is worth noting that Wright, the translator, shows a special interest in this question. For it cannot be by accident that he also translated into English and published in 1619 a Latin book by the Dutchman Martin Becanus, which he called *A Treatise of the Judge of Controversies*. Henceforth, emphasis will increasingly shift from the sufficiency of the contents of Scripture to its functional insufficiency. The former question refers to quantity and to the exhaustive universality of Scripture as the conveyor of divine truths. This rationale is implied in the "partitive" conception of Scripture and Tradition acknowledged, for instance, by Radford. On the contrary, the problem of Scripture's function invites no consideration of the quantitative or material extension of scriptural Revelation, but, shelving this secondary issue, it assesses the inability of Scripture to function as a judge applying the principles of Revelation to current controversies. Thus, discussion slowly gropes toward a dialectic of Church and Scripture; and the necessity of a dynamic relationship between these two if controversies are to be resolved begins to dawn in the darkness of polemics.

Gordon's seventh point admittedly maintains the perspective of the material insufficiency of Scripture, and his summary of the controversy on Traditions follows the same line:

> That, besides the word of God written, there is also necessarily required the word of God not written, that is to say, divine and apostolical traditions.[13]

Pickford, left the English College of Douai in 1618 to join the Franciscans at Gravelines.

[12] *A Summary of Controversies*, 1616, pp. 28, 33, 53, 54.
[13] l.c., p. 58.

Gordon's well-balanced point of view, however, is made clearer in another volume, also englished by Wright, his *Treatise of the Unwritten Word of God, commonly called Traditions* (1614). This is another version, in eleven chapters, of the same fundamental material concerning the theology of Tradition. Gordon Huntley presents a double viewpoint: on the one hand, all Christian doctrine is contained in Scripture implicitly; on the other, all is not expressly in it. The necessity for the existence of binding apostolic Traditions arises from this gap between the implicit and the explicit. Gordon provides several examples of these implicit Scriptural doctrines, the explicitness of which comes from Tradition. This enables him to coin some finely balanced dialectical statements, such as: "The Scripture consequently, mediately and virtually as in a general principle contains all things necessary to salvation";[14] "Our faith relies only of (*sic*) the word of God, but the Scripture only is not all the word of God";[15] "Wherefore all those places which do commend unto us the Holy Scriptures do also consequently commend unto us Traditions and the unwritten word of God, seeing that therein consists the principal part of Holy Scripture, to wit, the true sense of the words".[16]

Thus, Tradition with Scripture constitutes the whole word of God, because Tradition preserves and teaches the meaning of what is written in Scripture. This, as we shall see, is a frequent theme of the Catholic apologists of the seventeenth century. Yet one may go further. Between the implicit and the explicit contents of the written word, it would seem that there is not only room for a Tradition, in which the implicit is expressly known, but also for a movement of discovery and explicitation. Is there anything implicit in Scripture which is not yet expressly taught by Tradition? In other words, does the doctrine of the implicitness of Scripture entail a doctrine of the development of faith and dogma? One might think the question premature concerning an author of the beginning of the seventeenth century, although later chapters will show that several writers of the latter part of the century did indeed consider similar problems. The question is raised, however, by a few tantalising lines where Gordon opens an entirely new panorama without pointing clearly to the details of his vision:

---

[14] *A treatise of the unwritten Word of God, commonly called Traditions*, 1614, p. 32.
[15] l.c., p. 43.
[16] l.c., p. 57.

> And truly the Holy Scripture is so fertile and plentiful that many points of faith do as yet lie hidden and unknown therein, which hitherto has (*sic*) never been gathered together by any, but these things are contained virtually and not expressly in it.[17]

Such a sentence has two possible meanings. Either theological reflection has not yet found in Scripture all that Tradition contains explicitly; or some doctrines are implicit in Scripture which are not yet explicit even in Tradition. Which did Gordon mean? I would like to think that he was bold enough to envisage the latter; but I should admit that I cannot be sure.

The primacy of Scripture is unequivocally stated by several authors of the first years of the century, notably by one of the best known English theologians of the period, Matthew Kellison (1560-1642), who was a professor of theology for most of his life after his ordination in 1589. First a lecturer at the English College at Rheims and Douai, he became Regius Professor at the University of Rheims in 1601, Chancellor of the University in 1605; in 1613 he returned to Douai as President of the English College, where he had the ungrateful task of smoothing over the troubles caused by his predecessor Thomas Worthington. He remained at this post until his death.

In his *Survey of the New Religion* (1603), Kellison identifies the letter of Scripture with the word of God, as long as the letter is known with its true meaning:

> If they give us the letter with the true meaning, which is the formal cause and life of the word, we will reverence it as the word of God, and prefer it before all writings of Popes and Church. Wherefore, when the letter of Scripture is joined with the right meaning, then do we grant, though men wrote it, that it is the word of God, because it explicates his meaning who spake unto the holy writers in that meaning and directed their ears and hands in the writing of the same.[18]

Kellison's other work, *A Reply to Sutcliffe's Answer to the Survey of the New Religion* (1608), repeats similar propositions, sometimes quoting his previous volume verbally. Reviewing his former book, Kellison explains its double standpoint: "After a long commendation of Scripture and a great difference which I put betwixt the Pope's decrees and Scripture, I give the precedence and preeminence to Scripture. But yet I prove that the bare letter is no more Scripture

---

[17] l.c., p. 31.
[18] *Survey of the New Religion*, 2nd ed., Douai 1605, pp. 21-22.

than the body is a man without a soul".[19] This is the question of what he calls the "form" of Scripture:

> For I affirm here, the word is compounded of the sound or letter, and the sense or meaning; and that is as the matter, this as the form; that as the body, this as the soul; and so the word of God is not the letter only, but the letter with a true sense and meaning; and consequently the word of God cannot have a false meaning; but the same letter, as it may have a true and a false meaning, so with a true meaning it is the word of God, with a false sense it is the word of the devil.

The devil can give a false meaning to any writing. Truly, in the exchange between Christ and the devil, during the temptation in the desert, Jesus rebuked Satan with scriptural arguments. Yet "Scripture only convinced not the devil, but Scripture sensed by a lawful interpreter, as Christ was".[20]

The tone of Kellison's theology did not always remain as irenic as in the passages hitherto quoted. In 1616, Kellison published at Douai a long Latin volume of anti-Calvinist polemics, where he made it his avowed aim "rather to subvert and refute Calvinian doctrine than to assert and confirm the true and Catholic faith".[21] Yet the allusions to Catholic doctrines, which are made in the course of Kellison's careful though hostile examination of Calvin's works and ideas, point to the same conception of Scripture as his English works. Quite often, the Latin of the *Examen* is hardly more than a translation of the English of Kellison's earlier books. "Scripture", Kellison writes in a close approximation to his previous statement, "does not consist of the letter only, but of the letter and the sense; that is as the matter, this as the form; that as the body, this as the soul and life".[22] The heretics indeed, be they the innovators of the past or those of the present, use the Scriptures but they do not have the Word; for Scripture is in their hands in its letter, not in its sense. "Take the sense away, and the letter of Scripture is no more the word of God than one body belongs to a man and to a corpse".[23] If Kellison admits the superficial presence of the letter among Calvinists, he withdraws from their midst the substance of Scripture. For "if they press upon us the letter of Scripture infected with and steeped in their false interpretations and glosses, we reject it as adulterous; we even lothe

---

[19] l.c., p. 23.
[20] *A Reply to Sutcliffe's Answer*, fol. 47 r.
[21] *Examen Reformationis Novae*, p. 23.
[22] l.c., p. 36.
[23] l.c., p. 47.

it more than the words of any men".[24] The hands of innovators have transformed the letter of Scripture out of recognition into the devil's instrument:

> We therefore grant the innovators that the letter of the word of God is with them, although truncated, defective and weakened; but we deny that the word of God is with them, and we say that what they boast of is simply the word of the devil, for the letter which is taken in a heretical sense does not express the mind of God but the mind of the devil, who is the author and adviser of all the heresies.[25]

Behind these harsh judgements there lies a profound and rather modern notion of the Word. Kellison senses that the identity of Scripture and the Word of God, as it was traditionally expressed in Catholic theology before becoming the center of Protestant thought, rests upon an analogy between the divine Word, born eternally of the Father and eventually spoken to man in the Prophets and in the Lord Incarnate, and the word conceived in the human mind in the form of thought and for the purpose of communication. There was of course nothing fundamentally new in this: it is basic to Augustine's Trinitarian theology and to the Schoolmen's explanations of the procession of the Son. Yet by its emphasis on the communication aspect of the analogy, Kellison's development of this point comes nearer to our modern concerns. For this reason it should be quoted at length, at the cost of belaboring the obvious:

> The word in general is that which expresses the speaker's mind: for the mind's thoughts are hidden, and are expressed by words acting as signs and symbols. The human word expresses a man's mind; the word of God expresses God's mind; the devil's word expresses the devil's meaning. Just as man is not only a body or only a soul but something made of both, likewise the divine word is not the letter only but the letter united to the meaning that God himself intended.[26]

In this approach what essentially constitutes a word is its symbolic aspect, by which it communicates a truth or, to speak in a less intellectual context, by which it bridges the gap between two persons, opening the mind of the one to the other. Accordingly, a word does not exist as word as soon as it has been pronounced or written, but when it has been heard or read,—and this not absent-mindedly, but so as to be understood. A word functions as word rather than as

---

[24] l.c., p. 46.
[25] l.c., p. 47.
[26] l.c., pp. 43-44.

agglomerate of sounds or letters, when communication has been effectively established through it.

Applying this to the Word of God, Kellison concludes that the Scriptures cannot be the Word until God's purpose has been fulfilled through them in the reader's understanding of their divine meaning:

> When the right meaning accrues to Scripture, then we confess that it is the word of God, in spite of being written by a man, for then it expresses God's mind, who guided the sacred writer in uttering and writing it.

Once the sense of Scripture is known, the holy books brook no peer. In both his English and his Latin works, Kellison does not hesitate to pursue the comparison of Scripture with the other writings used in the Church, and he determines their scale of authority by the different degrees to which they are guaranteed by God: "Wherein a difference is put betwixt Scripture and the definitions of the Church, Pope or Councils. Because they are assisted by the Holy Ghost only that they may define the truth, and so the sense of a Council's definition confirmed by the Pope is of the Holy Ghost, but it is not necessary that every word or reason in a Council proceed from the Holy Spirit of God".[27] This even leads Kellison to an obvious exaggeration. God's assistance to the Councils does not dispense these from the proper human care and the necessary research into the problems they are concerned with: "However God does not assist the conciliar Fathers to the point where they may not apply diligence and make enquiries".[28] Thus *Acts, ch. 15*, reports that, at the Apostles' Council in Jerusalem, "there was a great debate"; men argued and God assisted them to reach their conclusion. "This diligence being applied, God assists them infallibly, that they may not err in their definition". So far, so good. But Kellison goes one step further and, placing the sacred writers on a totally different plane than the Council Fathers, denies the necessity of any human process of investigation on the part of the scriptural authors, who thus become, as it were, robots mechanically guided by God:

> But God infallibly assist a canonical writer without any care, study or diligence on his part, so that he does but passively uttering or writing what God has revealed to him.

---

[27] *Reply to Sutcliffe's Answer*, fol. 49 v.
[28] *Examen. . .*, p. 45.

This conception of divine inspiration has often undergirded much Catholic and Protestant reading of Scripture, although it has seldom been expressed so excessively. One easily perceives Kellison's purpose in so doing: he wants to ensure Scripture's supremacy over all ecclesiastical writings. For "not only the sense of Scripture, but also the words, not only the words but also the dots, and the arguments, and all that is in it, are acknowledged to be dictated by the Holy Spirit". Kellison nonetheless does not wish to disparage papal or conciliar authority. He is not a conciliarist; and a Council's definitions stand for him only insofar as they have been confirmed by the Pope. Yet both popes and councils belong together on one side of a profound dichotomy, Scripture occupying the other side. There is an essential distinction between the authority wielded by papal or conciliar documents and that which belongs to Holy Writ:

> Wherefore, as I said, let them not charge us with contempt of Scripture, for our opinion and estimation of Scripture is most venerable, if it be indeed Scripture; yea, we avouch that in itself it is of far greater authority than is the Church or her definitions, because, though God assists both, yet after a most notable manner he assists holy writers in writing of Scripture, because he assists them infallibly, not only for the sense and verity but also for every word which they write and every reason and whatsoever is in Scripture, whereas he assists the Popes and Councils infallibly only for the sense and verity of that which they intend to define, but neither for every word, nor for every reason, nor for everything which is incidentally spoken.[29]

The verbal inspiration of Scripture extends much further than God's guidance of papal and conciliar definitions: in the latter the truth only, in the former the words also are guaranteed by God.

Since Scripture, fully understood as divine word, is not the letter but the meaning of the holy books, one should know how to ascertain that meaning. In principle, the apostles, who received the letter from God, received also its meaning, which is now transmitted by the Church: "I confess also that our faith is principally grounded upon the Prophets' and Apostles' writings, which are God's word, but how shall we know that these writings are God's word, or thus to be understood, unless the Church and her pastors preach it and propose it?"[30] Kellison answers in *The Touchstone of the Reformed Gospel*, a somewhat superficial book of popular polemics: "Prophecy

---

[29] *Reply to Sutcliffe's Answer*, fol. 50 v.
[30] l.c., fol. 6 r.

according to the Rule of faith is one of the gifts which God bestows on his Church. Therefore there is in the Church one, and that an infallible, rule, for understanding to the holy Scriptures".[31] The living Church's kerygma provides the meaning of Scripture:

> So Scripture, which is of itself of more authority than the testimony of men, and faith also, which has God's word and authority for her ground, foundation and formal object, in respect of us depends of preachers, revelations not being ordinary, and not only of inward inspiration but also of outward hearing.[32]

Scripture, being "a law, not a judge", does not interpret itself. The law is, in an often recurring metaphor, "a mute magistrate, lacking tongue and speech".[33] It needs a living voice to formulate its meaning and pronounce its sentences. Yet this voice cannot belong to everybody. To fancy that God will reveal the meaning of Scripture to every Christian is a delusion, the mother of illuminism and enthusiasm. Revelations may be possible; they are "not ordinary". The ordinary way is to listen to the Church. "Our best will be... to listen to the common received, that is, the Roman Church, who, as she has ever had the custody of the book of Scripture, so it is most like that she best knows the meaning of it, having this book from the apostles and, with it, the apostles' and their successors' interpretation".[34]

In this perspective the bold language of Catholics who say that Scripture depends on the Church becomes acceptable. Kellison carefully qualifies it, yet endorses it in the light of an analogy taken from Christ's own relation to his witnesses:

> We reply that although it is plainly absurd that Scripture in itself should be dependent on the Church, since it itself is the word of God and receives its truth and solidity from God alone: yet it is not absurd that it should be dependent on the Church in relation to us, since the Church is better known to us than Scripture. Just as Christ in and by himself was not dependent on any man's testimony, since he was himself the truth; yet in relation to the Jews, to whom John was better known than Christ, he was dependent on John and received his testimony, as also the apostles. Thus Scripture in and by itself is not dependent on the Church but on God alone, whose word it is; yet in relation to us it is dependent on the Church, for the Church is

---

[31] *The Touchstone of the Reformed Gospel*, 4 th ed., 1634, p. 15.
[32] *Reply to Sutcliffe's Answer*, fol. 6 v.
[33] *Examen. . .*, p. 37.
[34] *Survey of the New Religion*, p. 33.

better known to us than Scripture, and was established and known in the world before Scripture.[35]

One might expect Kellison at this point to identify tradition with the Church's transmission of the sense of Holy Writ in her preaching and teaching. This would correspond to modern concepts: the Church proclaims doctrine through papal and conciliar definitions, which are themselves infallibly protected as to their sense and truth, though not in their style, language and vocabulary. Indeed, the proper interpretation of Scripture is so transmitted: "For since the apostles handed on the understanding of the same Scripture to the first bishops and Christians, the genuine sense of Scripture is certainly the one that has been transmitted from hand to hand and from the the ancients to their successors".[36] Yet Kellison's formal definition of Tradition maintains the older and less sophisticated equation, common in the Middle Ages, of "tradition" and "inherited custom": "Tradition is nothing else but an opinion or custom of the Church, not written in Holy Writ, but yet delivered by the hands of the Church from time to time and from Christians to Christians even into the last age".[37] In the rendering of the *Examen*, the focus is on doctrine rather than on custom: "Tradition is nothing else but a doctrine not expressly contained in Scripture, but transmitted from the ancients to their successors in continuous fashion".[38]

The word "tradition" still retains some ambiguity in Kellison's language: it denotes custom and doctrine, interpretation of Scripture and ecclesiastical practice. This is logical enough, since all of these have been transmitted. Tradition means transmission before connoting what has been transmitted. It conveys both "opinions", which are obviously less than the Word of God, and the Word itself. Of some traditions it is true to say: "This Tradition is no less the word of God than Scripture itself, although it is not written but transmitted".[39] Or, in the sharper tone of *The Touchstone of the Reformed Gospel*, "It is clear that some Traditions were delivered to the Thessalonians by word of mouth, and those of equal authority with what was written, if not of more; for the Holy Ghost does name them first (as they were indeed the first in being); yea it is certain that before the New Testament was written the apostles delivered all by

---

[35] *Examen*. . ., p. 31.
[36] l.c., p. 39.
[37] *Survey*. . ., p. 357.
[38] *Examen*. . ., p. 34.
[39] l.c., p. 33.

Tradition and word of mouth. Therefore apostolical traditions are to be received and do oblige us".[40]

Here as in his broad approach to Scripture and Tradition, Kellison remains conservative: his rationale is pre-tridentine, and he is concerned with the active aspect of Tradition as delivery more than in the passive viewpoint of its contents. Although he occasionally slips into the polemical snares set for him by the questions and denials of his antagonists, he persistently rejects the option placed before him: either to give up the supremacy of Scripture, or to deny that Traditions also may be the Word of God. His theology follows one of the dominant strains of Catholic thought in England under Queen Elizabeth, that of Harding, and strikes a very different note from the opposite trend, which had its ablest representative in Thomas Stapleton.[41]

The primacy of Scripture, qualified in a Catholic sense, which we have found explained in Kellison, was also championed by an otherwise controversial and perhaps doubtful personage, Thomas Worthington (1549-1622?). As a priest, Worthington was involved, with the blessings of the future Cardinal Allen, in the hopeless ventures of Sir William Stanley, a military gentleman who had formed an English regiment at the service of the King of Spain. Worthington served as chaplain to Sir Stanley's troops for several years. As President of the English College at Douai from 1599 to 1613, he provoked dismay among many of the English refugees by placing Jesuits in prominent positions at the College: the ensuing difficulties finally occasioned his removal from Douai, where his place was taken by Kellison himself. He then returned to England, and, in his last years, devoted himself with great credit to theological controversy, with a short polemical piece, *Whyte died Black* (1615), and above all with the three volumes of *An Anker of Christian Doctrine* (1622), a work remarkable for the author's serenity and irenic concerns, a serenity which the years spent in Stanley's regiment would not have led to expect. A token of this may be seen in the argumentative method adopted. Instead of trying to swamp his adversaries under the cumulative weight of all sorts of arguments, as so many contemporaries do, Worthington focuses the debate on the only arguments

[40] *The Touchstone. . .*, pp. 29-30.
[41] M. R. O'Connell, *Thomas Stapleton and the Counter-Reformation*, New Haven, 1964.

that Protestants understand, that is, on Scripture alone. The very title of the second part of *An Anker* makes this explicit:

> ...wherein the most principal points of Catholic religion are proved by the only written Word of God. Not rejecting Divine or Apostolical Traditions, Authentical Councils, Popes' Decrees, Ancient Fathers nor other Ordinary proofs, but Abstracting from them in this Encounter: For better satisfaction of those who will admit no other trial of true religion but Scriptures only.[42]

It is from the Word of God, rather than from the Scriptures themselves, that Worthington starts. For, if he admits some form of the principle of the sufficiency of Scripture, as he certainly does, this is within the context of a broader theology of the Word. The Catholic Church, Worthington writes in *Whyte died Black*,

> teaches that the word of God is to limit and confine our faith, and that nothing is to be accounted as matter of faith which receives not its proof from thence. Hereupon it teaches further that this word is either written, which is commonly called the Scripture, or else delivered by Christ and his Church, and this comprehends Traditions.[43]

Both aspects of the Word of God enjoy "infallible authority", for, as Worthington continues, "the true and inward reason why the Word of God is the Word of God is not because it is written rather than delivered by speech, for this is merely extrinsecal to the point, but because the same word proceeds from them who were infallibly and immediately directed therein by the assistance of the Holy Ghost".[44] The infallibility of the Word extends to the Scriptures and to the Church's Tradition, which delivers the Word. Yet this is not enough, and it would provide Worthington with no ground on which to argue with Protestants unless the infallibility of Scripture also entailed its sufficiency for salvation. To Worthington's credit, he perceived the strength of the idea that the spoken or written Word of God, once received, is enough. "What then", does he ask in *An Anker of Christian Doctrine*, "do we say that Holy Scripture are insufficient?" His answer is unambiguous;

> No. God forbid; for they are most sufficient, and do contain, either expressly or implicitly, all doctrines necessary to salvation, yea incomparably and by infinite degrees more sufficiently than any other written work or book contains what art or science soever.[45]

---

[42] *The Second Part of an Anker of Christian Doctrine*, 1632.

[43] *Whyte died Black*, pp. 149-150.

[44] l.c., p. 150.

[45] *An Anker of Christian Doctrine*. First part, 1622, p. 62.

Or, as Worthington's previous book says it more tamely,

> The Catholics do ascribe all due reverence, estimation and respect to the Scripture whatsoever, acknowledging it to be God's ambassador, which unfolds unto man upon earth the sacred will and pleasure of our heavenly King; as also that it is the spiritual tenure by the which we make claim to our eternal and celestial inheritance. In like sort they willingly confess that Scripture is Scripture and the Word of God before it receives any approbation from the Church; as also that this or that is the true sense of any particular text of the Scripture before the Church do confirm the same.[46]

Admittedly, these statements, taken at face-value, look more sweeping than they are intended. Neither would Worthington dream of denying that certain Christian customs, practices and even doctrinal articles, especially in the sacramental realm, are not accounted for in the Scriptures; nor would he question the necessity of the Church to interpret the Word. The above passage continues in these terms: "Notwithstanding, seeing the true sense of the Scripture is as it were the very soul which informs the body of the letter, and that the Scripture is to be understood by the reader with that spirit with the which it was written, to wit, the spirit of the Holy Ghost, therefore do we hold that so far as concerns our taking of notice that this or that is the Scripture or God's word, or that this is the true sense of such a passage thereof intended by the Holy Ghost, we are to recur to the authority of the Church, which we believe to be directed and guided therein by the same Holy Ghost, according as the Scripture itself in several places assures us".[47]

When all is said, Worthington wants only to maintain that the prerequisites of salvation are clear in Scripture, and that everything else in the Church flows, by one channel or another, therefrom. He readily admits in the preface to *An Anker* that "some points of Christian doctrine are not expressly and immediately written in the Holy Scriptures, but supplied in those things which the apostles learned otherwise, either of Christ or of the Holy Ghost".[48] Neither the Lord nor his disciples wrote all they taught, so that Christian doctrine includes in fact "things not expressly written in particular".[49] Yet these are themselves not extrascriptural or alien to the Word of

---

[46] *Whyte. . .*, pp. 154-155.

[47] l.c., p. 155.

[48] *The Second Part. . .*, p. 87.

[49] l.c., p. 88.

God. For, as Worthington says of the seal of baptism, "this doctrine being not expressed in the Holy Scripture, yet is it deduced from there". He then proves this by comparing baptism and circumcision, thus drawing on the analogy of the two Testaments for the scriptural proof that might be lacking in the New Testament alone. Likewise, Worthington recognizes, in relation to Confirmation, that "many things were done and said by Christ and received by his Apostles, and by them delivered and taught by word without writing";[50] nonetheless, perpetual Tradition and general practise amount to sufficient scriptural support, for "that such perpetual Tradition and general practise is an infallible proof of Christian doctrine, is evidently declared in the first part of this work by many express texts of Holy Scripture".

In other words, Worthington bases the sufficiency of Scripture upon the fact—which he establishes with abundant references to the New Testament—that the Scriptures teach the necessity of Tradition. "Now let us see some examples and other testimonies of the written Word of God for Traditions, which the Church calls the unwritten Word":[51] this invitation shuns the Protestant position by accepting its point of departure—the sufficiency of Scripture—yet denying its conclusion—the irrelevance of Tradition. The two principles of Scripture and of Tradition are inextricably intertwined in such a statement as the following, which is typical of Worthington's theological method:

> Now because we undertake by Holy Scripture to prove all Christian doctrine more clearly and certainly than our adversaries can prove doctrine and practise, which indeed neither they nor we can do in some points immediately, but must recur unto approved Traditions: as well for their help therein as our own (for we all profess to rely principally upon Holy Scripture), it remains, for complement of this article, that we set before our eyes certain clear places which expressly remit us for further instruction to the testimonies, customs and traditions of former times and of our predecessors, who testify the judgement of the Church in their time.[52]

This corresponds to the complex programme briefly outlined at the beginning of the *Second Part of the Anker of Christian Doctrine*:

> And this we shall do for most part by the express written Word of God in clear and manifest terms; the rest also, no less assuredly by

---

[50] l.c., p. 101.
[51] *First Part*, p. 45.
[52] l.c., p. 51.

other Holy Scriptures, not only according to the understanding and judgement of the teacher of truth, the only known Church for many ages (which we do not so much urge in this present trial) but also we shall verify our belief herein by the most apparent sense and conference of other places against all that our adversaries can alledge of the sacred text to the contrary. . .[53]

Thomas Worthington is thus respectful of the appeal to Scripture alone, which he endeavors to emulate as far as is feasible in the framework of his theological principles. Thus, Catholic thought at its best is brought to an inter-crossing of motives with Protestant thought. For while Worthington pledges himself to a strictly scriptural argumentation, he discovers that Protestants do in fact, despite their statements to the contrary, use the method of Tradition. The point that Protestants themselves appeal to Tradition is frequently made by our authors, and often far less courteously than by Worthington. William Bishop's contrasting of the Catholic and the Protestant recourse to Tradition is more indicative of the temper of the times: ". . .it may be concluded that even as we Catholics have learned of the Apostles and ancient Fathers, our noble progenitors, to stand fast and hold the Traditions which we have received by word of mouth, as well as that which is written: even so the Protestants have received as it were from hand to hand, of their ignoble predecessors, old condemned heretics, to reject all Traditions and to fly unto the only Scriptures".[54] "In fine" Sylvester Norris exclaims in his *Antidote* (1615), "all you who profess the exact following of the written word, against the same written word embrace the Tradition and practise of the Church",[55] the case in point being that of abstaining from blood and strangled meats, and of worshipping on the Lord's Day instead of the Sabbath. Whatever the differences of language the remark, that Tradition is inevitable even for Protestants, is commonly made and adds fuel to the Catholic cause. Moreover, "all sectaries", Worthington notices, "plead general authority given by Christ to institute diverse particular forms which are not expressed in the Holy Scriptures".[56]

It is in the context of the necessity of the Church and the Traditions for interpreting Scripture that Worthington occasionally uses a

---

[53] *The Second Part* . . ., (Pages are not numbered, in the copy I have used, before page 17).

[54] *A Reformation of a Catholic Deformed*, 1604, p. 22.

[55] *The Antidote*, p. 35.

[56] *The Second Part* . . ., pp. 316-317.

"partitive" vocabulary, as when he writes: "God's Word is partly written in the Holy Bible, partly known and kept by Tradition".[57] We may gather from this that use of the expression "partly partly" constitutes no sufficient gauge of an author's conceptions. Much more significant is his vision of the ties that bind Tradition and Scripture. That Tradition acts as a complement to Scripture is a constant Recusant doctrine, the minimal meaning of which is that "some Holy Scriptures are hard and require authentical interpretation".[58] Such a complement cannot be additive for those who, like Kellison and Worthington, uphold the sufficiency of Scripture. Rather, Tradition is a necessary guide to understand the written word. Reading Scripture primarily consists in analysing and comparing its various texts, according to Worthington's view of exegesis:

> We must remember and consider that every word in the holy Scripture is true, and no contradiction can be in all the whole Bible, being all inspired by the Holy Ghost. And therefore all must be so understood and explained that all be verified. And when some words seem contrary toothers, by conference of all, the truth must be sought.[59]

In some cases, this investigation will lead to say that all this, "according to the very sacred letters and express terms, do testify the Catholic belief and doctrine";[60] in others the evidence will not be so blatant, yet the texts of holy Scripture, "though not all expressly, yet by agreeable deduction, may suffice together with the apostolical Tradition".[61] Like many others of his time, Worthington is not critical enough when he judges certain practises to stem from apostolic Traditions. "Because all Christians do so observe it", he says of the Lenten fast, "or know that others do so observe it, and have done in all former times, no adversary being able to show any other beginning of Lent's fast: which is a plain and assured proof that it was begun by the Apostles of Christ and doubtless by Christ's warrant".[62] Such a reasoning is justified by the assumption that, "else the beginning of so universal an observation would have been noted and recorded, when and by whom it was first ordained". Thus grounding Tradition in common sense (for we cannot speak here of historical certainty), Worthington also observes that the

---

[57] *First Part*, p. 38.
[58] l.c., p. 55.
[59] *The Second Part*, p. 104.
[60] l.c., p. 121.
[61] l.c., p. 247.
[62] l.c., pp. 251-252.

Scriptures frequently justify recourse to Tradition. Then, the rule of apostolic Tradition ought to satisfy both the rational requirements of the mind and the Christian desire for scriptural evidence. Tradition does not become such a guide as to supplement the deficiencies of Scripture, for Scripture, in Worthington's theology, is far from deficient; yet it turns out to be a necessary key to the meaning of Scripture. In the concrete, Worthington identifies this Tradition with what has always been done in the Church: the joint rules of universality and of antiquity surely warrant apostolic origin.

The principle, shared by Kellison and Worthington, of the primacy of Scripture in the Church was not universally upheld by their English Catholic contemporaries. A transition to a theology of another type will be provided by the works of William Bishop (1554-1624), a puzzling character if there was one, who, alone of all the authors studied in this chapter was, not in name only but in reality, a bishop, having been consecrated to the See of Chalcedon in 1622 or 23 and given jurisdiction over all Catholics in England, Wales and Scotland. Long before this he had composed several theological works, polemical pieces in the old style. The main one, *A Reformation of a Catholic Deformed*, appeared in two parts, the first in 1604 and the second three years later. Unlike most of the works mentioned so far, this was not addressed to Protestants in general, being specifically aimed at a prolific and not too interesting Anglican controversialist of Puritan orientation, William Perkins (1558-1602).

The very first chapter, entitled "Of Traditions", deals with our topic, thus showing again that this problem loomed large in the mind of the Catholic controversialists. Bishop's plan, in spite of the polemical tone of his work, is not entirely unirenic: it presents, firstly, the consensus of Perkins and himself, and, by implication, of Anglicanism and Catholicism ("Our consent") and, secondly, "The difference". Here, Bishop follows the older and soon to be outmoded method of citing his adversary's own words at length before refuting them ("The answer"). After a number of exchanges pro and con, in which Perkins's doctrine is described and assailed, Bishop lets his antagonist speak once more, explaining, this time, the Catholic position and his objections to it, to which Bishop gives final "replies".

In this instance, the Catholic doctrine takes the form of six arguments in favor of Tradition. As we shall not examine them in detail, we may list them briefly here:

1° The Apostle enjoins the faithful to "keep the ordinances which he taught them either by word of mouth or by epistle"; [63]

2° the list of scriptural books is not in Scripture; [64]

3° some books of Scripture and "the necessary doctrine contained in them" have been lost; [65]

4° both the Old Law and the civil law admit the force of unwritten custom; [66]

5° several "principal articles of the Christian faith and most necessary to be believed of the learned" are not "in express terms written in any part of the holy Bible"; [67]

6° "sundry places of Holy Scriptures be hard to be understood, others doubtful whether they must be taken litterally or figuratively", to understand which "considerate men have recourse unto the Traditions and ancient records of the primitive Church, received from the Apostles and delivered to the posterity as the true copies of God's Word, see the true exposition and sense of it, and thereby confute and reject all private and new glosses which agree not with these ancient and holy commentaries".[68]

These arguments are of unequal value, and only the last two (the argument from content, and the one from the necessity of inter-pretation) seem to me to be fully relevant.

Be that as it may, the consensus that Bishop finds with Perkins does not reach very far: "We", that is, Catholics and Protestants, "hold that the word of God was delivered by Tradition from Adam to Moses" and that, similarly, "the history of the New Testament... went from hand to hand by Tradition till penned by the apostles or, being penned by others, was approved by them".[69] This unwritten Tradition lasted, Bishop thinks, from eight to twenty years—far too short a time, really, for composing the New Testament as we now see it. Bishop also finds a partial consensus on two other points: Perkins agrees that "the prophets, our Savior Christ and his apostles spake and did many things good and true which were not written in the Scriptures but came to us by Tradition", although he excludes these from the prerequisites of salvation. Perkins also recognizes that "the Church of God has power to prescribe ordinances and traditions touching time and place of God's worship, and touching

---

[63] *A Reformation of a Catholic Deformed*, p. 11.
[64] l.c., pp. 12-13.
[65] l.c., p. 15.
[66] l.c., pp. 15-16.
[67] l.c., p. 17.
[68] l.c., p. 17.
[69] l.c., p. 1.

order and comeliness to be used in the same"; yet, mistakenly believing the Church able to order "childish or absurd" regulations, he qualifies this with conditions that are incompatible with the nature of the true Church.

On another item, which reaches nearer to the heart of our problem, William Bishop records a consensus: all Protestants insist on the reading of Scripture by all the faithful. At this point Bishop exclaims, in *A Reproof of M. Abbot's Defense of the Catholic Deformed by M. W. Perkins* (1608):

> What says he that we say not? We hold with him that the want of knowledge of the Scriptures is the cause of heresy: for he that knows and understands well the holy Scriptures can never fall into error or heresy.[70]

Bishop, admittedly, is more eager to discover differences than consensus. He rather pointlessly protests that his opponent, who has defined Traditions as unwritten, has also applied that name to practices mentioned in the *Acts of the Apostles*: but "that which is of record there", Bishop, who accepts the definition, objects, "cannot be termed a Tradition".[71] This semantic touchiness, which incidentally contradicts the modern use of the term, betrays a strict, narrow conception, for which Traditions must remain completely outside the written Word instead of being possibly written in Scripture itself. There are three kinds of traditions, divine, apostolical, ecclesiastical, these last being "instituted and delivered by the Governors of the Church after the Apostles' days". Bishop clarifies the authority of these unwritten ordinances:

> And of these three kinds of Traditions we make the same account as of the writings of the same authors, to wit, we esteem no less of our Savior's Traditions than of the four Gospels or any thing immediately dictated from the Holy Ghost. Likewise, as much honor and credit do we give unto the Apostles' doctrine unwritten as written. For ink and paper brought no new holiness nor gave any force and virtue unto either God's or the Apostles' words; but they be of the same value and credit uttered by word of mouth as if they had been written.

The unwritten is equated with the written insofar as both stem from the same root. Bishop never identifies unwritten words of the Church with the written word of God, and his distinction of three kinds of

---

[70] *A Reproof of M. Abbot's Defense of the Catholic Deformed by M. W. Perkins*, p. 217.

[71] *A Reformation . . .*, p. 2.

Traditions ensures that the ecclesiastical is not mistaken for the apostolical or the divine. Yet his main purpose is not to stress their differences but to show that at each level the unwritten is on a par with the written. As he points out, the controversy between Catholics and Protestants arises chiefly about the divine level: "Here the question is principally of divine Traditions, which we hold to be necessary to salvation to resolve and determine any matters of greater difficulty".

In Bishop's view, the written Word suffices for simple fundamental points of faith. "We deny not", he confesses, "but that some such principal points of faith (which the simple are bound to believe under pain of damnation) may be gathered out of the Holy Scriptures, as for example that God is Creator of the world, Christ the Redeemer of the world, the Holy Ghost the Sanctifier, and other such like articles of the Creed".[72] And again, in a more affirmative vein:

> All things necessary to be believed of every simple Christian under pain of damnation, that is, the articles of our belief, are contained in the Scriptures, but not the resolution of harder matters, much less of all difficulties which the more learned must expressly believe if they will be saved.[73]

For these harder questions the Scriptures, lacking capacity and clarity, are "profitable to make the man of God absolute, but not sufficient".[74] This, according to Bishop, is St Paul's doctrine and is therefore scriptural.

To establish the insufficiency of Scripture, William Bishop analyses its structure: it is letter and meaning, body and soul, reading and interpretation. "For the written word of God consists not in the reading but in the understanding. . .that is, it does not consist in the bare letter of it but in the letter and true sense and meaning joined together; the letter being as the body of Scripture, and the right understanding of it, the soul, spirit and life thereof: he therefore that takes not the written word in the true sense, but swerves from the sincere interpretation of it cannot be truly said to receive the written word as a good Christian ought to do".[75] The letter does not suffice; and in order to ascertain the meaning, most men need the advice and help of other elements than the text itself. This is

---

[72] l.c., pp. 2-3.
[73] l.c., pp. 8-9.
[74] l.c., p. 6.
[75] *A Reproof* . . ., p. 114.

also borne out by common sense, to which, like Thomas Worthington, Bishop appeals here: "It cannot be but most evident to men of
any judgement that the Scripture itself can never end any doubtful
controversy without there be admitted some certain Judge to declare
what is the true meaning of it".[76] This argument is strengthened by
the experience of human courts of law, in which there would be
"bloody debate and perpetual conflict" [77] unless judges were appointed to pass sentecnce, and by the example of the Old Covenant,
which instituted such judges. Bishop concludes on this peroration:

> Shall we be so simple as to suffer ourselves to be persuaded that in the
> glorious state of the Gospel, plotted and framed by the wisdom of
> God himself, worse order should be taken for this high point of the
> true understanding of the holy Gospel itself, being the life and soul of
> the rest?

If one cannot bear the idea of such a "worse order" for the Gospel
than for the Law, one must approve Vincent of Lerins who, when
he refers to the perfection of the Canon of Scripture, does not sever
it from the Church, but maintains that "no heresy can be certainly
confuted and suppressed by only Scriptures, without we take with
it the sense and interpretation of the Catholic Church".[78]

Scripture is therefore, to a degree, "sufficient", while being insufficient from another point of view; yet it is not the only sufficient
statement of Christian doctrine. The Apostles' Creed also, in Bishop's
eyes, may "be called the key or rule of faith, because it contains the
principal points of the Christian religion, and does open as it were
the door unto all the rest, and guide a man certainly unto the knowledge of them by teaching us to believe the Catholic Church, which,
being the pillar and ground of truth, directed and guided by the
Spirit of truth, will always instruct her obedient children in all
truth necessary to salvation".[79]

One could wonder here if this instruction, in Bishop's mind,
implies more than a repetition of what the Church has always taught.
The "generality, antiquity and consent" of Vincent of Lerins may be
taken to mean that all the faith must have been explicitly formulated
once for all. Whether this has been done in Scriptures or in the
Fathers' writings changes the locus of the freezing of doctrine, but

---

[76] *A Reformation . . .*, p. 18.
[77] l.c., p. 19.
[78] l.c., p. 9.
[79] *The Second Part . . .*, p. 3.

not the principle that doctrine has become a finalized datum. William
Bishop perceives at least one dimension of this problem. For he
states, against the biblical fixity of doctrine that Perkins defends:
"We say that some articles of faith were at first believed generally
by an infolded faith, which afterward, being by General Councils
unfolded and declared to be articles of faith, were believed expressly".[80] The development which is indicated here remains within the
implicit — explicit categories, but this is a more open position than
the denial of all unfolding. Here again, the Scriptures are shown to be,
in themselves, insufficient as regards the explicitation of faith.

Bishop's treatment of the question of sufficiency makes it clear
that, ultimately, it is neither to Scripture nor to the Creed that sufficiency accrues, but to the Gospel. On the one hand, the Gospel is
equated with "all our Christian doctrine, written and unwritten",[81]
although this is tantamount to begging the question, for it assumes
the point under discussion, namely that there are unwritten doctrines.
On the other, Bishop sees the Gospel as proclaimed by "our celestial
law-maker" in the form of a "law not written in ink and paper but
in the hearts of his most faithful subjects", who have been endowed
"with the blessed Spirit of truth and with a most diligent care of
instructing others, that all posterity might learn of them all the points
of Christian doctrine, and give credit to them as well for the written
as unwritten words, and more for the true meaning of the word than
for the word itself".[82] In this text, Bishop raises the apostolic and
ecclesiastical charisms of celestial guidance and visible succession to
the level of personal holiness: to his "most faithful" disciples Jesus
gave the Spirit of truth. The "true successors" of these faithful
disciples are themselves "lively oracles of the true and living God".[83]
What Bishop terms "the sentence and declaration of the Apostles,
scholars and successors" depends on official empowerment, but also
on spiritual insight; for the holy man, like St Augustine, "does not
trust his own skill and judgement" but consults the Catholic Church's
"antiquity, generality and consent".[84] Being a law inscribed in the
heart, the Gospel may be known with certainty only by those whom
the Spirit enlightens. When therefore Bishop affirms that "apostolic

---

[80] l.c., p. 144.
[81] *A Reformation* . . ., p. 7.
[82] l.c., pp. 19-20.
[83] l.c., p. 20.
[84] l.c., p. 21.

Traditions are as well kept in the mind of the learned as in the ancient Fathers' writings",[85] he has in mind the learned in the things of God who remember the Gospel by the thoughts of their heart, not insisting on scholarship and excluding a purely documentary Tradition committed to intellectual memory. In these conditions it is not surprising, shocking as the formula may sound, that in case some parts of the Scriptures would disappear, there would be "no great loss in that, according to our opinion", for "Tradition might preserve what was then lost": [86] it would know the whole Gospel by virtue of the holy memory of the most faithful hearts.

There clearly is an ambivalence in Bishop's approach to Scripture—one which may well pertain to the core of the Catholic view of the Word. Bishop may say with equal seriousness that "it is not of necessity for the simple sort and ignorant people to read the holy Scriptures and to go fish their faith out of that profound ocean",[87] and that "it is expedient to all men either to read the Scriptures or to hear them: to read them themselves if they be men of judgement, and indeed with a lowly spirit ..." All others should have the Scriptures read and explained to them "by their lawful pastors and approved preachers".[88] But the issue is not so much a matter of ignorance as of malice. For Bishop adds: "We would have none other debarred from reading them but wavering, wilful and perverse fellows".[89] Bishop entertains no doubt that the Scriptures in themselves testify to the truth: "The true knowledge of them delivers us from all error and heresy and settles us in the sound doctrine of the Catholic Roman Church". Yet the experience of his age shows the danger of letting everyone read the Scriptures for himself. "A sword is a good weapon, but put it into the hand of a madman, it will do more harm than good: so if some men get a smattering in holy Scriptures, they will use it madly".[90] What is needed in practise is sound advice on the part of "godly and prudent ghostly fathers".

The contrast between the Kellison-Worthington line of thought and that of the bishop of Chalcedon is not very striking. They all accept the fundamental principle that all simple points of doctrine required of all the faithful are included in Scripture. Kellison and

---

[85] l.c., p. 10.
[86] l.c., p. 16.
[87] *The Second Part* . . ., p. 143.
[88] *Reproof* . . ., p. 217.
[89] l.c., p. 218.
[90] l.c., p. 219.

Worthington go further, applying this to all points, whether hard or simple, for the learned only or for all Christians: these are at least implicitly in Scripture, whence they may be brought to light with the help of interpretative Tradition. Neither line, let us admit it, contains anything truly original. On the contrary, they prolong the theologies of former times, which were already constituted in the last decades of the sixteenth century in England.

In the context of the seventeenth century and its polemics, this contrast was so little an opposition that a much sharper one could well be found in the ideas of one and the same man. As an example of this, we may scan the main works of John Percy, S.J. (1569-1641), better known in his life-time, especially in the course of his debate and his subsequent controversy with Archbishop William Laud, as Mr Fisher the Jesuit. Percy's adventures as a Catholic missioner in Elizabethan and Stuart England left him little leisure to produce long well-organized theological volumes, and by and large, his books are immediately controversial, aiming at specific adversaries with whom Percy had, more often than not, orally debated. In spite of this somewhat unprofessional approach which gives Percy the tone of a debater rather than a systematic theologian, his volumes contain most valuable insights which should suffice to give him a place in the first rank of English theology. One point in particular may be mentioned, although it will not be pursued at this time: Percy, especially in his work *Reply Made unto Mr Anthony Wotton and Mr John White* [91] (1612), belongs to a series of authors who, in the course of their explanations of Catholic doctrines, proceed to a careful, nearly classical, analysis of the act of faith. After Edward Maihew, yet before Sylvester Norris, James Mumford and the great Henry Holden, Percy contributed to a theology of faith which would be worth a careful comparative study.

The *Reply* opposes to Percy's opponents a concept of Tradition which echoes the pre-Tridentine emphasis of Albert Pighi, making much of the existence of non-scriptural points of faith.

Percy does not wish to undermine Scripture. On the contrary, he extols it in its own order: "True it is, there is the virtue and power of God in the Scripture; there is purity and perfection of matter, majesty of speech, power over the conscience, certainty of the

---

[91] Signed with the initials A. D.

prophecies, etc. . .".[92] Were one to insist that Scripture is sufficient, as other Catholics have done, this could also be admitted as long as a proviso is maintained: "If it import sufficiency, it is not meant that *alone* sufficiency of which our question is, but at the most sufficiency *in suo genere*, in a certain limited kind, to wit, of written Scripture".[93] Scriptural sufficiency must be limited on several counts, in that the inner qualities of Scripture which Percy willingly contemplates

> do not shine like light to our understanding till it be illuminated with the light of faith. . . nor then neither unless those things be propounded duly, mediate or immediate, by the authority of the Church; upon which, being like a candlestick, the light of the Scripture must be set, or else it will not, according to the ordinary course of God's providence, sufficiently shine and appear unto us in such sort as to give infallible assurance that it is the word of God.[94]

The necessity of the act of faith makes Scripture insufficient, for it is directly from God Himself that the act of faith proceeds in us. The task of the Church in proposing the contents of revelation introduces another intrinsic limitation to the sufficiency of Scripture: the Church must intervene by presenting the object of faith.

This function of the Church leads Percy to a more radical limitation of Scripture's authority, in regard to the question of unwritten revelation, concerning which Catholics and Protestants differ deeply:

> Now the question is betwixt us and Protestants, whether God did reveal anything to the Prophets and Apostles, manifested by their means to men living in their times, and necessary to be believed of men living in succeeding ages, which was never written or at least which is not now expressed nor so contained in the Scriptures, that by evident and necessary consequence, secluding all Tradition and Church authority, it may be gathered out of some sentence expressly set down in Holy Scriptures.[95]

The problem concerns revelations duly made to the apostles and transmitted, since then, outside of Scripture. What is in Scripture, for Percy, must be explicitly stated in specific verses or may be logically deduced. At the basis of Percy's further explanations of tradition there lies too narrow a concept of the "virtually revealed" He must logically conclude that few doctrines are explicitly stated in Scripture or may be deduced in strict Aristotelian logic; in this

---

[92] *Reply made unto Mr. Anthony Wotton and Mr. John White*, p. 188.
[93] l.c., p. 190.
[94] l.c., p. 188.
[95] l.c., p. 67.

case another channel must exist for the doctrines that cannot be related to Scripture in such a precise way.

Thus Percy arrives at the notion of extrascriptural traditions: "By this little which I have said, it is apparent enough that the divine Revelation whereupon Christian faith is to be grounded is not contained only in the bare letter of the Scripture, but is also found in the unwritten Traditions of the true Catholic Church".[96] Similar statements recur many times, e.g.: ". . .the divine Revelation, made first to the Prophets and the Apostles, partly recorded in Scriptures, partly preserved in unwritten Traditions";[97] "The words of the text [Jn 10:27] are not limited to signify only the written word, but speak in general of the voice of Christ which, as I have shewed, is partly unwritten";[98] "the Revelation of those things, contained partly in Scriptures, partly in unwritten Traditions".[99] Percy had already made this point in an early volume, *A Treatise of Faith* (1600), which he reprinted in 1614: "The first conclusion is that Scripture alone, especially as it is by Protestants translated into the English tongue, cannot be this rule of faith which here we seek for".[100] In his *True Accounts of Sundry Conferences* (1626), Percy records a debate held in 1622 with the future Archbishop Laud: "I asked how he know Scripture to be Scripture, and in particular Genesis, Exodus, etc. These are believed to be Scripture, yet not proved out of any place of Scripture",[101] a question which he glosses in the following words:

> The Jesuit did not ask this question as doubting of the divine authority of Scripture, but to make it seem that beside Scripture, which the bishop said was the only foundation of faith, there must be admitted some other foundation to wit, unwritten tradition, and this of infallible authority, to assure us infallibly that these books are divine; which to be divine is one point infallibly believed by divine faith, and yet cannot be infallibly proved by only Scripture: therefore "only Scripture" cannot be said, as the bishop said, to be the only foundation of faith or of every point believed by faith.

Laud could not eschew this question by simply answering that "the books of Scripture are principles to be supposed, and needed

---

[96] l.c., p. 73.
[97] l.c., p. 92.
[98] l.c., p. 115.
[99] l.c., p. 128.
[100] *A Treatise of Faith*, 2nd ed., 1614, p. 21.
[101] I quote the text as reprinted in *The Works of William Laud* (Library of Anglo-Catholic Theology), vol. II, Oxford 1849, p. 70.

not to be proved",[102] for a *praecognitum*, in faith as in science, must also be *primo cognitum* without any other *prius cognitum* anticipating it, or Tradition could never "be known first and be an introduction to the knowledge of Scripture",[103] which would be negated by the facts and opposed to what Percy's antagonists readily admit.

If "partly... partly..." seemingly sums up these conceptions neatly, Percy is by no means a determined upholder of the two-source theory of Revelation in the conventional sense of these terms. The Scriptures and the unwritten traditions do not, for him, give us the contents of revelation without the help of a third element:

> This little which I have here said may suffice to show that, besides the divine Revelation made first to the Prophets and Apostles, partly recorded in Scriptures, partly preserved in unwritten Traditions, Church proposition of matters of faith, or the teaching of the present living Pastors of the Church, in such sense as I declared, is necessary; and that there is in it some absolute authority; and that this authority is infallible.[104]

Percy's explanation clarifies the difference between the authority of revelation, contained in Scriptures and traditions, and the authority of the Church that protects and proposes them: "For the written and unwritten word, being the divine Revelation itself, concurs to the assent as the formal reason of the object; whereas Church proposition or affirmation is only a condition, by the ordinary law of God, necessarily requisite to our infallible supernatural assent".[105] In other words, the Scriptures and the traditions contain the revelation, and are the word of God. Yet, in the ordinary course of things, it is by the testimony of the living pastors that the faithful know for certain what is and what is not stated in the Scriptures and the traditions. The magisterium is a condition, but not the object, of faith. It is the guide chosen by God to interpret Scripture and tradition:

> The same Church, which, by the assistance of God's Spirit, has hitherto preserved and shall be always able to preserve true divine Scriptures and to assure us which they be and to distinguish them from apocryphal books... has been and shall always, by the assistance of the promised Spirit, be able to preserve and to assure us which be true divine unwritten Traditions, and to distinguish them from all human

---

[102] l.c., p. 131.
[103] l.c., p. 132.
[104] *Reply* . . ., p. 92.
[105] l.c., p. 95.

inventions, though never so colourably pretended to be divine Traditions.[106]

Percy's insistence on this is couched in terms that anticipate the theology of the nineteenth century: "In the Church, besides the divine infallible written Scriptures, there must be admitted some divine infallible unwritten traditions, and some always living Magistrate".[107] Besides the Scriptures, there must be "unwritten traditions, which are the best ordinary interpreters of Scripture, and some living Magistrate, having infallible authority, who may, when controversies arise, infallibly declare which is the right sense and who by that authority may compel men to take them in that sense". "By doctrine of the Church (I understand) divine doctrine, including therein both the written divine Scriptures and the unwritten divine Traditions, and the true divine interpretation of them both, as by word, writing, sign or otherwise it is or may be propounded and delivered to us by the authority of the Church".[108]

The Church is not extraneous to Scripture and tradition. Rather, these together constitute the Gospel, which is intimately related to the Church: "I shew to my adversaries. . . that, if they do not admit Tradition and Church-authority, they have no sufficient means to know infallibly that the Gospel itself is Scripture. The force of which argument is grounded in the mutual connexion which is betwixt the Gospel and Church-authority, either of which bears witness of the other, as our Saviour did bear witness of St. John Baptist and St. John Baptist of our Saviour".[109] Percy adds that by divine infused faith one "may be assured both of the authority of Scripture and of the Church, and of the mutual connexion which they have one with the other, and of the reciprocal proof and testimony which they give and receive from the other".

So far, John Percy's conceptions represent a rather sophisticated approach to the problem of Scripture and tradition as seen within the larger question of the nature of the act of faith. By placing this question in the context of the theology of faith, Percy was opening new ground. By seeking a solution in the inseparable interrelationship of three terms, Scriptures, traditions, and magisterium, he was also

---

[106] l.c., p. 74.
[107] l.c., p. 184.
[108] l.c., p. 203.
[109] l.c., p. 99.

anticipating later developments. His division of revealed doctrines into two kinds, written and unwritten, was, in the writings that have been mentioned, unequivocal, and expressed in the expression "partly, partly", which had been discarded at the Council of Trent. In this matter Percy fits the commonplace view of Counter-Reformation theology, exalting the magisterium at the expense of the primacy of Scripture and of the originality of tradition.

However, the clarity of this "Counter-Reformation" view may be more apparent than real. For an anonymous volume of 1626, which is also ascribed to Percy-Fisher, the epistle dedicatory being signed I.F., adopts a different position. In this, *The Answer unto the Nine Points of Controversy Proposed by Our Late Sovereign unto M. Fisher, and the Rejoinder unto the Reply of D. Francis White, Minister*, the sufficiency of Scripture is unhesitantly acknowledged in a Catholic sense: "The Scripture, to them that know Tradition, is abundantly sufficient, but without Tradition not".[110] With sufficiency, there goes a primacy of Scripture in the Church, which the author formulates clearly in explaining a sentence of the medieval schoolman Durand de Saint-Pourçain (*Ecclesia, licet Dei dominationem habeat in terris, illa tamen non excedit limitationem Scripturae*): "His meaning is that the Church, though it have the authority of God upon earth, yet the same power is in some cases restrained and limited by Scripture. In which respect the Church cannot dispense in many things wherein God might dispense".[111] The Church is bound by Scripture, which her authority does not give her the power to contradict.

Yet the primacy of Scripture, or the limit that Scripture imposes to Church authority, cannot make Scripture sufficient by itself. As Percy adds, "Now what is that to the purpose of proving that men are bound to believe nothing but what is clearly contained in Scripture?"[112] The insufficiency of Holy Writ's clear contents is well expressed in Percy's exposition of the thought of the Tridentine theologian Pedro Soto: Soto "delivers two things: First, that the things concerning matters, not only of faith, but also of good life that are common and must be known of all Christians, are largely delivered in Holy Scripture. Secondly, that *post haec omnia*, after the knowledge of all these common substantial matters, as for other

---

[110] *The Answer unto the nine points of Controversy*, p. 141.
[111] l.c., pp. 137-138.
[112] l.c., p. 138.

particular things, they are to be learned by Tradition more than by Scripture".[113] These "other particular things" are "not the main duties of latria and religion, but reverential carriage and ceremonies to be used in the administration of the sacraments".

---

[113] l.c., p. 148.

CHAPTER TWO

THE JUDGE OF CONTROVERSIES

The authors we have hitherto surveyed treat our topic occasionally, according as the debates of their times raised the problem of authority in the Church. In the first decades of the century, however, there already started what was to become a remarkable series of monographs and even treatises on Scripture and on Tradition, a series which, as we shall see, gives great if unacknowledged importance to the English seventeenth century in the history of the Catholic theology of Tradition. The works of two men should be analyzed now, before we arrive at the longer studies that appeared toward the middle of the century.

Edward Maihew (1570-1625) a secular priest educated at Douai and Rome like so many of his contemporaries, joined the Order of St Benedict in 1607 while he was missioneering in England. He later functioned as Prior at Dieulouard in Lorraine for several years. Trying his hand at theological controversy, Maihew achieved better than the average, with *A Treatise of the Grounds of the Old and New Religion* (1608). The "grounds of religion", as outlined by him, extend much further than what most of us would understand by these terms, to the point of including a detailed explanation of the obvious. Thus the three "principal grounds" of the "old religion" are: that there is a God (Ch. 1); that the soul of men is immortal (Ch. 2); that Christian religion is the true worship of God (Ch. 3). At the fourth ground (Ch. 4) we enter the controversial field of the Catholic-Protestant disputes: "that among Christians, they only that profess and embrace the Catholic faith and religion are in state of salvation and do truly worship God". The remaining chapters of the first part of the book (chapters 5 to 12) explain this principle in a wisely progressive way, initiating the readers to "the definition and conditions of true faith" (ch. 5), to "the supreme and infallible authority of the Catholic Church" (ch. 6), and to the "particular grounds of Catholic religion", which are the Holy Scriptures (ch. 7), the Apostolic Traditions (ch. 8), the General Councils (ch. 9), the "decrees of the supreme visible pastor of the Catholic Church" (ch. 10), and the "consent of the ancient Fathers" (ch. 11).

After a short conclusion (ch. 12), Maihew passes to the more polemical section of his treatise, where he examines the grounds of the "new religion". This second part purports to show that Protestants in fact deny the principal grounds of the old religion (ch. 1), wreck the faith (ch. 2), destroy the Church's infallibility (ch. 3), deny all particular grounds of Christian religion except the Scriptures (ch. 4 to 8), and even, contradicting themselves, do not abide by the Scriptures (ch. 9). A short conclusion follows (ch. 10).

These two parts carefully balance each other, the same questions being covered with more serenity in the first than in the second, which features a more negative approach than the first.

The general outlay of Maihew's thought appears clearly from his plan. In order to guide us over the principal grounds of religion, God has granted us "our holy Mother the Catholic Church, the sacred spouse of Christ and his mystical body",[1] who has been endowed with "life and reason" and is therefore "apt to instruct and judge". To achieve this, the Church has been given "in her sacred bosom other more particular but divine and infallible grounds, besides his holy written word, whereby we are to be directed in faith". Maihew's method, like that of James Gordon, uses three points of reference: the Scriptures ("I bring forth proofs out of the Holy Scripture"), the Fathers ("I allege the ancient Fathers and writers, such as lived and wrote in the first six hundred years after Christ, which some Protestants challenge to have been of their faith and religion and therefore allow of their testimonies"), Protestants themselves ("I cite moreover the sentences of diverse sectaries of these our days"). Maihew, who is more fair-minded and objective than most of his colleagues, excludes all those who are "commonly by Protestants censured to be heretics", and adduces only the opinions of such as are "usually by all sorts acknowledged to be writers of their Protestant family and members, as they say, of their Reformed Churches".[2]

No difficulty, according to Edward Maihew, arises regarding the authority of most biblical books. The points about which there is "much difference" [3] between us and our adversaries, concern "the means by which we know the holy Scriptures. . . to be the true word of God", "the true sense and interpretation" of Scripture, which is

---

[1] *Treatise of the grounds of the Old and New Religion*, 1608, 1st part, p. 3.
[2] l.c., p. 7.
[3] l.c., p. 62.

"a far greater controversy",[4] and finally the existence of a "certain and infallible guide".[5]

The first point is taken up in the usual way: only the Church can tell us which books are canonical. Under Maihew's pen, however, this comes as a statement of fact rather than of principle. For when he further ponders over the reason why "we prove the Scripture to be canonical by the authority of the Church", he answers simply that this is "surely for no other reason than because the Church is better known to us than Scripture".[6] The Church, visible, historically established, testified to by so many well-known witnesses, constitutes an obvious source of information about the Scriptures. In terms of causality one could not claim that the Church is the "formal cause", but only a "conditional cause" of receiving the Scriptures.[7] To say that belief in Scripture is founded on Tradition is tantamount to the same: "For the certainty of the Tradition of the Church and of the testimony of the ancient Fathers depends on this that the Church cannot err".[8] In spite of appearances, however, Maihew has mixed two arguments here: the factual idea that the Church does act as a visible guide to know what Scriptures are canonical; and the different notion, which he has previously established (ch. 6), yet which certainly escapes the order of the visible, that the Church cannot err. In any case, Maihew underlines the principle of the supremacy of the Scriptures. That we enquire of the Church about the Scriptures is no more a disgrace to them, "than it was unto Christ that the Apostles gave testimony to him, because they were better known than he".[9] "Neither is this", he insists,

> anyways prejudicial to the dignity and authority of the holy Scripture: for this notwithstanding, we confess that the said Scripture is of far greater authority than the Church or her definitions be; which is manifest because although the Holy Ghost assist and direct the writers of Holy Scripture and the Church; yet certain it is that he has assisted and directed the first after a far more excellent manner than he does the second. . . .[10]

God's assistance protects only the infallible truth of what a general Council or the Bishop of Rome "intend to define", whereas it guaran-

[4] l.c., p. 67.
[5] l.c., p. 75.
[6] l.c., p. 62.
[7] l.c., p. 65.
[8] l.c., p. 67.
[9] l.c., p. 63.
[10] l.c., p. 62.

tees "every sentence" in the Scriptures to be "of the most certain
verity". This distinction between the Spirit's watchfulness over the
Church and his inspiration of the sacred writers will often be found
expressed by our authors.

The sense and interpretation of Scripture raises a much more
complex problem which lies at the root of what Maihew deems to be
the central controversy between Catholics and Protestants: it ushers
in what English Catholics in the seventeenth century will increasingly
see as the main question behind all disagreements on Scripture and
Tradition, namely, Who is judge of controversies in religion? "A
far greater controversy there is between us and the new sectaries",
Maihew explains, "concerning the true sense and interpretation of
holy Scripture, who is the judge thereof, and of whom we are to
receive it".[11]

The problem, as described here, stems from a series of facts on
which every one agrees: [12] the obscurity of the biblical language,
"sundry words" of which admit many senses and are therefore of
doubtful interpretation; the variety of "*genres*", since "many sentences'
are "prophetical, many parabolical, many metaphorical, which
commonly are full of obscurity"; the multiplicity of "senses under
one letter". With most medieval theology, our Benedictine holds
that the literal sense of the Bible, "which is that which the holy
writers first intended", and which—a source of compounded mysti-
fication—may be signified by the words used, either properly and
literally or improperly and figuratively, may itself be manifold.
With all Catholic theology to date, he also seeks for "a spiritual
sense, which is that which is signified by the things under the letter",
and he lists the usual trilogy: "This sense is either moral, which is also
called tropological, when it tends to manners; or allegorical when it
tends to faith or the Church; or anagogical when it tends to heaven
or life everlasting". It does happen—and, if we are to believe Maihew,
"not seldom"—that several of these senses together are intended by
the Holy Spirit in one and the same sentence. In these conditions we
may well exclaim with him: "And what a difficult matter is it to
discern them?" Adding to this the inner intricacy of the spiritual
mysteries revealed by Holy Writ and the bent of individual minds to
error, we can only agree that understanding the Scriptures implies
untying a very hard knot.

[11] l.c., p. 67.
[12] l.c., pp. 68-69.

In order to grasp the meaning of Scripture, one should in the first place compare the different passages that may refer to the same mystery, bearing in mind that "all the Scripture was penned by the instinct of the Holy Ghost and consequently is true: wherefore, if something more be said in one thing than in another, the one is not to be corrected or altered by the other, for both may be very well consonant unto truth".[13] The principle that all is true goes hand in hand with the fundamental axiom, that there can be no real contradiction between Scripture and the Church. Accordingly, since the better known should throw light on the lesser known, and the Church is better known, it follows that "the Scriptures ought to be interpreted according to the rule of faith, that is, the whole sum of Christian religion preserved as a *depositum* in the Church".[14] Both knowledge of the rule of faith and light from the Holy Spirit are therefore required to understand Scripture. Exegesis becomes a prophetic experience. In the second Epistle of Peter "the word prophecy signifies the interpretation or exposition of holy Scripture".[15] But "prophecy according to the rule, proportion or analogue of faith is one of the gifts God bestows upon his Church".[16] Should a private person boast of this gift, one should, on St John's advice, "prove the spirits if they be of God". Yet this will be a difficult judgment to arrive at for a man who is himself subject to error, so that the safest way to reach a sound conclusion concerning the gift of prophecy is to judge a man by his fruits. And among the fruits of Christian life one must count humility and obedience: "He that has the knowledge of God by true supernatural faith, hears and obeys the Church".[17] In conclusion, Maihew paraphrases Peter ("No prophecy of Scripture is made by private interpretation", II Peter 1:20), in these words: "No exposition of Scripture ought to be made according to any man's private fancy, but according to the doctrine and sense of the Church",[18] whom God "has warranted from error, whose authority he has made the rule of our belief, who has the custody of holy Scriptures and from whom we receive them, and infallibly know them to contain the true word of God".[19] Not only does the New

---

[13] 2nd Part, p. 141.
[14] l.c., pp. 151-152.
[15] 1st Part, p. 70; see pp. 75-76.
[16] l.c., p. 75.
[17] l.c., p. 71.
[18] l.c., p. 76.
[19] l.c., p. 77.

Testament itself teach this hermeneutical method; the Fathers also have constantly advocated it and the church has used it in the "condemnation of all heretics together with their false translations and erroneous expositions of the said Scriptures".

The analogy or rule of faith, which Maihew also calls the *depositum fidei*, serves as the touchstone of scriptural prophecy or interpretation. The Church, endowed with the Spirit's gift, is the judge, so that all private expositors must look to her and read Scripture in keeping with her doctrines. This will ensure, "by the divine censure and approbation of the Church", that "both the letter and the sense are of divine authority".[20]

If therefore Christian doctrine is indeed present in Scripture it cannot reside in "bare words" as Maihew points out through the following reasoning:

> The rule and ground of Catholic faith ought to be one (that is, not diverse), certain and manifest: but the bare words of Scripture alone cannot be such a rule, because the Scriptures are obscure, may be falsely and erroneously interpreted, etc., wherefore the sense of them is not one, certain and manifest: therefore the bare words of Scripture are not the only rule and ground of Catholic faith.[21]

Maihew finds that not all Protestants explain the principle of *Scriptura sola* in the same way. For some, the bare letter contains all doctrine clearly, which is, to him, an absurd thing to believe, for, were it true, there could be no disagreement among Protestants. Others "fly to deduction out of Scripture, and answer, that although the words are not expressly found in the Bible, yet that the mysteries themselves are expressly in it contained and delivered; and consequently that the words aptly signifying the said mysteries, and deduced out of the word of God itself, may very well and conveniently be used".[22] This is actually a very good description of how Catholics may conceive the inclusion of all Christian doctrine in Scripture: if it is not there in so many words, it is adumbrated in the scriptural presentation of the mysteries that doctrine expresses. However, the Protestant handling of this view leaves Maihew dissatisfied: "I reply that this is not sufficient". One misses here a correct understanding of who is able to effect such a deduction: one has thus been

---

[20] l.c., p. 78; see 2nd Part, p. 83, pp. 151-152.
[21] 2nd Part, p. 80.
[22] l.c., p. 75.

brought back to the question of what judge is to pass sentence in case disputes arise.

A private man, left to his own devices, may make a "wrong exposition, erroneously gathered out of the letter of holy Scripture, or made upon the same". Then, we have "not the word of God, but the word of man; yes, sometimes the word of the devil".[23] This is a strong proposition, yet is well expresses the basic conviction that "the Scripture is the true word of God in that sense only which was intended at the penning of it by the Holy Ghost". In other words, only he who knows the sense of the Spirit, which is the Catholic doctrine, can find it with certainty in the Scriptures; and, in ultimate analysis, the Church alone knows it immediately, and only those who follow her can eventually light upon the true meaning of the Scriptures.

It may of course still be asked in what way the meaning of Scripture is known to the Church, by what paths the doctrine of revelation comes to her and in what form it subsists there. Maihew answers: "The principal means for the entire preservation of it in the Church without corruption or depravation, ordained by God almighty, is the continual assistance and direction of the Holy Ghost, who always remains in the Church and directs her in all truth".[24] Yet to rely on the Spirit's guidance does not solve the problem of what form this guidance takes once it is embodied in the human actions of the men who constitute the Church. Edward Maihew's reply to this type of question surfaces in a description of Tradition which, though long, deserves to be cited in full:

> What then did the Apostles and disciples expressly set down in those their monuments which are contained in the New Testament? A part only, without all doubt, of the whole sum of Christian belief, in which part they ratified and confirmed the supreme and infallible authority of the Church, of whom the rest was to be learned and to whose custody they committed their said monuments: so that the whole sum or *depositum* has been kept and preserved in the Church, not all and only in express terms in holy Scripture, but the whole by Tradition, and a part of that whole also by writing, another part by only Tradition, by which likewise the said Scripture itself came to our hands. And after this sort the whole corps of Christian religion without any alteration descended unto us. This may be proved by that which has already been said concerning the true sense and exposition of holy Scripture: for, as I have shown, the Scripture ought to be interpreted

---

[23] 1st Part, p. 72.
[24] l.c., p. 87.

according to the analogy or rule of faith, that is to say, according to that belief which the Church by Tradition has received from Christ and his Apostles; wherefore the letter of the holy Scripture is not the whole direction of the faith of the Church; but the faith of the Church, the perfect and full direction of the said letter of the holy Scripture, of which it follows that the faith of the holy Church might have remained sound and entire by Tradition, although no such letter had been published.[25]

In reference to the recent problem of the "material sufficiency" of Scripture—a scholastic phrasing which I prefer to avoid—Maihew's central position would appear to be pithily expressed in the words: "the whole by Tradition, and a part of that whole also by writing, another part by only Tradition".[26] Regarding the form in which the deposit has been transmitted, the focus would seem to be on the fact that "the whole corps of Christian religion without any alternation descended unto us"; in other words, an unchanging set of doctrines has been handed down from the Apostles. Here, Maihew's insights, keen as they were, did not extend so far as to perceive that doctrine might develop. Yet, as regards the mutual relationships of Church and Scripture—which, I believe, raise the real problem underlying all others—Maihew penned a beautiful epitome of his thought in the statement that "the letter of the holy Scripture is not the whole direction of the faith of the Church; but the faith of the Church, the perfect and full direction" of the letter.

In this rationale, the Scriptures do remain so important a factor in the "direction" of the faith, that Maihew, afraid lest his formulation has gone too far or may lead others to undermine the dignity of Scripture, adds this corollary:

> Neither does this our doctrine any ways diminish the authority of holy Scriptures: for this notwithstanding, we affirm that the wonderful providence of almighty God most wisely ordained that the Scriptures of the New Testament should be written, that he moved the penners thereof thereunto, and directed them by his divine inspiration; and this both for the conservation and preservation of the faith and Tradition of the Church; and also that the said Tradition might with ease come to everyone's knowledge and that everyone by such monuments might learn to discern the true Church, of which he was to be instructed concerning all matters of faith and religion.[27]

---

[25] l.c., p. 78.
[26] l.c., p. 89.
[27] l.c., p. 91.

Maihew does not explain as clearly as desirable in what manner Scripture, besides referring readers to the true Church for their enlightenment, helps to preserve faith and Tradition. Yet the relation of Scripture and Tradition acquires a more definite shape if, with Maihew, we see a major difference between the distinct and certain status of the articles of faith in the Church's Tradition, and their infolded condition within Scripture: "I say, it is one thing probably to deduce an article of faith out of the Scripture, another thing to be expressly and plainly contained in it. We only by probable conjectures prove some Traditions out of holy Scripture, especially against heretics which deny Traditions and approve the Scripture. Nevertheless, by supernatural faith we believe them, because they are such Traditions".[28] In other words, faith is not founded on the scriptural seeds of all Christian beliefs, but on their clear blooming in Tradition. Faith believes Tradition, and theology illustrates it with Scripture. The first "particular ground" of Christian religion stems directly from the Spirit for the Church's enlightenment, but the second "particular ground", although it derives, not directly from the Spirit, but from the Church with He guides, turns out to be more universal and, accordingly, more fundamental than the first.

Maihew is lucid enough, and knowledgeable enough with Protestant writing, to recognize that the Catholic position lies open to a major criticism, which he voices and rebuts most carefully. Catholics, their adversaries claim, argue in a circle:

> For in this chapter I have affirmed the canonical Scriptures and their true interpretations to be known by the infallible authority of the Church; whereas before I proved the authority of the Church to be infallible by the testimony of holy Scriptures; wherefore it may seem that I have made a circle or, as M. Field calls it, a circulation.[29]

At this point, Maihew breaks relatively new ground by connecting the theology of Scripture and Tradition with the theology of faith. For the proposed objection raises, by implication, the question of the structure of the act of faith. "The full solution of this objection", Maihew writes, "depends on the resolution of a question which to some appears very intricate and hard, to wit: unto what we lastly resolve our faith, whether to the authority of the Church or of the Scriptures, or to some human motives?"

---

[28] l.c., p. 96.
[29] l.c., p. 78.

Our learned Benedictine outlines two theologies of faith, which we may identify briefly. In the one, which he connects with Stapleton, faith is led first by human reasons, by "inducements or arguments of credibility",[30] until God creates the formal cause of it by inserting a divine light into the mind, which is thus enabled to believe super-naturally what it was hitherto led to accept for human motives. In this case, faith is ultimately resolved and grounded in the divine revelation to which assent is given thanks to the divine light. Both Scripture and Church count among the elements the consideration of which urges man to believe. Obviously, such a theology undergoes no circular reasoning; it is divine revelation which makes the authority of the Church, as an article of faith, known by reading Scripture, just as it also makes the truth of Scripture known through the Church's authority. Divine revelation itself is not reducible to anything else.[31]

The second opinion, which Maihew favors, willingly upholds the apparent circle to which adversaries object, inasmuch as it affirms "both that we believe the authority of the Church to be infallible because it is revealed in holy Scripture; and also that we infallibly know the Scriptures to be canonical because as canonical they are propounded to us by the Church".[32] Yet Maihew refuses to see a vicious circle in this, for the meaning of 'because' is not the same on both sides. The causality in question denotes a formal cause, divine Revelation, only in the first case, where the Church's authority is formally revealed in the Scriptures. In the second case, the Church is not a formal cause but only a necessary condition of the knowledge of Scripture.

Thus, "the respects be diverse in the proof of the infallible authority of the Church by Scripture, and of Scripture by the infallible authority of the Church".[33] One may still wonder if perceiving Revelation in Scripture is not formally caused by something else. But Maihew is adamant: "Not by any other divine Revelation, because this is the last".[34] "The cause why we believe such a Revelation is no other Revelation but itself". The Church acts only as a condition or means. The edge of the objection is further dulled by the fact that "the objects of these two reasons yielded of our belief are diverse";

---

[30] l.c., p. 85.
[31] l.c., pp. 78-82; 85.
[32] l.c., p. 82.
[33] l.c., p. 83.
[34] l.c., p. 84.

scriptural Revelation shows "the verities or things as themselves revealed and believed", whereas the Church's proposition bears on "the revelations themselves contained in said Scriptures". Thus, although belief in Scripture and belief in the Church are grounded in one another, the experience of faith, far from turning upon itself in a circle, follows a straight line: the Church points to the Scriptures so that we may find Revelation in them, and we discern this scriptural Revelation thanks to the light of Revelation itself.

Faced with this accusation of circular reasoning, Matthew Kellison's *Examen Reformationis Novae* (1616) will give a slightly different answer, denying that the circle in question is vicious: "In a demonstration *quia* and *propter quid* there is a circle, by which we prove the cause by its effect and the effect by its cause. Yet it is not a vicious circle. For since the effect or result is better known to us than its cause, it is correct to prove the cause by the effect. And since the cause is naturally better known than the effect or result, it is correct in a demonstration *propter quid* to prove by a cause that the result is inherent in a subject." [35] It is only when both are equally known that the circle is logically objectionable because it contributes nothing to knowledge. The problem is therefore practical rather than speculative: Catholic knowledge of Scripture and of the Church is not based on a circle. Yet Catholics should be careful to find out what kind of person they are talking to before attempting to establish the authority of Scripture by that of the Church or vice versa, for their argument has no value if these are on the same level in the mind of their interlocutors.

Sylvester Norris, who will be considered next in this chapter, gave a more complete answer in *The Guide of Faith* (1621), where he followed more closely Maihew's problematic. Here also, the objection is refuted on the basis of "the last resolution of our belief", which is neither, for Norris, the Scripture nor the Church, but "the divine authority, which is the formal object of faith and of infinite force and ability to persuade immediately by itself without the help of any other formal inducement whatsoever".[36] The Catholic Church is only the proposer of the articles to be believed on divine authority;

[35] *Examen Reformationis Novae*, 1616: *Nam inter demonstrationem quia et propter quid reperitur quidam circulus quo causam probamus per effectum et hunc etiam per causam, qui tamen non est vitiosus, quia cum effectus seu passio notior sit nobis quam causa, recte potest per effectum probari causa; et quia causa est notior natura quam effectus vel passio, rectissime in demonstratione propter quid probamus passionem inesse subjecto per causam* (p. 39).
[36] *The Guide of Faith*, p. 68.

and its reliability is established by arguments of credibility. "Thus no round or circulation is made, because the selfsame thing is not proved but after a diverse and several manner".[37]

Norris, however, adds three other ways of escaping circular reasoning. The second way is the same as Kellison's practical consideration: arguments from only Scripture are valid for those who accept Scripture and deny the Church, and reverse arguments are good in the opposite case. Thirdly, "that idle circle is declined when we canonize the Scriptures by the testimony of the present Church, and prove the Church by the interpretation of Scriptures not made by the same Church which now is or lately was in the Council of Trent, but so expounded by the ancient Church in former days".[38] Finally, no absurdity attaches to an apparent circle if this is not the only reasoning in favor of Church authority, for in that case the scriptural arguments are supported "with such evident reasons or persuasible motives as are prudently judged to proceed from God".[39]

As we shall see, the objection of circular reasoning was there to stay, and other authors will try to answer it.

To return to Maihew, it would seem that his view of the relationship of Scripture and the Church would also apply to Tradition and the Church: the Church brings us the apostolic Revelation contained in Tradition, and we believe it in the light of Revelation itself. In neither case is there a circle, for the ecclesiastical Traditions which orient us toward the apostolic Traditions are no more equated with these than with the Scriptures: in one of his rare falls from perfect courtesy, Maihew indignantly retorts to the Anglican Field that "that which he says, that we make Traditions ecclesiastical equal with the written word of God, is one of his ordinary untruths".[40] In a more academic vein, he remarks that the mutual support which Scripture and Tradition bring to each other in Catholic theology has a name in good logic: "It is not called a circulation but a demonstrative regress".[41]

With Edward Maihew the quarrel concerning Scripture and Tradition has been raised to a higher level than would have been possible in the more polemical orientation of most of his colleagues. Above

---

[37] l.c., p. 69.
[38] l.c., pp. 69-70.
[39] l.c., p. 70.
[40] *Treatise of the grounds of the Old and New Religion*, 1st Part, p. 96.
[41] l.c., p. 85.

all, the problems are now being narrowed down and focused toward essentials. For Maihew the main hinges of the Catholic position concern the dialectic of spirit and letter; scriptural interpretation; Tradition as the whole in which Scripture has a part, and indeed the most important one; and the act of faith as the setting where the mutual inherence of Scripture and Church implies no vicious circle.

One point has been touched upon several times already without being exploited to the full. This is the question, already set at the center of the stage by James Gordon and his translator, of who is "judge of controversies" in matters of religion. One of Maihew's contemporaries, writing a few years later, happily pursued this line of enquiry and brought the debate one step forward. Sylvester Norris (1572-1630), alias M. Smith, or, in the usual signature of his books, N.S., had been ordained in Rome in 1596, was arrested in England and exiled after the so-called Gunpowder Plot (1605), entered the Society of Jesus in 1606 and spent most of his remaining years doing missionary work in England.

Norris left several polemical works, of which the most important, *An Antidote*, published in three parts in 1615, 1619 and 1621, is an ambitious project, the comprehensive design of which is well suggested by its full title:

> *An Antidote, or sovereign remedy against the pestiferous writings of all English sectaries, and in particular against D. Whitaker, D. Fulke, D. Bilson, D. Reynolds, D. Sparkes and D. Field, the chief upholders, some of Protestancy, some of Puritanism—divided into three parts, in which the chiefest points of faith, called in question by the Protestants of our times, is* (sic) *explained, defended and their principal objections answered.*

In 1623, Norris pursued his publishing ventures with a volume in which he developed some of the arguments of the *Antidote*: *The Pseudo-Scripturist, or a treatise wherein is proved that the written Word of God (though most sacred, reverend and divine) is not the sole judge of Controversies in faith and religion, against the prime sectaries of these times who contend to maintain the contrary.* The following year, our author also published *A True Report of the private colloquy between M. Smith and M. Walker,* which need not detain us here.

Norris's project and its wide scope are clearly explained at the beginning of the *Antidote*: "My purpose is not severally to encounter any one particular adversary, but to trace the steps and jointly to descry the errors of many. . . for my intention is to wade, with God's help, into the main ocean of all the greatest and most difficult questions controverted at this day between our English Protestants and us".[42] Norris selects the ablest Protestant authors he can find for each point, so that, the best being overthrown, all their adherents be "put to flight". His own arguments he intends to draw mainly "out of the Word of God, the heavenly treasure and touchstone of truth, out of the ancient Fathers, and for the most part also out of general Councils, out of the secret bowels and instinct of Nature, out of the discourse of reason, and lastly out of the undeniable writings and testimonies of our adversaries".[43] Norris divides his subject-matter into a series of "controversies", the first two of which, fundamental to all the others, deal with our problems: "That the Holy Scripture itself cannot be judge of controversies, against Doctor Whitaker, Doctor Reynolds and all other Protestants", and "That all things necessary to salvation are not contained in Scripture, against D. Reynold, D. Bilson and D. Field".

The Pseudo-Scripturist covers the same ground in a different way. In the first part "it is disputed *categorice* and absolutely that the Scripture is not the judge of Controversies";[44] in the second, "it is disputed *hypothetice* that, supposing for the time that the Scripture (as it is simply considered in itself) were the judge of Controversies", Protestants are in the worst position to gain from its judgements.

With his deep mistrust of Protestants, Norris contrasts most unfavorably the Reformers' reliance on *Scriptura sola* with the Catholic recourse to Scripture. The former do "appeal in all matters of controversy to the sole and silent majesty of God's sacred style",[45] but they pursue a deceitful goal, for they only want to "cloak their new device under the mysteries of Holy Writ"; they use Scripture as a "cunning and new device to avoid indeed all manner of trial". This is totally different from what Catholics do when, following the Church Fathers, they "maintain the sufficiency of Scripture in all necessary points of faith",[46] an expression which, in a Catholic mouth, is liable to have four possible meanings. *First*, it may mean "that the Scripture is taught to contain all things necessary to salvation, as the universal ground, seed or root from which whatsoever we believe

---

[42] *An Antidote* . . ., Epistle to the Reader, n. 3.
[43] l.c., n. 5.
[44] *The Pseudo-Scripturist*, preface.
[45] *An Antidote* . . ., p. 2.
[46] l.c., p. 40-41.

may either mediately or immediately be gathered": this Norris attributes to Cyril and Chrysostom. A *second* interpretation of the sentence is that "it teaches and directs us to the authority of the Church and doctrine of her pastors, by which every point is or may be particularly and clearly explained": this is traceable to Vincent "and others". *Third*, it may also suggest that "nothing besides the Scriptures is to be admitted, to wit, no private customs or particular traditions not agreeable or repugnant to the written word": this sense may be found in Basil, Cyril, Jerome and Augustine. *Fourth*, Scripture is quite sufficient "to conclude, even in plain and express words, certain main principles of our faith", like the creation of all things by God (Tertullian) or the condemnation of idolatry (Athanasius); and one may admit, with Augustine, that "It clearly comprehends the chief articles of our Creed and ten commandments".

These interpretations are not mutually exclusive. None of them hints or implies that Scripture can be fully understood without the Church's assistance, which is the main point to exclude in order to read the sentence in a Catholic way. Yet the second and third play on the word "sufficiency", taking it in less than its average strength. The first and the last on the contrary uphold a true sufficiency of Scripture, which teaches plainly and expressly the main points of faith and morals, implicitly and remotely all others. This is the usual sense of the term in Catholic writing, patristic, medieval or modern, which is summed up in *The Guide of Faith* (the special title of the third part of *The Antidote*) in these words:

> Faith is by hearing; neither do the Scriptures expound themselves or express the meaning of their hidden mysteries, but everywhere sends (*sic*) us to our pastors and teachers to hear from their mouths and suck from their lips the stream of life.[47]

In *The Pseudo-Scripturist*, Norris drives the same point home in a different way. The Scriptures are given their due as "the spiritual conduits whereby are derived to us the highest mysteries of our faith";[48] their sense is "a most powerful physic against the poisonous receipts of all heretical distillations".[49] Yet, in the first place, the true faith is not to be found "in the leaves of the words but in the roots of the sense", which points up the need for a "true and in-

---

[47] *The Guide of Faith*, p. 39.
[48] *The Pseudo-Scripturist*, p. 2.
[49] l.c., p. 3.

dubious interpretation". In the second place, Scripture belongs in a wider context: "We grant that the written word is *regula partialis*, but not *regula totalis* of faith and religion". This brings Norris to a minimal formulation of the scriptural principle: "We admit some things *praeter Scripturam*, but nothing *contra Scripturam*; that is, we approve some things not expressly found in the Scripture, but not any thing contrary or repugnant to the Scripture".[50] In a rather long but clear passage, Norris concludes to the relative sufficiency of Scripture as he understands it:

> They (i.e., the Catholics) grant that in the like reserved construction the Scripture may be said to deliver all things sufficiently which belong to faith and religion: and this not only because it delivers evidently all those articles of faith which are simply and absolutely necessary for all men to know (as the articles of our Creed, the Decalogue and those sacraments which are more necessary) but also in that all other points whatsoever, concerning either the true exposition of the written word or faith and religion in general, are warranted by the infallible authority of the Church, which infallible authority is proved and commended to us by the holy Scripture. And thus on the one side the Scripture warranting the Church's authority, and on the other the Church setting down and approving the true sense of the Scripture, it may hereupon be justly said that both these (I mean the Church and the Scripture) do interchangeably receive their proof out of the proof they give.[51]

Such a position does not mitigate the Catholic regard for Traditions. For evidently the sufficiency of Scripture is to be understood in the context of its function, which consists in being, in Norris's words, "the written or outward rule by which sentence is or ought to be guided".[52] In this analogy of the lawbook and the judge, which our Catholics borrow so frequently, the scope of Scripture remains universal: it functions as the "written law" does "in all courts, commonwealths, or public tribunals". Yet it would remain a dead letter unless a judge proceeded "to expound and deliver the true meaning of the law". Thus one may stress the high dignity of Scripture in this universal role, as well as its lacking the qualities required in a judge.

Norris does both. He does not shrink from singing this splendid yet carefully qualified encomium:

---

[50] l.c., pp. 3-4.
[51] l.c., p. 4.
[52] *An Antidote . . .*, p. 3.

Thus we are so far from derogating from the prerogative of Holy Writ, as we grant it is a perfect light and lantern to our feet. The entire rule and square of faith. The supreme and absolute judge of controversies. Thus we grant that it is the mine of truth, the fountain of life, the sea of wisdom, the armory of the Holy Ghost. It is the promptuary of God fully stored with all spiritual treasures: yet such are to be dispensed by the stewards of his house. It is, as Optatus noted, the will and testament of Christ, yet to be interpreted by those his executors whom he appointed to expound his mind and dispose his legacy. It is the book of heaven signed with seven seals, as Origen says, but not to be opened by any but by the Lion of the tribe of Juda, or them to whom he gave commission. It is, as another avers, the light of the world, not to be hidden under the bushel of any private or fantastical brain, but to be placed on the candlestick of God's Church to give light unto all her obedient children.[53]

The analogy of the law-book and the judge was so central to Norris's understanding of the function of Scripture that he dedicated *The Pseudo-Scripturist* "to the right honorable and reverend judges of England, and the other grave sages of the Law", deeming these, as he explained in his preface, particularly able to understand the true place of Scripture and the exact function of the Church as Judge of Controversies. Admittedly, Norris was willing to call Scripture a Judge, but only "in a restrained sense", insofar as "it appoints and sets down who is that Judge, to wit, the Church".[54] He was also willing to consider seriously the hypothesis that Scripture is the sole Judge, and to abide by the result. For, as the title of one of the chapters of *The Pseudo-Scripturist* has it, "That supposing the Scripture as Judge, yet the Letter thereof is more clear and perspicuous for the Catholics than for the Protestants".[55] In the main, however, the analogy of the law-book and the Judge points to the built-in qualifications of any Catholic acknowledgement of the sufficiency of Scripture. In vain do some Protestants object that "the voice of God" speaking in Scripture is the sole sovereign judge of controveries. For "the voice of God as speaking in Scripture is no way distinguished from the Scripture"; it states the law, it formulates the Gospel, it sows the seeds of all Christian doctrines, yet it still needs another voice to apply it and to solve the doubts arising about it. "Therefore", Norris reasons, "as besides the king speaking in his law, either himself speaking in a more lively manner, or some other

---

[53] l.c., p. 27.
[54] *The Pseudo-Scripturist*, p. 4.
[55] l.c., 2nd part, ch. 8, p. 95.

judge is requisite to satisfy the doubts which arise of the law; so besides the Holy Ghost speaking precisely by Scripture, either himself speaking in a more distinct and public fashion, or some other infallible judge is necessary to end the controversies which arise out of Scripture".[56] This theme recurs in *A Guide of Faith*: the Scriptures are "the outward law, the compass, the square"; yet the law is dumb, the level and square "not able to direct without the guide of the architect".[57] If we insist on calling Scripture a Judge, we then must say:

> The Scriptures are the dead and silent, the Church the lively, speaking and intelligible Judge, more easy than the Scriptures, more ancient than the Scriptures, more necessary than the Scriptures. . . Therefore although the Scriptures have a kind of judgement (as the inanimate law can judge) together with the Church, yet the Church is the principal, primary, supreme and most irreprovable voice in this spiritual consistory or court of religion.[58]

Sylvester Norris thus looks for a living voice applying and explaining the written text. Whereas this by no means restricts the universality and binding force of the text, it demands someone or something other than the text, which, in conjunction with it, will constitute the ultimate tribunal of Christianity. This judge of controversies should be endowed with qualities which are lacking from Scripture. For he must be "infallible", yet "albeit the Scriptures be so in themselves, yet in respect of us they are fallible: they may be erroneously printed, corruptly translated, falsely suborned, not well expounded, not rightly understood".[59] He must be "clear and facile", whereas Scripture is "hard, dark and hidden". He ought to "deliver his mind in all ambiguous cases as the parties in strife may evidently know when they hear his censure", whereas "neither Scripture nor the Holy Ghost as he speaks by Scripture, is ever able to pronounce such sentence".[60] We may now guess where this will eventually lead: the Judge of controversies, in order to meet all the requirements of a judge, must be a living body, the Church, speaking through its governors. In a similar demonstration in the third part of his *Antidote*, Norris adds the all-important proviso that the Church is

---

[56] *An Antidote* . . ., p. 4.
[57] *A Guide of Faith*, p. 67.
[58] l.c., pp. 67-68.
[59] *An Antidote*, p. 5.
[60] l.c., p. 7.

not just a convenient judge, suitably equipped for his task, but rather that in judging controversies the Church acts in Christ's name, for she "is the treasury or storehouse of God to which he commits all his heavenly ministries. . . his mouth or oracle. . . his trumpet or cryer. . . the messenger which reveals his will, the witness which gives testimony to his words. . . the vice-gerent. . ." But Christ, Norris remarks

> was sent from the throne of his Father with most ample power to decide all doubts in matters of faith. Therefore the Church succeeds him in this sovereign authority; she baptizes now in his person; sacrifices in his person, teaches in his person, governs in his person, excommunicates in his person; so she determines with infallible assistance and judges all controversies in his person. . . Therefore she judges of the apostolical doctrine, of the sacred Canon; she judges what is consonant to the divine Spirit of God and what is dissonant thereunto.[61]

One cannot dodge this conclusion by suggesting that the Spirit himself solves difficulties and controversies by speaking "inwardly", through "private motions", in the hearts of the faithful.[62] The doctrine of the private spirit, which is refuted at length both in the *Antidote* and in *The Pseudo-Scripturist*,[63] offers no stable position, for it simply pushes the issue further back: the inward spirit also needs to be proven true. Nor does it suffice to say that "the analogy of Scripture" constitutes a suitable test of the spirits, or that "the spirit ought to be tried by the Canon of Holy Writ so that, comparing men's interpretations with the Scriptures themselves, we may judge of their fidelity".[64] Piquantly enough, Norris retorts that this implies a circle, thus hitting on the very point which Maihew and he himself so carefully refute when Protestants object it to Catholics: it is "nothing else than to allow the circle so often hissed out of schools: by the Spirit to interpret the Scripture, and by the Scripture to discern the Spirit".[65] Or, in the more forceful language of *The Guide of Faith*: "This is a dotage gross and absurd, to prove the unknown word by a hidden motion, and the motion hidden by the word unknown. This is to dance the round so often reprehended, and to labor in darkness

---

[61] *A Guide of Faith*, pp. 64-65.
[62] *An Antidote*, p. 17.
[63] *The Pseudo-Scripturist*, 1 st part, ch. 2, pp. 6-14.
[64] *An Antidote*, p. 20.
[65] l.c., p. 21.

without hope of delivery".[66] Vainly does one answer that the Spirit is self-evident, that "he needs not the touchstone of Scripture, but may by itself be descried as black from white, light from darkness".[67] This, for Norris, contradicts the Scriptures, which enjoin us to try the spirits; and it runs foul of the notorious fact that many have confused the Spirit of Truth and the spirit of darkness.

Yet the doctrine of the private spirit is but a distortion of the Catholic conviction that the Spirit guides the Church and all the faithful together. To the Church God has entrusted the safe-keeping of both the letter and the sense of Scripture, the "inward kernel" and the "outward rine", the "bone" and the "marrow of his word".[68] Whereas the externals may be found written on paper, the inward reality resides in the hearts: "He preserved that more safe in the hearts of his faithful than the other in the rolls of paper; and so, as you take the bark and outward letter from the tradition of our Church, much more ought you to borrow from her the true sense and sap and heavenly juice".

Indeed, Scripture itself says: "My sheep hear my voice"; "The spiritual man judges all things". These quotes do not bring down the Spirit in the hearts of the faithful to the level of each private individual. They mean that the "sheep of Christ hear his voice", yet "not all times, not when they listen, but how and when it pleases God. Sometimes by secret inspiration, other while outward hearing or reading his Word".[69] At any rate, whenever the voice of God is heard, by mystical grace or in the faithful reading of Scripture, "they have never infallible certitude thereof, but when it is confirmed by extraordinary revelation or by the public judgement and approbation of the Church, by whose authority the spiritual man judges all things". Norris has thus turned the argument around, giving a totally new meaning to "the spiritual man" of St Paul. Feeling maybe that he has tried to prove too much, he opens still another possibility: "Or he may be said to judge all things, not infallibly, but prudently and discreetly, as the testimony of his conscience and instinct of the Holy Ghost shall teach and persuade him". Here surely, Norris comes much closer to his adversaries than he knows. Ultimately, as he is quite prepared to confess, "the evangelical law (is) more fit to

---

[66] *A Guide of Faith*, p. 70.
[67] *An Antidote*, p. 21.
[68] *A Guide of Faith*, p. 53.
[69] *An Antidote*, pp. 24-25.

be infused into the heart by the unction of the Holy Ghost, than to be uttered by words or imprinted in books". In this sense ought we to understand this other quotation: "All shall be docible of God".[70]

It follows that Scripture is always to be coupled with the judge of controversies in order fully to know Christian truth. In such a context the Word of God, to which faith is related, as St Paul says, by hearing, is "partly written, partly unwritten".[71] What the judge of controversies decides about Scripture is, by hypothesis, not written in it, although it may be obscurely and implicitly insinuated. Sylvester Norris, moreover, finds it obvious "that the Apostles thought it not expedient to set down all things in writing, that they often refer us to unwritten Traditions, that reason convinces the necessity of them, and the Fathers mention many which we must need embrace".[72] There is little originality, however, in the way he expounds his demonstration. His list of points known by Tradition alone ranges from the Scriptures themselves, their various books and their true sense, to the baptism of infants, the perpetual Virginity of Mary, the *Filioque*, the celebration of Easter on Sunday, the unbegottenness of the Father, the consubstantiality of the Father and the Son. Nonetheless, having provided this list, Norris returns to his conception of the universality of Scripture: the function of Tradition regards "the precise terms and clear explanation, the subversion of error and light of our profession", not "the substance of some of these points", which "be darkly insinuated in Holy Writ".[73] The actual opposition of Protestants and Catholics is therefore not so great as it would seem, for if Catholics recognise unwritten Traditions as "darkly insinuated" in Scripture, Protestant themselves "to refell their adversaries run to the supply of unwritten Traditions". "Why," Norris asks, "appeal you to Scripture alone and yet subscribe to such and so many points of faith not comprised in Scripture?" [74] One cannot answer that the Reformation tried to exclude "human traditions" opposed to the word of God whereas Catholics "rely upon human interpretations and uncertain Traditions". For it is "a great wrong" to say "that we cleave to human and uncertain traditions".[75] Catholics also claim to exclude these: "We anchor on such as are

---

[70] l.c., p. 26.
[71] l.c., p. 37.
[72] l.c., p. 31.
[73] l.c., p. 34.
[74] l.c., p. 36.
[75] l.c., p. 39.

divine, certain and infallible, authentically warranted. . . to descend from Christ or the Church, his holy and undoubted Spouse".

By his own admission Norris does not intend to treat the problem of Tradition as a whole: he excuses himself from doing so in *The Pseudo-Scripturist*, for it "would require a reasonable large treatise alone".[76] He prefers to "remit the reader to such Catholic writers as have most learnedly handled this subject"[77] and is satisfied with the method of the *Antidote*: "to set down, and consequently prove the said doctrine *a posteriori*, certain points of Christian faith which have no clear and convincing proofs out of Scripture, and yet are believed no less by the Protestants themselves than by us Catholics". However, he has taken time to state briefly what "the doctrine of Traditions" is:

> The doctrine of unwritten Traditions teaches us that all the articles and points of Christian religion have not their express proof out of Scripture but that some of them are believed only by force of Tradition and of the continued and uninterrupted practise of God's Church.[78]

Further on in this book, Norris points out that St Paul's declaration to the Thessalonians ("Brethren, hold the traditions which you have received, whether it be by word or by epistle", 2 Thess. 2:15) "do immediately and necessarily (without any help of strained consequences) imply a division or partition of his doctrine, which (no doubt) was God's word".[79] In two other places, he briefly alludes to the Fathers' support of "unwritten precepts and Traditions".[80]

Our study so far has brought to light a dominant line of thought, which is well illustrated by Kellison, Worthington, Bishop, Maihew and Norris: Scripture, as the only inspired word of God, holds primacy in the Church, provided it is understood in its right sense, which is ultimately identical with the doctrines of the Catholic Tradition. No sooner has this been affirmed as the central point of the Catholic faith and system of thought than it becomes possible to take up the question from complementary points of view: since Tradition is known to the faithful previously to their reading of Scripture, it is by Tradition, and not by the written word, that knowledge of Revelation is available to them. Scholars may find all

---

[76] *The Pseudo-Scripturist*, pp. 42-43.
[77] l.c., p. 43.
[78] l.c., p. 42.
[79] l.c., p. 101.
[80] l.c., p. 114; see pp. 128-9.

Christian doctrines in one form or another, explicitly or implicitly, in the Scriptures; but they would not see them there unless they were enlightened by the Spirit, and the test of this heavenly guidance is the convergence of their exegesis with the actual teachings of the Church.

Yet there are great differences in approach between these men. Kellison and Worthington, interesting as they are, present little originality in comparison with their predecessors of the 16th century. Maihew brings the debate forward by squarely facing the issue of circular reasoning and by shifting his ground from the theology of Scripture and the Church to the theology of the act of faith. Although this more existential consideration has not yet brought about any radically new problematic, it has at least set the stage for further reflection. Norris, in a rather different direction, also brings new water to the mill of the discussions by focusing attention on the question: Who is Judge of Controversies?

Thus a shift of focus is slowly taking place. Already the famous John Percy, Mr Fisher the Jesuit, cared little to meet the Anglicans on the partly shared principle of the sufficiency of Scripture. With Sylvester Norris also, the main emphasis is passing from Scripture to Tradition, by way of the question of the Judge of Controversies. This is not exclusive of a high regard for Scripture. Both Percy and Norris still use the vocabulary and the categories of the older perspective. Yet the sufficiency of Scripture is more openly qualified and even, with Percy, denied, although it is not negated in the sense in which other Catholics accept it.

CHAPTER THREE

THE ISSUES SHARPEN

The controversies between Anglicans and English Recusants continued unabated in the 1630's, very much along the same lines as before. The story, however, presents the gratifying aspect of a sort of flowering of theological thinking or at least writing between 1630 and 1634, when several important works came to light. In the main, little truly new appears in these essays, though previous perspectives are sharpened and our polemicists actively follow some of the lines opened by their predecessors, so that the period offers the spectacle of a focusing of attention on some of the key issues in the debate between the partisans of the "old religion" and those of the reformed Establishment. These years are especially relevant for Catholic developments concerning Scripture and Tradition, for the major works of anti-Protestant argumentation hinge around the question of how to read Scripture.

In 1630 a new figure appears on the scene, a man who, like so many of his colleagues, managed to fit one noteworthy contribution to the intellectual defense of the faith in the multiple pastoral activities of a priest during penal times. James Sharpe (1577?-1630), who also went by the name of Francis Pollard, was ordained at the English College of Valladolid in 1604, joined the Society of Jesus in 1608 and afterwards did missionary work in England except for a period of banishment. In 1630 he published his volume of controversies, to which he gave a title indicative of his concerns: *The Trial of the Protestant Private Spirit*. The somewhat long explanation of the title which, in the manners of the times, follows it, conveniently sums up Sharpe's purpose and method: *Wherein their doctrine, making the said spirit the sole ground and means of their belief, is confuted by authority of Holy Scripture, testimonies of ancient Fathers, evidence of reason drawn from the ground of faith, absurdity of consequences following upon it against all faith, religion and reason.* Thus, the author intends to investigate scrip ural interpretation with the purpose of confuting the protestant hermeneutical system, founded, as he understands it, on the private spirit of man over against the common spirit of the Church. Although it does not affect the relevance of his work, this is only the "second part, which is doctrinal", of a longer project. As Sharpe's preface explains it, the second part was conceived and written first; it then occurred to the author that refutation of the Protestant private spirit ought to be preceded by a demonstration that Protestants do ground their religion on such a spirit. While the second part contains the refutation, the first is to provide "a proof or declaration that the same spirit is such a ground to the Protestants". Unfortunately, the conditions in which English Catholics have to work make publishing so difficult that, if "this part gets breath and birth and comes to light before the first", it is only because "like to two twins they struggled at birth" and, several midwives being brought in to help, "this fell to the lot of one more ready and skilful".[1] Sharpe finally expresses the wish that the sales of the second part might help to publish the first, hoping that this "may give thee (the reader) content, and thy content give vente, and the vente help on to the birth of the other". The problems of an author have changed little since then, in spite of the passing of penal times. As a point of fact the first part came posthumously to light, in a printing of the entire work in 1640: *The Examination of the Private Spirit of Protestants*.

The ten chapters of *The Trial of the Protestant Private Spirit* start with the theology of faith (ch. 1) and proceed to "confute" the private spirit on eight counts: by Scripture (ch. 2), by the Fathers (ch. 3), by reasons drawn from the difficulty of discerning the spirits (ch. 4), by "true infallible authority and means of interpreting Scripture" (ch. 5), by reasons drawn from "the nature of a judge of faith" (ch. 6) and "from the nature and certainty of faith" (ch. 7), by "circular absurdities" (ch. 8) and "doctrinal absurdities" following upon it (ch. 9). At the end, some Protestant retorts are briefly answered (ch. 10).

The Catholic faith has four characteristics, which the Protestant faith lacks: it is "for probable testimonies accepted as credible, by Church proposed as infallible, by an infused habit effected as super-

---

[1] *The Trial of the Protestant Private Spirit*, preface.—Who wrote *The Trial*...? The book is signed J.S., which can mean John Spenser (1601-1671) or James Sharpe (1577-1630). John Spenser (see next chapter) wrote *Scripture Mistaken* (1655), *Questions propounded for resolution* (1657), *Schism Unmasked* (1658), which were published more than 25 years after *The Trial*... I treat *The Trial* as being the work of Sharpe on account of great differences in style, method, and theological orientation between this book and the works of Spenser.

natural, by divine verity revealed as truth infallible and necessary to be believed".[2] Faith is described along the lines of the first theology outlined by Maihew, due importance being given to a judgement of credibility. Yet it is not a purely rational assent, it is "infused" and "supernatural", bearing on "revealed truth". It is also, and this has relevance for the Catholic-Protestant debate, "the beginning and ground of justification, the way and gate to salvation, upon which the Church of Christ is founded, and is as the life and soul of it". Faith "certainly and infallibly" believes "either expressly or *implicite* all whatsoever articles of faith God has revealed to his Church by his Apostles". Briefly summarising the decree of the Council of Trent on Justification (January 13, 1547), Sharpe calls this faith "a necessary mean, instrument or disposition to our justification and salvation, without which none is justified and by which, informed with charity, all are justified".[3] Several aspects of faith, material and formal, exterior and interior, subjective and objective, converge in this short definition: "Faith is an inward assent of the mind which we give to that which God, who is the prime verity and can neither deceive nor be deceived, has revealed to us by means of the preaching and teaching of the true Church".[4] Yet, although Sharpe does justice to the Tridentine concern, so misunderstood by Protestants, for faith as the central element in the process of justification, his descriptions remain over-intellectual. This would be neither here nor there, as far as our study goes, had it not colored Sharpe's approach to the Scriptures. It is precisely as included in the "material object" of faith that Sharpe views Scripture, strongly objecting to what could be a legitimate, but very different, angle of vision, by which "untruly and fraudulently the Protestants do generally aver that in the Scripture the Spirit of God is, and is to be sought and found; and that by industry and reading of the words and text the Spirit is to be found". Granted that this pneumatic principle would require considerable elaboration before acquiring a Catholic meaning, search for this sense would provide a suitable meeting ground for Catholic-Protestant dialogues. But Sharpe's purpose is to refute, not to meet. He will accordingly look at Scripture as from the outside: it then appears, not as a locus of the presence of the Spirit in the Church, but as part of that which is to be believed, confronting the faithful as an object does a subject,

---

[2] l.c., p. 9.
[3] l.c., pp. 9-10.
[4] l.c., p. 122.

or as a matter waiting for the form—here, the faith—that will give it life and being.

Thus, the contents of faith are described as follows:

"We Catholics do profess to believe, first, all that which has been written by the Apostles or Prophets in Holy Scripture, and that in the whole books of Scripture, as anciently as they were by a Council of Carthage, St Augustine and others, received, and all in that sense as it was by ancient Church expounded; 2., all that which has been by the same Apostles delivered to posterity by word of mouth and tradition; 3., all that which has been declared to us out of Scripture and Tradition, by definitions of general Councils; 4., all that which by continuance of practise has been by our holy Church ever revealed; 5., all that which by unanimous consent of holy learned doctors, Fathers, and saints, has been believed".[5] Both Scripture and Tradition convey or contain articles of faith; they therefore appear anteriorly to the faith of the individual, which is objectively patterned upon them, and yet they also follow his faith in the individual's subjective apprehension of their contents.

This provides Sharpe with one of his main assertions: "The knowledge or doctrine of faith is presupposed to the true knowledge and understanding of Scripture. . . Faith and the rule of faith is necessary before the understanding of Scripture".[6] Sharpe has forewarned us that when he speaks of understanding Scripture, he does not refer to the "sense and interpretation which is only probable and credible", but to that "which is certain and infallible". He thus rules out of consideration both the rhetorical use of the Bible in preaching and its scientific investigation with the tools of exegetical research. He prescinds from "that which is only for the pulpit and documents of manner, or which is for the schools or subtleties of divinity",[7] being interested in "that which is for doctrine of faith and articles of belief". In so doing, Sharpe accentuates a distinction, which is not so familiar to Protestant as to Catholic theology, between the province of faith in the strict sense, and those of piety or scientific and theological research. Sharpe's entire conception of the nature and purpose of Scripture is grounded in this distinction, as appears in the following passage, which epitomises his outlook on the whole problem:

[5] l.c., p. 24.
[6] l.c., p. 119.
[7] l.c., p. 124.

Out of all which it does follow that the words of Scripture and the
diligent and frequent reading or hearing of it are so far from being
a necessary means of faith, much less the sole and whole means of it,
that faith is a means necessary and presupposed to the understanding of
Scripture. For the Scripture consists not in the words and letters
only, but in the sense and understanding principally; and if the sense
depends not upon the bare words, but upon the ecclesiastical and
Catholic rule and Tradition of faith, as is proved, then must faith be
pre-required as a help and means to find out the true sense of Scripture. And they who read Scripture must bring faith with them,
as a help and means to understand Scripture, and not ground their
faith upon the reading of Scripture, which being diligently read,
though it may serve to confirm and nourish faith in oneself, or to
illustrate it or defend it to others, and in both being, according to the
rule of faith interpreted, a light to direct them in the way of piety and
to inflame them with the heat of charity, yet it can neither be a first nor
firm ground to cause and produce first and certain faith in any (for
a man must bring faith to believe it), nor a sufficient means to resolve
all points of faith necessary to salvation. . . .[8]

Sharpe seeks for an infallible interpretation, one which will indeed
reveal "the soul" of Scripture beyond any possible doubt. For,
true it is, Scripture "consists of words or text which is read or heard",
but that is "only the body, bark and covering of God's word".[9]
Not what is heard or read matters, but "the sense and meaning which
is understood and believed": this is "the life, soul and substance of
the Scripture". With undeniable insight, Sharpe esteems that Protestants generally tend to overstress the importance of the text
without showing enough concern for the sense. They "make the
words of Scripture, as they are heard or read, not only the organ or
instrument of faith as much as we make the sacrament instrument of
grace; but also the sole instrument, which with diligence read or
heard they prescribe as the only means to receive faith and salvation".[10]
If this last remark is an exaggeration, the reference to the quasi-
sacramental value of the text accurately pinpoints a constant tendency
of Protestant thought and piety.

As regards its sense, Scripture "is a book sealed with seven seals",
which no one can break open "but he who has the key of David",[11]
that is, anyone who is "faithful with David". Thus the substance of

---

[8] l.c., p. 124.
[9] l.c., pp. 122-123.
[10] l.c., p. 122.
[11] l.c., pp. 119-120.

Scripture is revealed by faith, which already knows it. Yet faith is not the only "means of expounding the holy Scripture",[12] and Sharpe counts four rules of interpretation, namely, besides faith, "the practise of the Church, the consent of the Fathers, and the decrees of the Councils".[13] These are of course based on the fact that, since "the Church itself cannot err",[14] her constant practise as well as the doctrines of her Fathers or the decrees of her Councils express her mind. Of these three, the "most infallible means" of expounding Scripture is a general Council, although not all that a Council says or does has infallible relevance, but only "whatsoever is not *obiter*, by the way, not as a proof only, but on set purpose and as a conclusion or definition delivered or defined that is, without all question or examination, to be received as a certain, infallible and authentical sense of Scripture".[15] Following the inner logic of his position, Sharpe seeks for official means and interpretations of Scripture. Nevertheless, he does not disregard, although he hardly does justice to, the wisdom of employing normal resources of critical reading. He admits that "there be other helps which are good and profitable, as the consideration of the antecedents and consequences of places, the conference of one place with another, the observation of Scripture-phrases, and the skill and examination of the original texts".[16] Yet these methodical devices ought to remain at what he deems to be their inferior place: "Because they are neither certain nor infallible, but only probable, yes, often doubtful, and sometimes deceitful, nor yet proper nor peculiar to Christians, but common to Jews, pagans, heretics and all sorts, and also not to our purpose for the present: there we will omit them. . .". This admittedly cuts short the long task of sharpening Catholic exegesis; yet it tallies with Sharpe's concentration on the authentic and infallible interpretation of Scripture.

This infallible interpretation, destined to unveil the substance of Scripture, which is no other than the articles of faith, cannot belong to fallible individuals, to anybody's private spirit. What was written under the Spirit's impulse, must also be interpreted under his influence. Sharpe even speaks of "inspiration" in both cases:

---

[12] l.c., p. 125.
[13] l.c., p. 130.
[14] l.c., p. 125.
[15] l.c., p. 128.
[16] l.c., p. 130.

As the holy men of God, the Apostles, inspired by the Holy Ghost
spoke and dictated the word of God when it was made; so the interpreters of the same word ought not to bring in any exposition of the
same word of God upon their own will and sense, but upon the
inspiration of the same holy Ghost, when by them it is interpreted:
so that we should receive the sense of Scripture from the same Spirit
from which we received the text of Scripture.[17]

In spite of the language he uses, Sharpe runs no danger of mistaking
false mysticism for inspired interpretation. Admittedly, he upholds
the privilege of the spiritual man to judge spiritual things, but only
"according to such rules and directions as everything is to be judged".[18] What is already certain, he judges in keeping with this
certainty; what is still obscure, "according to the rule of faith and
the authority and testimony of Councils, Fathers, Tradition and
the Church". For the principle of the Spirit rests on the unity of the
Spirit. "Because truth and faith is not private to one nor singular in
any, but common to all and generally received by all the faithful. . .
so also the Spirit of truth is not private to any one but common to
all the faithful".[19] Therefore, ultimately, the "judge of faith", the
"judge of controversies of faith", the "judge of the sense of Scripture" cannot be any particular individual man, however inspired
he may be: the final judge on earth is that through which the Spirit
speaks, the Church. The Spirit of God, to whom the sense of the
Scriptures is entrusted, is "a Spirit common and general to all the
faithful, uniting the shepherd with the flock and the flock to the
shepherd, both in the fold of Jesus Christ in unity of one Spirit and
faith".[20] Were one to ask who or where is this Church who can
pronounce the Spirit's sentence, Sharpe would try to pinpoint the
necessary qualities of the Judge that we are looking for. Carefully
sifting out several theories, he finds that only one possible "judge"
cannot be eliminated. He rules out "the whole body of the Church",[21]
secular Princes, lay people, the Scriptures, the private spirit. Only
"bishops and prelates" have been given authority and power to judge
controversies.

This attempt to discover the only possible judge of faith is centered
on the nature of the Scriptures. That these cannot be the judge is

---

[17] l.c., p. 139.
[18] l.c., p. 386.
[19] l.c., p. 139.
[20] l.c., p. 140.
[21] l.c., p. 148.

proved, according to Sharpe, by five considerations, the convergence of which provides a convincing argument. Firstly, they themselves "in respect of us" need a judge "to determine and assure us which is the true Canon, true original text, true translation, true sense and the rest".[22] Like most of Sharpe's arguments, this is not a theoretical but a practical one, borrowed from well known facts of the history of Scripture and its interpretation. Secondly, Scripture has never yet decided any of the "greatest difficulties... the mainest questions... or the hottest contentions". Adding to his list of facts, Sharpe states, thirdly, that "the Scripture is mute, dumb and unable to speak, hear or pronounce sentence" and therefore is apt to be "drawn, wrested and interpreted to contrary senses and opinions". Fourthly, it is "neither clear and evident, nor does evidently and expressly contain and declare all the senses of itself, all the mysteries of belief, all the questions of controversies, all doubts in divinity". Fifthly, many have been converted without reading Scripture.

Such a line of thought is no doubt acceptable in the limits of Sharpe's factual argumentation. The basic principle that Scripture cannot be a judge because it does not itself speak is self-evident. Yet to insist on this betrays a singularly crude conception of the ways in which the Spirit may possibly work. If the principle has already been accepted that the true judge is the Spirit, it should follow that the Spirit can devise his own ways of reaching his ends, without necessarily modeling his instruments on the practices of human tribunals. The analogy of the judge, legitimate as it is, can therefore, in the hands of our Catholic apologists, be used more univocally than analogically, as Sharpe certainly does in this discussion. However this may be, Sharpe pursues his point to its logical end by showing that "neither the letter nor the spirit" of Scripture is the judge of faith: "the letter because the letter, or the words in the bare literal sense, are occasion of error and heresy"; "the internal sense", because "this true sense intended by the Holy Ghost is often obscure, hard and uncertain".[23] The upshot of this is that "Scripture-sense is the thing in question and contention, therefore is the thing to be judged and decided, not the judge who is to give judgement".

James Sharpe exploits with singular sharpness, even though with a tendency to overstress his points, the two themes of the structure of faith and of the judge of controversies. His demonstrations appear

---

[22] l.c., p. 156.
[23] l.c., pp. 158-159.

to be singularly negative, in that he is concerned with refuting the Protestant concept. Yet the Catholic position underlies all he says. And the result is, in his mind, totally positive, for it establishes beyond the shadow of a doubt that the Catholic Church in her bishops and prelates is the judge of controversies in religion: these alone have been entrusted with the only possible foundation of an absolute judgement about faith. Still refering to the analogy of the secular judge, Sharpe points out that judges pronounce sentences according to a rule or law. An infallible judge "must have some rule, likewise infallible and certain, by which he may be directed in his judgment, and some solid foundation upon which he may build his definitive sentence".[24] The rule in question must be endowed with a number of remarkable qualities, exactly commensurate with its function. It must be "so certain and infallible that it can neither deceive nor be deceived"; "so continued and not interrupted that it cannot decay or perish"; "so firm and immutable that it cannot be changed or corrupted", "so known and visible that it may be discerned" by all who need it; "so markable and notable that it may be a sign distinctive"; "so necessary and important. . ."; "so universal and general. . ."; "so fundamental that it be contained among the chief articles of the Creed or plainly expressed in Scripture"; "so sufficient that it be able to explicate and determine all articles and doubts in religion"; "so complete that it contains virtually and be able to resolve plainly, all questions and conclusions of faith. . .". Faith is "one and certain",[25] "entire and Catholic", "Catholicly and universally believed".[26]

So far, Sharpe has hardly touched the concept of Tradition directly, although he has alluded to customs, practices, traditions, and to the word of God, "not only that which is written in paper, but also that which was delivered in preaching by the Apostles".[27] Yet his solution to the question of the rule or foundation of the judgment of faith comes near to being a description of the deposit of Revelation in the Church's unchanging Tradition. Furthermore, the idea of a universality of faith implies a notion of Tradition as the continuous preservation of the same faith:

---

[24] l.c., p. 147.
[25] l.c., p. 187.
[26] l.c., p. 188.
[27] l.c., p. 360.

It must likewise be catholicly and universally believed, that is, what was by the first faithful, the Apostles and others in the first ages believed, must also by the succeeding faithful in the next ages likewise be believed; and what is in most places and countries and has been by the most faithful in most countries generally believed, the same must also by others likewise faithful in other countries be generally believed.[28]

This leads to what is, in the context of the Catholic notion of Tradition, a beautiful conclusion: "By which belief of the same doctrine in all or the most places, persons and times, is made one Catholic Church among all persons, in all places and all times".

One question which has already drawn the attention of the Benedictine Edward Maihew remains to be asked, concerning the Catholic arguments. Does Catholic thought run in a circle, proving A by B and proving again B by A? This accusation is met squarely by James Sharpe, who provides a slightly different answer from Maihew's. Whereas Maihew rejected the idea that there is a circle, Sharpe admits the fact, but finds shelter in Aristotle, for whom some circles are logically acceptable: the Catholic circle is one of them. Having said this in self-defense, Sharpe attacks Protestant positions on the same ground of logic, and finds that Protestant circles are logically unacceptable and, furthermore, that there are a multitude of them: between Scripture and Spirit, Spirit and faith, election and understanding of Scripture, spirit of everyman and general Council. His defense of the Catholic circle will alone detain us.

That there is a circle is readily acknowledged: "Ask a Catholic how he knows the Scripture to be infallible and true, he will answer, because the Church tells him so; ask him how he proves the Church to be infallible and true, he will answer, because the Scripture says it is so; and so he proves the Scripture by the Church and the Church by the Scripture".[29] Yet this is no logical catastrophe, for the Catholic circle does not ruin the Catholic conclusion.

Sharpe meets the objection directly, analysing the structure of faith in order to show that it entails no circular grounding. Unlike Maihew, however, he does not distinguish between two theologies, but brings Maihew's two analyses into one. Faith, according to Sharpe, implies "a preparation, to prepare us to accept the things believed as credible and in prudence worthy to be believed".[30]

---

[28] l.c., p. 188.
[29] l.c., p. 200.
[30] l.c., p. 201.

These "credible motives" or "credible testimonies" are "miracles, consent, sanctity, antiquity, and the rest...". They occasion a "human faith" by which "we settle our preparation or acceptation of faith and the credibility of it". The credibility of the Catholic faith rests on a prudential judgement of credibility, which itself presupposes an objective examination of the claims of the Catholic faith and Church. As to the "actual assent and belief", it rests upon "the habit of faith, and depends upon the divine revelation of God, declaring in Scripture or Tradition, and proposing by holy Church what and why we are to believe".[31] The "last resolution" of faith is settled on this revelation, which guarantees its supernatural certainty. Again, there is no circle at this point. Admittedly, assent rests on the authority that has been recognised in the Church on the basis of revelation. Yet this "reciprocal testimony and proof" [32] does not amount to a vicious circle, for the two elements, Church and Scripture-revelation, fulfil dissimilar functions. Scripture-revelation acts as the formal cause of the "infallibility of Church-proposition", whereas "Church-proposition is only conditional, as *conditio sine qua non*, to know Scripture-revelation". Scripture or, as Sharpe says it better, Scripture-revelation, includes the Church, of which it is an *a priori* proof, a "formal precedent cause", whereas the Church, or Church-proposition, is *a posteriori*, coming logically after the Revelation which reveals it: it is a "subsequent annexed condition".

Moreover, Aristotelian logic accepts the validity of reciprocal proof whenever "the one is not the total and sole cause of knowing the other". But the previous analysis has already shown that if the Church is revealed supernaturally by Scripture, it is also known naturally by the credible testimonies already mentioned. The conclusion may then be proved "by another medium than by the premises",[33] and this proof is valid in another order than the act of faith, namely, in the order of credibility. In this case, the circle in question is not "bad and unlawful" in Aristotelian logic.

Sharpe's merging of the two theologies of faith into one has placed him at an advantage: the two answers that Maihew presented as alternatives have now become one compounded reply. This is apologetically more effective.

Apologetic effectiveness is, on the whole, the mark of Sharpe's

---

[31] l.c., pp. 201-202.
[32] l.c., p. 202.
[33] l.c., p. 203.

polemical essay. His *Trial of the Protestant Private Spirit* constitutes, by and large, a powerful approch to the question of how to read Scripture. No doubt, the problematic how lost breadth; the horizons are narrower; one problem has been isolated from the whole set of pending issues. However, within these limits the dialectic has been singularly sharpened.

Laurence Anderson, or Anderton (1576-1643), also known as Scroop, entered the Catholic Church while he was at Cambridge University, and he may have been, although this is not certain, a clergyman of the Established Church. He joined the Society of Jesus in 1604 and spent the rest of his life as a missionary in Lancashire.[34] Among his several books we may mention a largely historical survey of the origins of Catholicism and Protestantion, *The Progeny of Catholics and Protestants* (1633). But his main title to fame accrues to him from a long, anonymous volume of controversies, entitled: *The Triple Cord, or a Treatise proving the truth of the Roman Religion by Sacred Scripture taken in the litteral sense, expounded by the ancient Fathers, interpreted by Protestant Writers* (1634). This important publication, which includes a major dissertation on Tradition, purports to have been born of an attempt to discover a new method (another one) of converting Protestants. This new method consists in proving Catholicism with the help of the literal sense of the Bible and of the Protestant interpretation of Scripture, or rather, by the interpretation of Scripture by selected Protestant authors. These two elements, the literal sense, and the Protestant interpretation, together with the testimony of ancient Fathers, constitute the "triple cord" to be used. In all this, Anderson forgets neither the Catholic appeal to Tradition nor the Protestant recourse to the Fathers.

Actually, this method is not so new as Anderson seems to believe. James Gordon, William Norris, Richard Broughton, Richard Smith, make considerable use of Protestant testimonies, while Richard Smith also prides himself on proving the Catholic faith by the literal sense of the Bible.[35] Whether or not Anderson knew these

---

[34] One must not confuse Lawrence Anderson with James Anderson (d. 1613), alias John Brereley, the author of *The Protestants' Apology for the Roman Church* (1st edition, 1604, often reprinted; Latin edition in Paris in 1615, translated by William Rayner, *Joannes Brerelei . . . pro Romana ecclesia adversus novam protestantum doctrinam libri tres*). There also was a Roger Anderson who wrote *Miscellania, or a Treatise containing 222 Controversial animadversions* (1640); see below, ch. 9.

[35] On James Gordon, see ch. 1; William Norris, ch. 2; on Richard Broughton, ch. 6; on Richard Smith, ch. 4. Let us mention Ignatius Goodwin (d. 1667),

authors, it would seem natural that, in the circumstances of Recusant polemics, several men could independently forge similar tools of argumentation.

The fundamental methodological principle of the work is well explained in the preface, in which Anderson makes it clear that, in his opinion, the triple theological cord he will wield should satisfy the most difficult reader:

> Now if the texts of Sacred Scripture taken in their proper and literal sense, and the answerable expositions made by the holy Fathers and sundry of the learned Protestant writers, do all of them conspire in making that sense of Scripture, which wholly agrees with the doctrine and practice of the Catholic Roman Church, I do not see what more can be required by any indifferent and understanding man for the making it appear clear, as the sun at noonday, that the written word of God is that which teaches us our Catholic faith, and confutes and condemns such errors as arise against it.[36]

The author's purpose evidently rests upon a certain conception of the literal sense, as in itself sufficient to establish the truth of the Catholic faith. This was already Richard Smith's contention. In Anderson's hands, however, this principle is used with more subtlety than by the Bishop of Chalcedon, who was easily contented with plain quotations which he did not trouble to analyse or explain. Anderson's theological introduction establishes the ground on which the entire book will be built, and its comprehensive title shows the scope of Anderson's design: "A preparative to the Triple Cord, wherein is proved the dignity and infallibility of the written word of God or Sacred Scriptures; as also the necessity of finding out their true sense intended by the Holy Ghost, with certain infallible rules for the finding out of the said sense". Under this title, the author examines "the true state of the question concerning the verity of the Sacred Scriptures" (Sect. I); he shows that "the Sacred Scriptures are the true word of God, divine and infallible" (Sect. 2 to 5); he then studies the senses of Scripture and their interpretation, reaching the conclusion that "the only certain rule" of interpretation is "the Church of Christ" (Sect. 6 to 10); and he ends by identifying the Church as the Roman Catholic Church (Sect. 11).

---

who wrote *Lapis Lydius controversiarum modernarum catholicos inter et acatholicos* (1656), in which he intended to prove more than three hundred points of doctrine *ex Verbo Dei scripto*.

[36] *The Triple Cord*, preface.

This comprehensive, though concise, essay of some twenty-four pages introduces Anderson's survey of the controversies with Protestants, the first of which pertains to our topic and covers approximately the same ground as the "preparative", since its subject matter is "the true state of the question in controversy between Catholics and Protestants concerning the judge of controversies in matters of religion".[37] Here, Anderson proceeds very systematically to examine the "true state of the question" about the judge of controversies (ch. 1), the Church's infallibility (ch. 2), the difficulty of understanding Scripture (ch. 3), the interpretation of Scripture and the problem of the private spirit (ch. 4), the canonical and apocryphal books (ch. 5), biblical translations (ch. 6) and finally the Traditions (ch. 7). As this sequence of chapters suggests, Anderson's approach takes account of previous literature: the focus remains on the judge of controversy; the point made by James Sharpe about the private spirit is duly emphasized and, as already noticed, the literal sense of the Bible is given its due especially for the purpose of theological argumentation, although the customary respects are paid to the spiritual senses as long as these convey a meaning intended by the Holy Spirit.

Anderson, however, does not simply summarise or copy his predecessors. Far from being a mere epitome of current controversies, his work tries to open new ground and betrays a finely original approach to some of the points in question. To begin with, Anderson takes a different stand from the position adopted by many Catholics, in whose eyes the validity of Scripture is not established by Scripture itself. There is no doubt, for him, that Scripture testifies to itself.

Scripture, as admitted by all, is "a principal ground of Christian faith and religion, the dignity and infallible truth thereof must necessarily be acknowledged. ... So that according to Catholics there is not any one sentence or text of Scripture which we are not bound to believe for most true and divine".[38] No Catholic has difficulty with the intrinsic dignity of Scripture. None would undermine the binding value of clear biblical statements, for they are for him the word of God. Yet Anderson is concerned lest Protestants continue to think that Catholics despise Scripture. He therefore intends his proofs from the Scriptures "only in this regard that the

---

[37] First Controversy, l.c., pp. 33-180.
[38] l.c., pp. 1-2.

world may know that we Catholics do so highly esteem them for
divine and infallible, as whatsoever is spoken, taught or to be read
therein, we in all disputes and controversies of religion do humbly
submit ourselves to the doctrine thereof".[39] The problem does not lie
in the theoretical strength of scriptural arguments in matters of
controversy, for these are final for Catholics even in controverted
questions. On this basic principle Catholics and Protestants stand
together. But a recurring problem concerns the sense of Scripture.
It is one thing to believe that Scripture is the word of God, and quite
another to know its true sense with certainty. Polemics and discussions turn sterile, and arguments fly at cross-purposes, if no agreement has been reached on the sense of the texts. Therefore, "that
which imports for the final and infallible deciding of controversies
arising from the Scripture is to find out the true sense thereof intended by the Holy Ghost, to which all parties will profess without
any tergiversations to yield and subscribe".[40]

That one of the possible meanings of the text is intended by the
Holy Spirit is the important thing. This may be "litteral or mystical",
for the Spirit may express himself through the plain meaning or
through a more abstruse content of the scriptural texts. Yet mystical
senses, since they are harder to determine, seldom indicate the true
purpose of Scripture. "It cannot be denied that a firm argument may
be taken from any sense, litteral or mystical, so long as it appears that
sense to be true and intended by the Holy Ghost; but because it is
most difficult to know and discern when these mystical and spiritual
senses are true and so intended by the Holy Ghost, therefore ordinarily speaking, arguments from this sense are weak, uncertain and
not sufficient absolutely to determine a point of faith".[41] Anderson
agrees in this with Thomas Aquinas and with all Protestant authors,
who, while admitting the possibility of spiritual senses, find that these
are seldom trustworthy. He may thus conclude to everybody's
satisfaction: "It is our general doctrine that, seeing it is certain, that
sense which is immediately gathered from the words to be the sense
of the Holy Ghost, that therefore from the litteral sense are we to
take arguments that will be efficacious".

Thus is again raised "the question in controversy between Catholics
and Protestants concerning the judge of controversies in matters of

---

[39] l.c., p. 3.
[40] l.c., p. 11.
[41] l.c., p. 14.

religion":[42] How does one interpret Scripture? At this point Anderson quotes the Council of Trent: "No man dare to interpret the Sacred Scripture contrary to that sense, which the holy Mother the Church has and does hold, to whom it belongs to judge of the true sense and interpretation of Holy Scriptures".[43] The opening words of this sentence shorten the actual text of the Council, although they adequately convey its meaning. The strength of this statement comes from its origin: "the Church of Christ in general Council". Anderson also justifies it in several ways. The Church has "power from Christ to discern the word of God from the words of men"; accordingly, she must also have "the like power of discerning in the words the sense and meaning of God from the sense and understanding of men". This is required for the preservation and announcement of the gospel. For "the true Gospel of God does not consist in the writing of words but in the sense": if the Church "had only the written word and not the true sense thereof, she had not the true Gospel of God, and so neither faith in Christ, which is had by the true Gospel, faith having relation not to the words but to the sense". This is a classical argument used time and time again by Anderson's predecessors. Another reason is that "Christ opened [the Apostles'] understanding, that they might understand the Scriptures, which certainly he did not for them alone but much more for his Church; and so accordingly the Apostles delivered to the Church the true sense thereof: for if they had delivered the words but not the sense, they had not preached the Gospel".[44] The sense of Scripture seems, then, to be kept through a sort of parallel transmission somehow duplicating Scripture, the words being preserved in one way and one place, the sense being kept in another way and another place. Yet what is important is not the double knowledge, of words and of meaning, implied here; it is the unity of both in the experience of "understanding the Scripture": "Seeing the Church is the pillar and ground of truth, and truth properly and truly is in the understanding of the Scriptures, not in the writing or words, but improperly and as in a sign, it evidently follows that she has a certain knowledge of the truths which are contained in the Scriptures".[45] The words of Scripture are signs of the doctrine which abides in the Church. Therefore, "the true and sincere sense

---

[42] l.c., p. 33.
[43] l.c., p. 21; see D.-S., n. 1507.
[44] l.c., p. 22.
[45] l.c., pp. 22-23.

of the Scriptures is to be taken from the interpretation of the Catholic Church." Knowing that many Protestants profess to find the sense of Scripture in the early Fathers, Anderson objects to their decision to limit this to the first centuries: "Neither may we in reason think that this gift of interpretation of the Sacred Scriptures ceased with the pastors of the primitive Church".[46]

This is the point where the "question between Catholics and Protestants" arises: "whether, besides the Sacred Scriptures, any other infallible authority and judge is to be acknowledged, by which the doctrine of faith and the true sense of the Scriptures may be proposed to the faith ful as revealed by God and to be believed".[47] Protestants in general hold that Scripture alone is the sole judge of controversies, although, as Anderson shows, many do appeal to the Fathers of the primitive Church, thus throwing the scriptural principle into jeopardy. Catholics maintain that Scripture cannot be the judge of controversies, because it does not reveal its own sense and cannot apply it to controverted questions. While Scripture is the word written, its meaning, known only through the Church, is the word not written. "Having hitherto proved that neither the Scriptures of themselves nor as conferred together nor yet as expounded by the private spirit, can be our sole rule of faith or judge of all controversies, it now next follows that I speak of the Word not written, but delivered from Christ or his Apostles by word of mouth".[48] Anderson adduces the text of the Council of Trent and concludes: "Here the Council receives and reverences with like piety the Word written and not written, to wit, the Traditions". From this approach it would seem that Anderson does more than identify the Scriptures with the written word, and the traditions with the unwritten word. The understanding of Scripture is only "improperly and as in a sign" in the written word; properly it is only in the understood word.

Thus the traditions are not presented as a second source, as a parallel series of documents to which we may have recourse in order to discover true doctrine. The traditions are to the Scriptures what the sense is to the letter. There is an analogy, in this matter, between the Old and the New Testament:

> Calvin replies that the doctrine of the Prophets and of the New Testament were not additions to the Law, but explications thereof, as being

---

[46] l.c., p. 60.
[47] l.c., p. 33.
[48] l.c., pp. 152-153.

taught or contained in the Law, though not in particular, yet in general. But I suppose Calvinists will not deny but that they believe more than is written in the Law, and no otherwise does the Law contain them than in general and, as it were, virtually: but so likewise are Traditions contained therein, and so no additions.[49]

If Calvin may receive the Prophets and the New Testament as implied in and fulfilling the law, one should by the same token receive the traditions as implied in and fulfilling the New Testament. Tradition is not an addition to Scripture, but a manifestation or unfolding of its meaning; it is not other than Scripture and distinct from it. One cannot have Scripture without a tradition that interprets it, for without tradition Scripture is a closed book, a meaningless written word.

This evidently makes tradition the ultimate rule of faith. This was true before the New Testament: "I proved before that in the time of nature and much also in the time of the Law, the faithful were instructed by Tradition not written. . . . . So, confessedly, Traditions have been and may be rules of truth".[50] In the Christian order of things the Church is also the rule: to "the Tradition and Judgement of His Church" [51] Jesus entrusted the gospel. Only there do we read the designs intended by the Holy Ghost. "The true sense and interpretation of Scriptures and thereby the deciding of all differences in religion, are to be known and taken from the Catholic Church, from General Councils and the unanimous consent of Ancient Fathers".[52] "Not the Scriptures alone, but the Church of Christ expounding the same, is to be acknowledged and received for our guide and judge in matters of faith".[53] One should therefore be wary, when interpreting the "nonwritten" of an author like Anderson, not to read more recent problems and conceptions into it. Thus, a statement like the following could be misinterpreted: "We understand by the doctrine of the Church such points of faith also as, not being written in the Scriptures, have been delivered by word of mouth, the Holy Ghost inspiring them or Christ being the author of them: and these we believe to have as infallible authority of truth as if they had been written in the Scriptures".[54] In the light of Anderson's approach, "not written" is not the same as "not implied" in Scripture. It means that besides

---

[49] l.c., p. 77.
[50] l.c., pp. 170-171.
[51] l.c., p. 161.
[52] l.c., p. 35.
[53] l.c., p. 52.
[54] l.c., p. 23.

the immediate connotation of the written word, which the Church knows in her heart, the Church's doctrine also contains points or practices which, without being, strictly speaking, the meaning of a written passage, nevertheless are "no additions", being contained in Scripture "in general and, as it were, virtually". These traditions, although remote from the literal meaning of Scripture, appear, in this perspective, similar to the "mystical and spiritual senses". They are difficult to determine by reading Scripture, yet quite certainly they are the sense of the Holy Spirit as soon as the Church proclaims them.

Undoubtedly, another analogy may also be made: the Church's knowledge of Scripture and of tradition originates in an inspiration by God. This is not far removed from the Calvinist notion of interior testimony. Anderson, however, distinguishes carefully between his appeal to the Church as the depository of the unwritten word or traditional meaning of the Scriptures, and the Calvinist appeal to the Spirit: "Some object that the Church receives from God inspiring her the right sense of Scripture, and so first decides the controversy in her mind before she can exteriorly decide what is to be believed: therefore the Spirit speaking in her heart is the supreme Judge, even to Catholics".[55] Notably enough, Anderson does not deny this. Yet he does not make the testimony of the Spirit to the heart of Church leaders the rule of faith: there is no rule of faith until their interior conviction of the sense of Scripture has been publicly endorsed by the Church in a judicial sentence: "The motions of the Spirit inspiring the pastors of the Church are unknown to others and to themselves uncertain, until they be outwardly decreed and subscribed by the head and members of the Church, and so are no judicial sentences or final decisions or rules infallible, either to themselves or others". Undoubtedly, the rule of faith cannot be a merely subjective persuasion in the hearts of bishops or popes. Only when the Church as a whole has spoken is the meaning of revelation known for certain. Yet this does not destroy the analogy between the testimony of the Spirit in the hearts of the faithful and his testimony in the heart of the Church. The former is the Calvinist rendering of the Catholic insight which the latter formulation expresses. The real difference lies in ecclesiology: either one identifies the Church with each faithful relationship to God speaking in his word; or, on the contrary, over and above his testimony in the heart of each Christian, the Spirit

---

[55] l.c., pp. 119-120.

gives a wider testimony in the heart of all, together mystically present in the supernatural structure of the Body of Christ.

In the same year, 1634, Matthew Wilson, S.J. (1582-1656), alias Edward Knott, published a book against Dr. Potter which is remarkable mainly for the fact that it provoked William Chillingworth's long answer *The Religion of Protestants, a Safe Way to Salvation* (1638). In his short essay *Mercy and Truth, or Charity Maintained by Catholics* (1634), Wilson does not treat the question of tradition in itself. Yet he devotes a few pages to the Protestant reading of Scripture. His main point, like that of Anderson, is that Scripture alone cannot be a judge of controversy in matters of religion—a point which he proves on the ground of the nature of a writing (chap. 2, nos. 3-5), the nature of Holy Scripture (nos. 6-14), the nature of biblical translations (nos. 15-16), the difficulty of interpreting the Bible (nos. 17-18), the nature of a judge (nos. 18-25), and finally the admissions of several Protestant authors (nos. 26-27).

The Catholic reverence for Scripture is affirmed from the outset: "No cause imaginable could avert our will from giving the function of supreme and sole judge to Holy Writ, if both the thing were not impossible in itself, and if both reason and experience did not convince our understanding that, by this assertion, contentions are increased and not ended".[56] Scripture is "a most perfect rule, forasmuch as a writing can be a rule"; yet Catholics deny "that it excludes either divine Tradition, though it be unwritten, or an external judge to keep, to propose, to interpret it in a true, orthodox and catholic sense". Since the unwritten word preceded the written word in the beginning, it is logical that both should continue now in the Church: "What greater wrong is it for the written word to be compartner with the unwritten, than for the unwritten, which was once alone, to be afterward joined with the written?" The Church does not only hand us a script to read; she also preaches and proclaims its meaning in her own doctrines. Matthew Wilson's position may, then, be summed up in this short statement: "If we receive the knowledge of Christ and Scriptures from the Church, from her also we take His doctrine and the interpretation thereof".[57] Whereas Scripture alone is an "inanimate writing", the Church is "a living judge".[58] Traditions derive

---

[56] I quote Wilson according to Chillingworth, *The Religion of Protestants, a Safe Way to Salvation*, Philadelphia, 1840, p. 87.

[57] l.c., p. 99.

[58] l.c., p. 102.

from the Church's function "infallibly to interpret Scriptures already written, or, without Scripture, by divine unwritten Traditions and assistance of the Holy Ghost, to determine all controversies".

The irony of the matter lies in Chillingworth's refutation of Wilson: Chillingworth admitted, like Wilson, the infallibility of universal unwritten traditions and saw no contradiction between this principle and the self-sufficiency of Scripture. Yet he complained that Wilson should have proven more: "You were to prove the Church infallible, not in her Traditions (which we willingly grant, if they be as universal as the Tradition of the undoubted books of Scripture is, to be as infallible as the Scripture is: for neither does being written make the Word of God the more infallible, nor being unwritten make it the less infallible); not therefore in her universal Traditions were you to prove the Church infallible, but in all her decrees and definitions of controversies".[59] Chillingworth believed he knew better than Wilson what was the Roman Catholic conception of "traditive interpretations", with the result that Wilson explained one doctrine and Chillingworth refuted another. The point, for Wilson, was that since Scripture cannot speak, it needs a living voice to pronounce sentence out of it, this judge under the Spirit's guidance drawing on the Church's memory of what the apostles said and did. But the correlation of Scripture and Church cannot be limited to controversies. Before these arise, such a correlation already exists and it rests upon the very nature of faith: "Scripture can be clear only to those who are endued with the eye of faith. . . . Faith then must not originally proceed from Scripture, but it is to be pre-supposed, before we can see the light thereof; and consequently there must be some other means precedent to Scripture, to beget faith, which can be no other than the Church".[60]

This was firmly traditional ground. But Chillingworth refuted something else, namely, the concept of tradition as a separate transmission of given doctrines by other than scriptural conveyance. He wrote, apparently without a smile, that the sense of Wilson's argument "must be this: when only a part of the Scripture was written, then a part of the divine doctrine was unwritten; therefore now, when all the Scripture is written, yet some part of the divine doctrine is yet unwritten".[61] The discussion went at cross-purposes. Matthew

---

[59] l.c., p. 217.
[60] l.c., p. 94.
[61] l.c., pp. 109-110.

Wilson explained the classical conception of the correlation between Church and Scripture, while Chillingworth argued against a position close to that which was later to be called the two-source theory.

Their misunderstanding is all the more unfortunate as the antagonists should have known better. Wilson's works do not reveal a great mind; he was a mediocre theologian; yet of his good faith no one can doubt. As he wrote in the "Epistle dedicatory to Prince Charles" at the beginning of *Christianity Maintained* (1638), "My scope and work, as I am saying, is only to maintain the authority of Holy Scripture, the mystery of the Blessed Trinity, the Deity of our Blessed Saviour, the infallibility of his Apostles, the power of his miracles, the necessity of his grace and of the absolute certainty of the Christian faith". All these points he felt endangered by Chillingworth's theology, and he devoted his rather pedestrian volumes to a defense of the traditional faith against a much better equipped, but strangely blinded adversary.

Of Chillingworth's high standing in the opinion of the Catholics who knew his character best there is ample evidence. Paulinus Cressy calls him "that extra-ordinary sublime wit and judgement" and regrets the necessity that has compelled him to criticize Chillingworth's theological opinions. His *Exomologesis* movingly points to the dilemma of friendship caught in conscientious disagreement:

> I shall have frequent occasion hereafter in this narration to weigh both his proofs and objections, at least such of them as were most powerful with me, but resolving to be extremely tender of his reputation; and if the inwardness which I had for many years with that worthy person does enable me to say any more of the like kind, yet the mutual friendship between us, the great obligations I have to cherish his memory, and the high esteem of his excellent parts make me so far from being willing to say anymore that I am sorry that I cannot with a good conscience blot out that which I have already written.[62]

Not all the theologians who entered the fray of the Chillingworth controversy thought so highly of their adversary. Many of them, like Wilson, professed to consider him either a determined propagator or an unconscious tool of Socinianism, which had become the bugbear of many traditional Christians, Anglican or Catholic. Yet Cressy's heartfelt expression of regrets may serve as a suitable epilogue to this chapter, which has seen the sharpening of theological issues— a good thing—through the always to be moaned, yet at times unavoidable, fire of polemics.

---

[62] *Exomologesis*, p. 141; see below, ch. 5.

CHAPTER FOUR

SCRIPTURE ALONE

The process of polishing the tools of polemics continued with Richard Smith (1566-1655) who in 1625 succeeded William Bishop as bishop of Chalcedon and Ordinary for the Catholics of England, Wales and Scotland. Unlike several of our authors, Smith is not the man of one book: in the course of his long life he wrote half a dozen important volumes of polemical theology, the first appearing in 1609 and the last nearly fifty years later, in 1653. Judging from his stormy episcopal career, which brought him into open conflict with the regulars, with the Catholic nobility and, finally, with the Holy See, which he sorely aggravated by refusing to resign, he must have been a singularly disagreeable man with a one-track turn of mind. It was largely in reaction to his intransigence that no successor was appointed when he died, and that English Catholics were left without a bishop until 1685, when John Leyburn was made bishop of Hadrumetum and Vicar apostolic in England and Wales.[1] Yet, considering his success as a professor at Valladolid and Sevilla and as President of the English Collège d'Arras in Paris, he must have enjoyed adequate intellectual and administrative abilities.

Richard Smith's main theological works follow a clear pattern conceived at long-range. In 1609 he publishes *The Prudential Balance of Religion*, the second part of which appears in 1622 under the title *A Conference of the Catholic and Protestant Doctrine with the Express Words of Holy Scripture*. These two parts of one project are unrelated as to contents. The first compares Augustine of Canterbury, the apostle of Catholicism in England, and Luther, the founder of Protestantism. The second, originally published, unlike the first, in Latin, compares both Catholic and Protestant doctrines with the Scriptures. Smith's idea was, first to help simple people with arguments borrowed from "the rules of true prudence and right reason", these being "the most general, most easy and most effectual for all

---

[1] See Basil Hemphill, *The Early Vicars Apostolic of England, 1666-1750*, London, 1954.

sorts of people",[2] and afterwards to help theologians with a deeper study of the basic conflicts between the Catholic and the Protestant faiths. Smith admits that only the second study does justice to the issues, for "Catholics and Protestants agree that to be the true religion of God which is most agreeable to his word". But he reckons that it would be unwise to use the test of the word in front of common people: "Since they neither agree which is his word (Protestants rejecting much of that which Catholics reverence for God's heavenly word), nor which is the sense thereof, they cannot be brought to agree about one balance of God's word whereby they may weigh their religion together".[3] If this is so even for learned doctors, it is obvious that, as "not only Catholics teach but also Protestants confess. . . the weaker sort of Christians cannot judge which is the true exposition of Scriptures". Smith is led to conclude that "to weigh religions to them by the balance of Scripture were to weigh one unknown thing by another".

With somewhat questionable optimism, Smith believes that "the weights of prudence and right reason are both common and evident to all": he is of course in this a child of his times, the age of Descartes and the *Discours de la Méthode* (1637). The 598 pages of *The Prudential Balance of Religion* are therefore devoted to a non-theological demonstration of the falsity of Protestantism in the light of the personality of its founder.

Smith was no doubt aware of the dubious aspect of this method, for he justified it in a Latin book, which was later published in English with the title *Of the Author and Substance of the Protestant Church and Religion* (1621), in which, among other things, he played the since then oft-repeated game of pinpointing the essence of Protestantism. In a word, he thinks that this essence resides in the principle of Justification by faith alone. Protestantism as Smith describes it is strict Lutheranism; other shades of reformed doctrine are not truly Protestant. Having shown this, Smith sets out to prove that Luther, who fathered Protestantism, cannot possibly have been guided by God.

The relevance of this essay in detection comes through in the preface of the work, where Smith explains that it is easier to argue over questions of fact than over points of doctrine. Catholic doctrinal

---

[2] *The Prudential Balance of Religion*, "Epistle to the most noble and renowned English nation", fol. 2 v.
[3] l.c., fol. 3 r.

proofs "are certainly theological demonstrations, because they are clearly drawn from the proper principles of divinity, to wit, from clear words of God confirmed by the Tradition of the Church and unanimous exposition of the Fathers".[4] Unfortunately, these proofs "take little effect" with heretics, who quarrel over the meaning of Scripture, or with the unlearned, who "hardly perceive what kind of proof is a theological demonstration and such as divinity can afford no greater, or which is the true sense of God's word, or how great the authority of the Church or Fathers ought to be". It is therefore better, wherever possible, to use demonstrations that are not only theological but also, "that I may so speak, mathematical". Smith explains this "mathematical" aspect in this way:

> They consist of one principle which is grounded not only upon the foundation of Divinity, to wit, the word of God together with the exposition of the Church and Fathers, but also is manifest by the light of reason.[5]

In Richard Smith's mind, this kind of demonstration does not bring true doctrine down to the level of purely rational philosophy. "Neither let any think", he warns us, "that that religion which is most agreeable to prudence and the light of reason is not also most agreeable to Scripture".[6] Using rather disparate metaphors, Smith calls reason and Scripture "words of different degrees" and "twins of one and the selfsame parent", who have "great sympathy and connexion together". He compares the relation of God's "word and faith" to "the natural insight which our understanding has of truth" with that of grace to "the natural inclination of our will to good". In their origin they are one; it is by their structure that they differ. Borrowing, yet distorting, traditional imagery, Smith significantly identifies the "word in the heart" with the light of reason:

> Reason and Scripture are both God's word and God's truth, the one natural, written by his own hand in our souls by creation, the other supernatural, written in paper with the hands of his holy scribes by revelation.[7]

Such language would seem to ascribe more importance to reason than to revelation; and there is little doubt that, at this stage, Richard

---

[4] *Of the Author and Substance of the Protestant Church and Religion*, 1621, fol. 3v.
[5] l.c., fol. 4 r.
[6] *The Prudential Balance . . .*, fol. 3v.
[7] l.c., fol. 3 r.

Smith tries to argue for the Church by the universal light of reason rather than the particular light of faith, on the basis of historical fact rather than of scriptural datum.

Yet this method is only destined to prepare the second half of his self-assigned task to refute Protestant doctrine and to help the Catholics engaged in controversy. The time must come to deal the ultimate blow to the Lutheran Reformation by challenging it, no longer at the level of historical fact and before the tribunal of reason, but on the very ground claimed by Protestantism as its own and before the courts of supernatural faith. The *Conference of the Catholic and Protestant Doctrine with the Express Words of Holy Scripture* (Latin edition, 1622; English translation, 1631) is undoubtedly, from the standpoint of Smith's conception of Scripture, his major work. True it is, little can be kept from the argumentation of the book: on the successive points considered, which number no less than two hundred and sixty, Smith merely quotes the Scriptures, thus constituting a chain of citations that may have proved useful to preachers and other popularizers of Catholic doctrine, but remain of little interest to theologians. The very reason why Smith was satisfied that this constituted a good method, however, is highly relevant to our investigation; and he explains himself at length in a long methodological preface to the reader, "wherein the scope, manner of proceeding and profit of this book is declared". Smith himself deemed this preface a necessary contribution to the arguments proposed, and he warned that it was "requisite to be read before the book".

The *Conference of the Catholic and Protestant Doctrine* fulfils the long cherished project, already announced in the preface to the book of 1609: after disproving Protestantism "by the weights of prudence and right reason", Smith wishes to do so again "according to their claims to the Holy Scripture and the express words thereof".[8] The present work aims at showing that "they have no reasonable or colorable pretense of Scripture, but that it makes expressly, clearly and directly against them and for Catholics, almost in all points of controversy".[9] But, and here Smith launches a revealing methodological discussion, two ways may be adopted for such a demonstration. The one proceeds "by conferring of diverse places together, by bringing the exposition of the Holy Fathers, decrees of Councils

---

[8] *A Conference of the Catholic and Protestant Doctrine*, preface, n. 1.
[9] l.c., n. 4.

and traditions of the Church": this method of exegesis backed up by patristic and historical references is the one "which hitherto Catholic writers have followed". In adopting another method, the bishop of Chalcedon is aware of pioneering a new approach: he will simply compare "the express words of Catholics and Protestants with the express words of Holy Scripture touching the same matter". The first reason given for selecting this kind of argument is purely pragmatic: Smith writes for the common people and wants to give them something geared to their capacity. The first method would be above their reach, while the second "is as clear for everyone to see as it is clear to see that Yea and Yea of the same matter agree, and that Yea and Nay do disagree". In spite of this concern for effectiveness, Smith's simplified method may be justified theologically, and the rest of the preface is devoted to demonstrate its legitimacy.

Two conditions are required, however, for the method to work. One regards the words or letter of Scripture, and the other their meaning or sense, for Scripture "consists of two parts, whereof the one is the word or letter, the other is the sense thereof". The first condition may well be judged superfluous: Smith wants "the words of Holy Scripture to be taken as they be in the Bible or book of God, without any addition, subtraction, or transposition: briefly without any chopping or changing whatsoever".[10] This would seem to be implied in the very idea of arguing from the bare words of Scripture; but I suppose some amount of redundancy may be pardoned when writers are caught in the fire of controversy. Smith must make sure that his purpose is understood. He nonetheless puts forward an interesting explanation for this self-evident condition: "Where God alone is Judge", he says, "there it is reason that all men be silent and only hearken what God says, nor interrupt or corrupt his words". Other reasons are, that since Protestants impose silence on the Church in matters of faith, "it were impudency for them to request to speak", and that, if they themselves speak, they contradict their own standard, for in that case, "they admit not the only word of God for judge of controversies, but partly also their own, and make one entire judge of them both". Smith concludes, in typical fundamentalist language,

> I will compare their doctrine with the Scripture, mere Scripture, only Scripture, and let them hearken to nothing but Scripture; let all their own words whatsoever be set aside; let the Scripture's pure and only words show and judge...

[10] l.c., n. 5.

The second condition is germane to the first, although Richard Smith, with more than necessary thoroughness, explains it at length. He wants to interpret the meaning of the words of Scripture at face-value: "That the pure written word of God may judge betwixt us according to the pure sense thereof, which (when it is spoken clearly or of purpose to tell us what God's meaning is) of itself and according to the usual acception of men it does afford".[11] In other words, the bishop of Chalcedon will carefully shun all exegesis. He will "set aside a while men's guesses or imaginations of the conference or exposition of this or that place of Scripture, with which we may weigh what we will and how we will, saying: This is the meaning; that is not the meaning; this follows; that follows not; this is true; that is false". To this hermeneutics, practised by Catholics and Protestants, and which is unavoidable if the Scriptures need explaining, Smith, sounding like a Puritan, opposes "the divine and pure scale of the pure meaning of God's pure word". Admittedly, he does not claim that all Scripture is clear; he simply intends to restrict the argument to clear passages, to places where Scripture "speaks both clearly and of set purpose for to express her meaning", to "that which is in plain terms and of set purpose spoken to declare one's meaning", to "plain and clear words, spoken of purpose, and in such sense as usually men understand such words".[12] But there are in his opinion, many such passages, enough, to be sure, to back up more than two hundred and sixty points of Catholic doctrine.

Smith will therefore "take that light which the Scripture of itself gives". To this beam from God he opposes Protestant exegesis, apparently unaware that his description could apply just as well to Catholic exegesis, because it simply describes the process of literary analysis. The effort to escape the pure word of God forces Protestants, Smith states,

> to say that much of the Scripture was not spoken of certain knowledge, or not according to the meaning of the speaker; to teach that most weighty sentences of the Scripture were spoken ironically, mimetically, and hyperbolically; to change the most universal propositions of the Scripture into particulars; to limitate speeches not limited by the Scripture; to alter absolute speeches into conditional; to make causal propositions not causal; to expound words in some sort, which were spake simply; which were spaken of one time, to interpret them of another; to make one saying of many; to understand words that signify the

[11] l.c., n. 6.
[12] l.c., n. 7.

doing of a thing, of an endeavor to do it; which signify working a thing, of the way or mean thereto; which signify that a thing is, to expound that it ought to be; words which signify a true thing, to expound them of a show or apparent thing. . . .

Admittedly, Richard Smith does not object to exegesis in principle when the Scriptures do need clarification. But he is eager to accept the challenge of Protestantism on the ground that, where Scripture is clear, the pure word of God ought to be enough to sort out true doctrine from false. Taking up the challenge amounts to a sort of theological gamble: "Either the Scripture in matters of controversy declares her meaning by herself without any help or exposition of man, or she does not". If she does, let us abide by her decision; if she does not, Catholic doctrine has nothing to lose, but the Protestant stance by Scripture alone has then been disproved: "For if by herself she does not clearly declare her meaning in matters in controversy without some help of man (especially without the help of one of the opposite parties who contend about her meaning) certainly she is not fit to be the only judge of controversies".[13] Thus Bishop Smith ultimately claims that the basic principle of Protestants, Scripture alone, proves the Catholic position.

To establish this paradox beyond doubt, he will borrow his statements of Catholic doctrine from the Council of Trent or its Catechism, or, if he finds no suitable passages there, from authors in good standing like Thomas Aquinas, Stapleton or Bellarmine. Texts will not be selected for their scriptural overtones but as good epitomes of Catholic doctrine; and Richard Smith is confident that, placing straightforward expressions of the Catholic faith besides the plain Scripture, "we may see that when the Catholic doctrine is to be set down most plainly and distincly by them who best know it, of its nature it requires to be delivered with the very same or the like words which the Scripture uses". Catholic formulations spontaneously fall into a scriptural pattern, and they urge men to pass from language to meaning and to gather that "the Catholic doctrine is in very deed one and the selfsame with the doctrine of the Scripture".[14]

Protestant doctrine likewise will be expressed in the words of recognised spokesmen for Protestant divinity, in Smith's words, of

---

[13] l.c., n. 6.
[14] l.c., n. 9.

"the first, chiefest and famousest Protestant preachers and leaders": [15] their comparison with plain and clear Scripture will show them up as "so many barkings of dogs against heaven, so many cries of Jews against Christ, so many blasphemies of damned men against God".[16]

As for the testimonies of Scripture, it will not be necessary to bring in many citations for each point, "since God is as much to be believed in one word as in many".[17] No attempt will be made to prove that the words of Scripture are clear: this should be, by hypothesis, self-evident and the Scripture self-explanatory.

There is no need to elaborate on the immeasurable profit which Smith expects from his book and its method: it will provide "a short and easy" way to make an end of all controversies;[18] it will constitute a manual for polemicists, containing a synopsis of Scripture, of Catholic and of Protestant authors; it will snatch away from Protestants their claim to follow Scripture; above all it will show that in almost all matters in controversy, "Catholics do stick fast to the very words of Scripture and religiously keep her letter and form of speech",[19] a point which Smith glosses in this way. As regard the letter: "What she calls faith, we call faith; what she calls the body of Christ, we call the body of Christ". As regards the form: "Where the Scripture affirms, we affirm; where the Scripture denies, we deny". As regards the sense: "Catholics in all these 260 points do admit that sense which the express words of Scripture, and they spoken of purpose to declare God's mind, do of themselves propose".[20]

Smith ends his preface with a short examination of some objections or "scruples", concerning the Latin Vulgate, the fact that Scripture at times seems to contradict itself in words if not in meaning, the allegation that some Catholics also have opposed the Bible, and the correlative contention that not all Protestants contradict Scripture. Then, carried away by the expected success of his demonstration of 260 points of Catholic doctrine, Bishop Richard Smith (he was a bishop at least when his English text was published) proclaims that everyone may see, as a result of his work, that the first Protestants taught "the word of the Devil", were "ministers of the

[15] l.c., n. 19.
[16] l.c., n. 10.
[17] l.c., n. 8.
[18] l.c., n. 11.
[19] l.c., n. 12.
[20] l.c., n. 14.

Devil... blinded from hell... apostates... wolves... (who) drew
Christians from God's truth to the Devil's lies, from the lap of the
Catholic Church to the den of thieves, from the assured path of
salvation to the open way of damnation".[21] Then, feeling perhaps
that this language may be too strong for the tender ears of Protestants,
he adds a less than irenic afterthought: "If at any time I use any
sharp words against Protestants" they are intended only for their
teachers and leaders. And he prays that God may open their eyes.

Some twenty years after the publication of the English version of
The Conference of the Catholic and Protestant Doctrine .., Richard Smith
returned to the problem which was at the center of his theological
and apologetical concerns, the question of Scripture alone, with a
long volume entitled *Of the All Sufficient Proposer of Matters of Faith*
(1653) which was signed D.R., Doctor of Divinity. Making a
distinction between a "proposer", that is, "an intellectual person"
who proposes faith, and a "proposal", namely, that which is proposed
to faith, he explains at length that the Church is properly to be called
the proposer, while Scripture belongs in the categories of proposal.[22]
The first book proves "that the true Church of God is the all-sufficient external proposer of matters of faith", whereas the second
shows "how Scripture is or is not an entire rule of faith". It is in the
second book that Richard Smith comes to the point which is of
concern to us, the function of Scripture. A short preface introduces
the problem in these terms:

> Because the letter of Scripture is a proposal of points of faith, though
> we cannot properly enquire whither Scripture propose all points of
> faith because that is the part of a proposer, yet we may enquire whether
> in Scripture or by Scripture all points of faith which are any ways
> necessary to be believed of any kind of men be sufficiently proposed, as
> Protestants commonly affirm and Catholics ever deny.[23]

The question if therefore not *where* Scripture proposes all the doctrines, but whether all the articles proposed by the Church are
contained in "the letter of Scripture as a proposal of points of faith".
The Protestant stance makes Scripture the proposer, and this Smith
will not discuss here because he has refuted it in the first book. He
will only examine whether Scripture, called proposer by the ones and
proposal by the others, does contain all points of faith.

---

[21] l.c., n. 19.
[22] *Of the All-Sufficient Proposer of Matters of Faith*, p. 311.
[23] l.c., p. 312.

More than half of this second book, however, is hardly relevant: it attempts to demonstrate the Catholic position by documenting the uncertainties, hesitancies, confusions and contradictions of Protestant authors. Each chapter comprises two sections: "Protestants sometimes affirm"; "Protestants sometimes deny", with the result that Smith, after one hundred pages of such a *sic et non*, can conclude:

> But now having shown the manifold and main uncertainties and contradictions of Protestants touching Scripture, let any judicious reader judge whether Protestants can rationally say or think that the Scripture is the only Judge or only Rule or only sufficient proposer of points of faith, appointed by God for to direct and guide us assuredly and infallibly in matters of assured and infallible faith.[24]

Thus psychologically prepared, the reader is now presented with the "Catholics' certain and constant doctrine concerning the same".

Richard Smith begins with a long exposé and demonstration of the negative aspect of the Catholic position. In the first place, Scripture "taken by itself alone without attestation of the Church that it is the letter or word of God, cannot sufficiently propose to men any thing to be believed with divine and infallible faith" [25] (ch. XIV). Previously to the proposal of faith, we need to be certain that Scripture is the word of God, and such a certainty comes from the Church and not from Scripture itself. In the second place, granted that Scripture is the word of God, it "does not sufficiently propose to men all points of faith" [26] (ch. XV), for unwritten Traditions of faith are known to all Catholics and are even acknowledged by many Protestants. From there on, Smith proceeds by successive mopping up of several aspects of the question. Scripture does not sufficiently propose all points of faith "to all men capable of external proposal" (ch. XVI), for the rather childish reason that the blind and the illiterate cannot read it.—Scripture has not proposed all points of faith "at all times" (ch. XVII), since there was no Scripture before Moses; or in all places (ch. XVIII), since St Irenaeus testifies that the Scriptures have not been translated in all the languages spoken by Christians.— Scripture does not propose all points of faith "clearly enough" (ch. XIX).—Finally the Scripture's proposal of points of faith

---

[24] l.c., p. 410.
[25] l.c., p. 411.
[26] l.c., p. 441.

"is not necessary, in ordinary course, to have divine faith" (ch. XX).
This leads to a good summary of Smith's argumentation:

> It is evident that (Scripture) is not the all-sufficient proposer in-
> stituted by God for to believe with divine faith. For first it is no
> intellectual person as doubtless a proposer of points of faith is. Sec-
> ondly it proposes not all points which God will have us to believe
> with divine faith. Thirdly it does not propose clearly enough all the
> points of faith which it proposes. Fourthly, it proposes not all points
> of faith to all kinds of men who are capable of external proposal.
> Fifthly it has not been at all times nor in all places when and where
> divine faith was. Sixthly, in ordinary course it is not necessary to have
> divine faith.

Smith fully realises the negative aspect of this approach, for he
immediately switches to the positive side: "But now having seen
what the Scripture is not, let us see what it is. For though it be not
the proper proposer of faith instituted by God, yet it has many excellent properties conducing to that end".[27]

Before we take a look at this complementary view of Scripture,
however, we ought to draw attention to some remarks made by
Smith in the course of his demonstration.

Richard Smith's main proof that Scripture does not establish the
fact that it is the word of God could easily be dismissed today because it appeals to the Aristotelian categories of matter and form:
one does not find in Scripture "the material object of divine faith,
which is God's saying that it is his Word";[28] and Scripture is in no
better position regarding the formal object of faith, "which is authority": "because authority is in an author, and an author is a rational
intellectual person saying something which for his authority or
credit we believe".[29] Matter refers to the content of Scripture (and
here more specifically to the belief in Scripture as the Word of God);
form to the authority on whose testimony we believe. If this is not
strikingly enlightening in regard to Scripture or to the structure of
faith, it becomes highly relevant in Smith's description of Tradition.
For Smith faces squarely a question which arises out of his demonstration that Scripture cannot sufficiently propose faith. Catholics do
not rely for this on Scripture but on Tradition. In these conditions,

---

[27] l.c., p. 483.
[28] l.c., p. 424.
[29] l.c., p. 425.

it is legitimate and unavoidable, to ask "Why is Tradition of itself credible, and not Scripture?" [30]

Smith's answer is couched in the categories of matter and form. And suddenly, out of his heavy-handed treatment of delicate questions, in the outmoded framework of Aristotelian notions, a spark of light shines, which anticipates some of the more modern developments of the theology of Tradition. "I answer", the bishop of Chalcedon writes,

> that if we speak of Tradition materially, that is, of the doctrine which we have by Tradition, that is no more credible of itself than is the doctrine which we have by the Scripture... But if we speak formally of Tradition, as it is an act of the Church, that is of itself credible, because that includes the delivery of doctrine by the lively or living voice of the Church. Which voice of the Church is evident to us, and her authority makes the doctrine which she delivers to us credible.[31]

This short text introduces the distinction, with which we are familiar today, of passive Tradition—called here "material"—and of active Tradition—called "formal"—. The formal Tradition or the formal aspect of Tradition is shown to be the more important, in that it gives credibility to the contents of Tradition. This formal aspect is furthermore set in an ecclesiological context: it is "an act of the Church". Finally, this act "includes the delivery of doctrine by the lively or living voice of the Church": thus the nineteenth century stress on the living Tradition is heralded. At one stroke we thus find aspects of later theology (passive and active Tradition, predominance of active over passive Tradition, Tradition as an act of the Church, Tradition as implying a living voice), clearly expressed in 1653. As the following chapters will show, Richard Smith was not, in the 1650's, a lone witness for a very advanced notion of Tradition. Especially with Christopher Davenport and Thomas White, he was one of several who opened the perspectives into which future theology was to enter. By the same token, one may well say that little has been discovered since these men wrote: we have only enlarged and re-affirmed some of their insights.

Richard Smith explains in three chapters the positive aspect of the Catholic doctrine on Scripture (ch. XXI-XXIII). Here as elsewhere he carefully limits the question to Scripture properly so called, the written Word. In this he is more careful, as he lets us know, than most

---

[30] l.c., p. 437.
[31] l.c., pp. 437-438.

Protestants and also, we may add, than many Catholics. For the expression, "the Word of God", may mean several things besides Scripture. In a list that is clearly not exhaustive, he remarks that "the word of God" may be "well understood either of the *word preached* (Gal. 1, 8) without which there is no faith (Rom. 10, 14) or of the *ingrafted word, which can save our souls* (James 1, 21) or of the *word written in the hearts of the faithful* (Jerome)".[32] I fail to see any difference between these last two meanings, but this is neither here nor there. Smith obviously wishes to emphasize the dynamic aspect of the expression "Word of God", which is not simply written in dead letters, but comes alive in the Church's preaching, is a source of salvation when it has been engrafted in the Christian soul, and is faithfully pondered over and kept in the hearts of the faithful. The problem at hand, however, is restricted to the written Word.

The bishop of Chalcedon has stressed time and time again, in the 483 pages of his book, that Scripture is not a sufficient proposer of the faith. Now, however, he adopts a dialectically opposite position: if Scripture does not propose all points of faith, nevertheless it "contains the sum of Christian faith and all things that are necessary to be believed of all kinds of men explicitly".[33] This title of chapter XXI stands in contrast with the great bulk of the previous demonstration, where Scripture was shown not to be sufficient a proposer of faith. Chapter XXII ("That the Scripture teaches plainly enough the sum of Christian faith and all things absolutely necessary to be believed explicitly")[34] is in contrast with that part of the exposé which has shown Scripture not proposing the points of faith clearly.

In spite of this, the bishop of Chalcedon is not contradicting himself and giving back to Scripture and to Protestants with the left hand what his right hand has taken away from them. His concern is to define the exact scope of the Catholic-Protestant disagreement, now that Protestants have been shown to be, by and large, wrong. And the difference between the two sides turns out to be much less than expected. Protestants maintain that Scripture proposes all points of faith; Catholics that Scripture does not propose yet contains them: "That the Scripture contains the sum of Christian faith and all things necessary to be explicitly believed of all kinds of men, is manifest".[35]

---

[32] l.c., p. 423.
[33] l.c., p. 485.
[34] l.c., p. 492.
[35] l.c., p. 485.

"It seems that both St John and St Luke profess that they wrote in their Gospel the sum of Christian faith and all that is absolutely necessary for salvation".[36] "And this the Fathers teach." Richard Smith, polemical as he can be elsewhere, becomes now very irenic and open, for he esteems that "this is all which some Protestants desire, though in words they will seem to say more".

There nonetheless remains between Catholics and many Protestants a wide rift, concerning which we could wish that Smith had been clearer than he turns out to be. The sentence where he defines "the true difference" is actually very obscure:

> Wherefore the true difference between us is not whether all things simply necessary to be explicitly believed, or all necessary to every one be in Scripture; but whether all things any way necessary, or necessary to any men, be in Scripture.[37]

Richard Smith's meaning hinges on the terms "every" and "any", "simply necessary" and "any way necessary". As I understand it, Catholics believe Scripture to contain "all things simply necessary", that is "necessary to every one", whereas Protestants, in Smith's rendering of their doctrine, teach that Scripture contains "all things any way necessary", that is, "necessary to any men".[38] For Catholics, the contents of Scripture delimit fundamental points without which no man can be saved; and some other elements of faith are not necessary to the salvation of every man. But Protestants, in Smith's words, "will have all points that are of faith to be either actually contained in Scripture or to be clearly inferred out of it. . .". Some of them even "will have not only all things necessary but also all things behoveful to salvation to be contained in Scripture". His restriction of the contents of Scripture to points absolutely necessary to salvation as distinguished from other points of faith, is reinforced by Smith's subsequent comments:

> We confess that it contains all which we acknowledge to be fundamental, that is, by God's institution absolutely necessary to salvation. . . I add also that the Scripture sufficiently teaches the far greater part of points of faith. . . . Moreover I add that the Scripture teaches mediately every point of faith, because it sends us to the Church, which teaches us all points of faith.[39]

---

[36] l.c., p. 486.
[37] l.c., p. 489.
[38] l.c., p. 490.
[39] l.c., pp. 490-491.

As a matter of fact, Richard Smith published in 1645 a book *Of the Distinction of Fundamental and Not-fundamental Points of Faith*, in which he gave the Catholic meaning of the doctrine of fundamentals: fundamental points refer to "principal or capital" points of faith, or to "such as are the foundations of other articles", or to such articles as "their actual belief is necessary to every particular person and to salvation", whereas the belief of not-fundamental points is only conditionally necessary, that is, "if they be sufficiently proposed".[40] Protestants on the contrary, as Richard Smith understands them, regard as fundamental articles the minimum required for Church unity, the profession of other points of faith being left to the discretion of each individual. Smith's volume on the *Fundamental and Not-fundamental Points of Faith*, however, does not enter the discussion of the function of Scripture regarding fundamentals, which he was to treat in his book of 1653 on the *All-sufficient Proposer*. . . .

Once the scope of Scripture is limited to the fundamentals of faith, the next point follows smoothly: Scripture teaches plainly what it teaches. The fundamentals are taught "in the plain and usual sense of these words, which is to teach plainly enough as can be by writing".[41] There is no need for complicated exegesis in order to arrive at all the points necessary to salvation. Scripture, however, may remain obscure in other parts and concerning other beliefs than those which are absolutely necessary.

In brief "Scripture is necessary to the better being of Christian faith".[42] In this sense Smith understands the statement of 2 Timothy 3,16: "All Scripture divinely inspired is profitable to teach, to reprove, to instruct". He suggests that this is really what Protestants mean by their exclusive emphasis on Scripture, thus implying that they ought to be satisfied with the positive aspect of the Catholic stand as he has explained it: "Indeed they make no greater necessity of Scripture than we do, whatsoever they pretend in words".[43]

How widespread among the Recusants was the theology of scriptural sufficiency upheld by the Bishop of Chalcedon? It clearly prolongs the lines of reflection that were instanced in our first chapter,

---

[40] *Of the Distinction of Fundamental and Non-fundamental points of faith*, (1645, signed C.R.), p. 95.
[41] *Of the All-Sufficient Proposer* . . ., p. 493.
[42] l.c., p. 496.
[43] l.c., p. 498.

where several authors tried to distinguish between two sufficiencies, the one being agreeable to Catholics and the other denied by them; yet it was in the middle of the century that this sort of investigation was pursued most thoroughly.

In 1655 the Jesuit John Spenser (1601-1671), alias Vincent Hattecliffe or also Tyrwhitt, published in Antwerp *Scripture Mistaken the Ground of Protestants and Common Plea of all new Reformers against the ancient Catholic Religion of England*. The seven points of controversies about which John Spenser wanted to correct the Protestant scriptural arguments are not especially relevant to our investigation. But the preface clearly outlines the task to be undertaken. Most Catholic apologists have followed a debating method which, though valid in itself, failed to dislodge Protestants from their basic stand:

> The Roman Church, even from the first challenge of her adversaries in these last ages, has given them the foil (nay quite defeated them) at the weapons of antiquity, universality, unity, succession, visibility, sanctity, miracles, Fathers, Councils; but these were so far and clearly her weapons that they (= Protestants) scarce ever durst lay claim to any of them, and so the victory (glassed in their eyes) seem either none or small because not gained with a weapon of their choosing.[44]

It still remains to win the victory with the Protestants' own weapon, namely, "the written word of God, the sole written word". Admittedly, the Church has never admitted defeat at the hands of Holy Scripture, and has always accepted to debate on this ground, requiring only the presence of able judges who would decide who has won the encounter. Yet even then Protestants escape, for their theory recognizes no judge but Scripture alone. It is with Scripture alone that Protestants must be vanquished. And this is precisely what Spenser attempts to do:

> I have endeavored in this present treatise to give my readers an essay of this kind of victory of the Roman Church, wherein I hope he will find it manifest that the texts which our adversaries usually allege against the Roman doctrine in such points as I have touched are not arguments but mistakes.

To this end, Spenser demands that Scripture be quoted in its original tongue, that the meaning, in keeping with "their principle of sole Scripture", be defined as that which appears "by the words of the original", by "the plain and proper sense of the words", without

---

[44] The pages of the preface are not numbered.

flying, as Protestants often do, "to tropes and figures and improprieties and shadows and obscurities". He plans to keep himself "close to Scripture in the whole process".

John Spenser's endeavor is obviously similar to Richard Smith's and it rests on the same principle that, although the Catholic faith is preserved by Tradition coming from the Apostles, its major points— and even, in the case of *The Conference of the Catholic and Protestant Doctrine* and of *Scripture Mistaken*, minor points—can nonetheless be established on the basis of Scripture alone. Yet one may feel that these demonstrations have been pragmatic polemical devices rather than theological commitments to the sufficiency of Scripture. At any rate the theoretical background to the method, which at least Richard Smith explains at length, would deserve to be described with less polemical overtones than it is, in order to arrive at a full-fledged formulation of Catholic doctrine on Scripture. Richard Smith has indeed placed us on the way and he has opened rich perspectives, which still remain to be looked into at greater depth than he has himself done.

The next few chapters will show this as in fact one of the major concerns of the middle decades of the seventeenth century. Other authors of importance and depth concurred with Smith and Spenser in their search for an argumentation based on Scripture as exclusively as possible, within the Catholic conception of the faith. Some of them advanced further in the direction of the sufficiency of Scripture.

CHAPTER FIVE

SEVERAL CONVERTS

The men we have studied so far were cradle-Catholics, or, if converted at one time from allegiance to the Established Church, they acquired sufficient familiarity with Catholic theology to express themselves, in turn, in the quiet manner of serene possession, even when their serenity was superficially marred by the polemical tone of their writing. In this chapter we shall make the acquaintance of some authors who cast their theological contribution in the form of apologies for their "return home". Thus a new angle of vision will be opened, whence we may look at the problem of Scripture and Tradition somehow with the eyes of those who experienced several systems of relationships between the two, and who were therefore able to compare them, if not with the dispassionate detachment of theoretical scholars (if there can be any in this field), at least with the commitment of those who have witnessed the two systems at work in their own existence. This should afford complementary light to the testimony of Chillingworth who, after testing the Catholic understanding of Tradition, went back to his Protestant past.

Thomas Vane, a clergyman and physician, reached relatively high rank in the Established Church since he was Chaplain to the King at the time of his conversion, around 1645. He entitled his book *A Lost Sheep Returned Home* (1645) thus placing it on the shelf of conversion literature. With Vane's apology for his conversion a gush of fresh air enters our Recusant writings, in that it is much more personal than systematic, at the risk of being, by the same token, less professionally theological and less satisfactory in its approach to controverted questions. The book was effective enough after its publication in Paris to have been included in the works that were re-printed in England by Letters Patent from James II by the printer Matthew Turner of Holborn, in the short period when advantage could be taken of the King's dispositions to print and sell Catholic books openly.

Vane sums up the process of reasoning that led him to accept all the teachings of the Catholic Church:

Having thus found out that the Church was she from whom I was to receive assurance what is the word of God; and that otherwise it was impossible for me to know it, and that she could not mistake or err in her directions. I conceived then that I was bound to believe all that she propounded to me as the word of God, whether it was written or not written (writing being no testimony to the truth of anything, seeing it may be false, as well as speaking), and that to doubt anything was to call all into question and to dissolve the whole nature of divine faith.[1]

It thus became evident to Thomas Vane that all Christian doctrine is not necessarily written in the Holy Scriptures, and that the entire substance of the faith derives from the Apostles, whose testimony is true. This derivation is called Tradition, which Vane defines as "a full report of what was evident to sense, namely, what doctrines the Apostles taught, what Scriptures they wrote". Such a report being evident, "it is impossible it should be false".[2] Vane's reasoning appears clearly through these few texts: the successors of the Apostles knew clearly the Apostles' teachings; this knowledge passed down successive generations, to that, knowing evidently what was taught by our immediate forefathers, we by the same token know the apostolic doctrines thus transmitted.

Thus Vane ascribeds all doctrine both to the Word of God and to Tradition: "Nothing is to be reputed a matter of faith which is not formally and expressly to be proved by the word of God either written or unwritten, and delivered by full ecclesiastical Tradition".[3] One may wonder how far Thomas Vane would go toward acknowledging Tradition as not only identical with the Word of God transmitted to and in the Church, but also as channeling divine truths unknown to Scripture. Writing, he has said, is no warrant of the truth of anything; yet one should obviously distinguish between ordinary human authorship and the writing of the Scriptures under the inspiration of the Holy Spirit. Besides, the testimony of the 2nd Epistle to Timothy is to be taken into account: "All Scripture is inspired of God and useful to teach, refute, redress, form to justice" (2 Tim. 3,16). Alluding to this text, Thomas Vane counter-balances his statements on Tradition with an equally clear acknowledgement of the sufficiency of Scripture:

---

[1] *A lost sheep returned home*, 1645, p. 56.
[2] l.c., p. 39.
[3] l.c., p. 54.

Thus indeed the Scriptures may be granted sufficient, joined with Tradition, but not alone. And whereas there are some places of the Fathers alleged by Protestants to prove the Scriptures to be clear in all substantial points, they are to be understood, as the Apostle's words are, with reference to such men who have been before instructed by Tradition.[4]

In the framework of the Tradition Scripture is sufficient, but not outside of it.

By far the most fascinating account of conversion written in the 17th century is that of Hugh Paulin de Cressy (1605-1674), also known by his Benedictine name, Serenus. A fellow of Merton College, Cressy was in Holy Orders in the Church of England and held benefices in Dublin before he was reconciled with the Catholic Church in 1646 under Davenport's influence. He then studied theology for some time in Paris, where he knew Henry Holden, an English docteur de Sorbonne who will claim our attention later. In 1649, Cressy entered the Benedictine Order at Douai, where he resided for most of the next ten years. Having returned to England in 1660, he was involved in several theological controversies, notably with George Morley (1597-1684), Bishop of Worcester, in 1662 and with Edward Stillingfleet in 1672.

Serenus Cressy's book, *Exomologesis, or a faithful narration of the occasion and motives of his conversion unto Catholic Unity*, published in Paris in 1647, is both a highly subjective story of the author's spiritual itinerary and an excellent comparative study of Catholic and Anglican doctrines on Tradition and Scripture. Far from being accidental, this conjunction of two strains in Cressy's theological autobiography corresponds to fundamental conceptions that slowly dawned on him during his Anglican days and flowered in his reception into the Catholic communion. For the whole issue between Catholics and Protestants, as our author understands it, boils down to four problems, the solution of which puts into place the four cornerstones of religion: What is the Rule of Faith? Who is Judge of controversies in religion? What is schism? Is the Church perpetually visible? The four "conclusions", which provide the structure of Serenus Cressy's reflections, are tantamount to the four answers he gave to these questions.

The *Exomologesis* is, in the first place, an apology and it could indeed be compared with Newman's famous *Apologia pro Vita Sua*

---

[4] l.c., pp. 52-53.

(1864). Cressy's conversion has been attributed, as he complains in
the preface, to "worldly ambition, discontent and melancholy",
by persons who "did assume to themselves the authority or rather
licence to judge of my inward thoughts and intentions".[5] Cressy
originally planned no rejoinder; but at a time when he was considering
entering the Carthusian Order, his spiritual adviser asked, or ordered,
him to "give some proof both of the mature advice and also reason-
ableness of my change".[6] Thus Cressy wrote the *Exomologesis*, as a
public confession of "former errors and schism, but withall joined
with a discovery of, no doubt, many imperfections in searching after
truth during the twilight of my doubtings and uncertainties, and
many weaknesses in defending the truth after I had found it". It was
also meant to be a thanksgiving, "a *tabula votiva* representing to the
world the tempest of schism and heresy from which I could not have
escaped the utmost danger of shipwreck, had not Almighty God, the
lover of souls, provided a secure haven for me in the Catholic
Church".[7] Like Newman, Cressy found no other way to do this
"than by discovering myself nakedly to my very thoughts".[8] In
keeping with this resolve, Cressy's volume abounds in personal
reflections and in descriptions of his state of mind during his pil-
grimage from the Church of England to that of Rome. Incidentally,
this spiritual journey was probably occasioned and at least hastened,
although no one can warrant that it was caused, by the events of
1644, when civil war between the King's party and his opponents
led Cressy into exile in France. The political aspects of this tragedy
were disquieting enough: Cressy found this war "an object not only
of horror but even of astonishment, as having never read or heard of
any other that could enter into comparison with it".[9] The religious
implications of the conflict turned out to be still more surprising.
For the issue of the political struggle became a matter of life and
death to the Church as by law established. The spiritual drama of
those who saw the Church of England on the brink of extinction was
of course lived in many different ways by the exiles who were biding
their time at St. Germain around the diminished Court of King
Charles II, and elsewhere. Whereas some, like John Cosin, found

---

[5] *Exomologesis* . . ., preface, p. 2.—On Cressy, see J. McCann, *Lives of Fathers
Sabin and Cressy*, London, 1932.

[6] l.c., p. 4.

[7] l.c., pp. 6-7.

[8] l.c., p. 5.

[9] l.c., p. 9.

friendship and understanding among the Huguenots, others appreciated Gallican Catholicism as germane to their own religious ideal. But while a staunch High-Churchman like Herbert Thorndike could bear with serenity the long gestation of his remarkable book, *Epilogue to the Tragedy of the Church of England* (1659), others felt in duty bound to leave a sinking Church for one that seemed more likely to survive. This was Cressy's case. "For the present", he tells us, "I was in quest of a church, that church wherein I had been bred ere this time being almost ready to expire".[10] His search appeared to him all the more reasonable as the situation that prompted it was the more absurd: "Who could imagine", he wonders, "that an inconsiderable number of peevish ignorant Presbyterians should ever come to be able. . . upon quarrels against episcopal tyranny, to accept of a Presbyterian tyranny infinitely more unreasonable and intolerable?"[11] Further considering the principal tenets of Presbyterianism, Cressy raises the following question, which serves to introduce his reader to the chief theological issue studied in his book:

> What is more unreasonable than that sects, whose essential grounds are Scripture alone with a renouncing of all visible authority to interpret it, should yet assume to themselves an authority to inforce their opinions upon the consciences of others?"[12]

Thus the main doctrinal debate of *Exomologesis* centers on the problem of Tradition, seen in the shadow of the Protestant emphasis on Scripture alone without authoritative interpretation. Let us note, in view of Cressy's position as it will be outlined, that when he investigated the Church's authority in quiet retreats near Paris, he made it a point to study the Catholic authors who wrote after "the new schisms gave Catholics the opportunity to study this controversy more exactly", for he felt, with considerable acumen, that older testimonies could not provide "the most qualified sense of the Church's authority",[13] the Council of Trent and the controversies of the 16th century having focused the problem and sharpened the theological approach. He also sought for the strictest theology of the matter, "abstaining from relying upon the suspicious moderateness of Cassander, Franciscus de Santa Clara, etc." and turning to "the judgement of our learned Stapleton", who has never been suspected

---

[10] l.c., p. 218.
[11] l.c., p. 10.
[12] l.c., p. 11.
[13] l.c., p. 363.

by any Catholic "of tergiversation, partiality or unsoundness".[14] Cressy thus acquainted himself with the spirit of the Counter-Reformation at its most militant, although he could not of course express it in these terms: to him Stapleton represented an uncompromising theology, and this was what, as an Anglican seeking to know more about Roman Catholicism, he was looking for.

In the process of his conversion, Paulinus Cressy reached these two conclusions, which dominate his *Exomologesis*:

> 1° The entire rule of faith, comprised in the doctrines delivered by Christ and his Apostles immediately to the Church, are contained not only in Scripture, but likewise in unwritten Traditions.[15]
>
> 2° It belongs alone to the Catholic Church, which is the only depository of divine Revelations, authoritatively and with obligation to propose those revelations, to all Christians etc., to interpret the Holy Scriptures and to determine all emergent controversies; and this to the end of the world, inasmuch as the Church by virtue of Christ's promises and assistance is not only indefectible but continually preserved in all truth.[16]

Catholic doctrine Cressy exemplifies by quoting the Council of Trent. Even though the citations are long, we should give them in full in Cressy's translation. He quotes first the main section of the Tridentine decree on the Scriptures and the apostolic Traditions:

> The most holy, etc., synod of Trent, etc., clearly perceiving that this truth and discipline (namely, the doctrine of Christ and his Apostles) is contained in books written and unwritten Traditions, which were received from Christ's mouth or delivered as it were from hand to hand from the Apostles, to whom the Holy Ghost dictated it, has arrived even to us: following the orthodox examples of the Fathers, receives and venerates with an equal affection of duty and reverence all books as well of the Old as New Testament, since one God is the author of both, as likewise the Traditions themselves, whether pertaining to Faith or Manners, as dictated either by Christ's own mouth or by the Holy Ghost, and by a continued succession preserved in the Catholic Church.[17]

Whereas the Council of Trent here follows the Church Fathers, the Protestants in the main knowingly oppose them: Cressy quotes, among other texts, article 6 of the 39 Articles of the Church of England.[18]

---

[14] l.c., pp. 363-364.
[15] l.c., p. 123.
[16] l.c., pp. 246-247.
[17] l.c., p. 130; see D.-S., n. 1501.
[18] On the Thirty-nine Articles, see below, ch. 6.

Cressy completes his reference to Trent with the main passage of the decree on the Vulgate and the interpretation of Scripture, where he finds the "substance of what the Church has defined" concerning Church authority in matters of scriptural interpretation:

> Moreover, to the end to restraint petulant wits, this synod decree that no man, relying upon his own skill and wresting Holy Scripture to his own senses, shall presume to interpret the holy Scriptures in matters of faith and manners pertaining to the edification of Christian doctrine against that sense which has been and is held by (our) holy Mother the Church, to whom it appertains to judge of the true sense and interpretation of Holy Scriptures, and against the unanimous consent of Fathers, although such interpretations were never at any time to be published abroad.[19]

These texts, rather than the opposite passages from Protestant authors, represent the faith of the ancient Church: this, in a word, is the point on which Cressy's enquiry bears, and to which he devotes large sections of his *Exomologesis*. "The Catholics of these days do shew themselves indeed sons of those Catholic fathers, exactly treading their steps in appealing to Scriptures and general Tradition from which there lies no prescription or appeal".[20] The Fathers did not argue against heretics with the help of Scripture alone. They extolled indeed "the fulness of Scripture",[21] yet in most instances they rested their case upon Traditions, "Traditionary doctrine",[22] "Catholic Tradition",[23] the Apostles' *depositum* both of the doctrines and discipline of Christianity",[24] "the Traditionary interpretation of many ages".[25] In cases where Scripture was silent the early Church based its decisions "on Tradition alone",[26] thus demonstrating what Cressy prefers to call the indefectibility rather than the infallibility of the Church. In an autobiographical reminiscence, he remarks how "unfortunate" the word "infallibility" was for him, when, taking it in the most rigorous sense, he despaired "of ever being able with a good conscience to enter into the communion of the Catholic Church". Besides, he could neither find that word in any Council, nor see why it has been "pressed upon us with so much

[19] l.c., p. 282; see D.-S., n. 1507.
[20] l.c., p. 143.
[21] l.c., p. 146.
[22] l.c., p. 148.
[23] l.c., p. 124.
[24] l.c., p. 157.
[25] l.c., p. 423.
[26] l.c., pp. 157-158.

earnestness as of late it has generally been in disputations and books of controversy". Protestant arguments against infallibility—and here Cressy thinks first of all of Chillingworth—"if that word were once forgotten or but laid by, would, I am convinced by mine own experience, lose the greatest part of their strength, and however appear not to endanger the Catholic Church at all".[27] Thus, despite his preference for Stapleton above the irenists, Cressy has experienced the edge of the Catholic language and he is not loath to blunt it.

As a former member of the Establishment, Paulinus Cressy is acquainted with the Anglican claim to follow the Fathers, which was embodied in Jewel's challenge of 1558 and in the writings of most Caroline divines, even during the eclipse of the Interregnum. Nonetheless, far from taking a milder view of English Protestants than of English Puritans or continental Calvinists, Cressy interprets their appeal to the Fathers in psychological rather than theological terms. He has "experience of the particular disposition of English Protestants' ; he may well have enjoyed happiness "in the acquaintance and friendship with many of the most considerable persons for learning, prudence and piety in that Church"; yet, out of this fount of personal knowledge, he is convinced that "there is no point of controversy which they are more unwilling to touch upon than this".[28] Eager as they are to attack church infallibility in a negative way, they prove reluctant to justify positively their teaching regarding "Scriptures being the only rule, and no visible judge to interpret it". One reason for this, according to Cressy, lies in their gratitude to the Fathers for supporting their form of ecclesiastical government against Calvinist criticisms: this makes them hesitate to disagree with the Fathers' testimony in favor of "traditionary doctrines and rites".[29] But there still is another reason why English Protestants abstain from careful enquiries into the grounds of the doctrine expressed in their sixth Article. Speaking, as Cressy says, "knowingly of myself and not a few others", he suggests that if Anglicans do not sufficiently examine their positive identification of "express Scripture alone" with the rule of faith, this is because they have been excessively impressed by the negative arguments against the only alternative, namely, "ecclesiastical Tradition which is to be received upon the authority or (as

---

[27] l.c., pp. 284-285.
[28] l.c., pp. 134-135.
[29] l.c., pp. 135-136.

the Schools call it) the infallibility of the Church".[30] At bottom, they are afraid of laying bare the weakness of their position. For then the two only possible alternatives (Scripture alone, or authoritative Tradition) could fall to the ground. Both foundations would shrink. "Christianity itself would become questionable and a way made for direct atheism".[31] "Shame or remorse" impels Anglicans "to defer somewhat to the ancient Church's authority, as it were excusing themselves that they dare not suffer themselves to be directed by her; for if by her as a visible Church, then by all Churches succeeding her to these our times".[32] "No third intelligible way of grounding belief" is conceivable besides "divine revelation proposed and interpreted authoritatively by the Church, or mere Scripture without any obligatory interpretation";[33] and since English Protestants have already made their choice against the first, they shrink from too close an investigation of the second.

Whatever we may think of Cressy's explanation of the Anglican bow toward the Fathers and the authority of the early Church, it does tally with the ambiguity of Anglican formularies, and especially of Article 6, which, as we shall see, one Catholic author, Richard Broughton, could criticise sharply, while another, Christopher Davenport, writing at approximately the same time, appreciated its meekness.

However, Paulinus Cressy's main contribution to a Catholic-Anglican dialogue lies elsewhere than in his psychological interpretation of fundamental attitudes, whatever the judiciousness of his observations and the authenticity of his experiences may have been: his investigation of the Tradition-Scripture alone issue includes a remarkable attempt to describe accurately what Tradition consists in. The Catholic doctrines on Christ's atoning death and on his "real unfigurative presence" in the Eucharist could not have been "more securely propagated and more clearly and intelligibly delivered to posterity in books written" than, "as they have been, in the Tradition and universal practise of the Church, and in a continual visible celebrating of those divine mysteries, where every action they did perform published the truth which they believed". Liturgical practices express the "confession of that Presence with

---

[30] l.c., pp. 137-138.
[31] l.c., p. 138.
[32] l.c., pp. 138-139.
[33] l.c., p. 139.

exclusion of all tropes and metaphors in the business". The meaning of faith is "conveyed more intelligibly and represented more exactly, lively and naturally by such practices and solemn spectacles than by bare words".[34] The Church treats these events of her life as an "express, impossible-to-be-mistaken way of propagating the mysteries of Christian belief".[35] Thus, Christian truth has been transmitted, "continued and daily everywhere preached, not so much in sermons (though so too) as in visible practise, and not so much written in books (though so too) as in the hearts of all professors of Christianity".[36]

What Paulinus Cressy outlines thus is no other than what recent authors have called a "real" as distinguished from a "documentary" Tradition. Cressy calls it "practical Tradition"[37] and describes it in well-coined formulas:

> This admirable way of conveying saving truths, as it is far more express than words alone, the natural sense of the mysteries being as it were construed and interpreted to the people thereby or (according to the prophet's expression foretelling this way of Tradition of the Gospel) being not written with ink and on paper but by the Spirit in men's hearts, by which means the sense sunk into their souls far more effectually than if words only had swom into their brains: so seems it to me also far more lasting than books, being scarce possibly obnoxious to be either extinguished or adulterated.[38]

More briefly, though hardly more simply, Cressy pictures Revelation as "conveyed not in formal expressions of words and phrases but, which was far more efficacious, in the natural sense and importance of them incapable of ambiguities by such a way of Tradition so impossible to be interrupted as long as Christians begot Christians".[39] And again, in another light: "The adequate subject (of Church authority) are all Catholic Christians, as well instructors as instructed: since Tradition is continued by them both, shining in the doctrines taught and received, in devotions exercised, and in outward practices and ceremonies celebrated by all Christians".[40]

In this "real" way, Christian belief passed from the Apostles to

---

[34] l.c., pp. 180-181.
[35] l.c., p. 181.
[36] l.c., p. 184.
[37] l.c., p. 204.
[38] l.c., p. 182.
[39] l.c., p. 187.
[40] l.c., pp. 346-347.

their successors, from the first to the second generation of the faithful, from the second to the third. And there is no reason for this process to stop, and no force able to bring it to a halt:

> Now what has been spoken of the second and third ages may upon the same grounds be verified of the fourth, fifth, and all following to the world's end.[41]

By the same token, the universality of Tradition is assured in substance no less than in time. For all Christian doctrines, and not only those toward which the liturgical life is more directly focused, have been handed on in this concrete, vital way. All Christian mysteries have been transmitted experientially rather than didactically. There are no exceptions. What Cressy shows about the Passion and the Eucharist "may and ought rationally be extended likewise to the whole body of divine revelations pertaining to the substance of Christian religion, how abstruse, how sublime, yea, how seemingly speculative soever".[42] "What has been exemplified in one or two supernatural truths revealed may be extended to all the substantial points of Christianity, all which, as I before demonstrated, arrive unto us by the same conveying hand of universal Tradition by several ways, as writing, public profession and practise propagated".[43] Such a Tradition is "oral", in the sense of not being committed to a set form of writing, although it may have been written somewhere and is not transmitted exclusively by word of mouth: it is channelled through events—the sacraments, the liturgy, the preaching—which entail the use of words, gestures and things.

A special place should be given, in this "practical Tradition", to the Creed. Cressy, here as elsewhere, is well-informed; instead of ascribing the Creed to the twelve Apostles, he considers it to be "an enlargement of that form of baptism prescribed by our Savior", to which "the Apostles or apostolic persons might afterwards adjoin the other articles following". This perfectly explains the differences presented by the form of the Creed in various parts of the ancient Church. For, such additions being made successively, "it is possible some persons might carry away in their voyages into Africa the briefer Creeds before they were so enlarged".[44]

---

[41] l.c., p. 465.
[42] l.c., pp. 184-185.
[43] l.c., p. 465.
[44] l.c., pp. 201-203.

Thus originating in the need for a baptismal rehearsal of the main items of Christian belief, the Creed—and here lies its originality in the complex of the Tradition—"seems to be of a middle nature between written books and oral Tradition: as a prescribed form of words, so it approaches to the former; but as committed by all to memory and actually repeated at baptism and other public devotions, so it partakes much of the latter".[45]

Tradition is therefore not conceived by Cressy as a simple logistic line, but as a system of interrelated processes through which the faith is transmitted from generation to generation. The experience of baptism, with *traditio* and *redditio symboli*, stands, even in its simplified forms of modern times, at the core of these processes. Tradition, seen as a whole, is constituted by the sum total of many diverse kinds of traditions, which vary in form and in certainty, though not in their common characteristic of being essentially public. Cressy entirely rules out the concept of "secret tradition" as self-contradictory: "Traditions are obvious to all men's eyes, and sound aloud in all men's ears, shining in the public visible practise and profession of the Church". In his reflection on this fundamentally public structure of all Tradition, handed on in public actions performed in the Church, Cressy becomes once again strikingly modern, and raises the question of the definability of points of faith hitherto undefined:

> The Church is so far from pretending (as Protestants would fain seem to fancy) that she has certain secret conservatories of these Traditions, out of which upon occasion she can draw some special ones to determine emergent controversies, and much less that the Holy Ghost suggests unto her in time of need any formerly vanished apostolic Revelation, that whatsoever is not expressly in Scripture or evidently apparent in the publicly received profession and practices of the Church are not perhaps determinable as points of faith, that is, as traditionary divine revelations.[46]

Cressy mentions the Immaculate Conception and "the subtle controversies between the Jesuits and Dominicans concerning grace and free will. . ." as perhaps incapable of precise decision. One will note the wise caution of this conclusion, which does not commit Cressy to deny the possibility of the Tradition maturing, so to say, at

---

[45] l.c., pp. 201-202.
[46] l.c., p. 194.

a given moment into total and unanimous certainty. The problem of the development of doctrine—another Newman trait—is thus hinted at.

A passage from Cressy's later volume, *Roman Catholic Doctrines No Novelties* (1663), may bring some light to bear on this. After insisting, as above, that the Church introduces no innovations into the Christian faith, Cressy remarks that she nevertheless may depart from the past in the wide area of matters indifferent:

> Indeed, in all matters left indifferent and no way commanded from the beginning, nor contrary to any divine Revelation, the Church of later times may vary, as she thinks fit, either from the practise or injunctions of the former.[47]

This keeps "matters of faith and divine Revelation" out of the scope of possible variations. Yet even here, Cressy recognises the possibility of changes that affect the outward form, though not the substance, of Revelation: the rule of following the ancient Fathers (Cressy is now referring to Jewel's old challenge, which has recently been repeated by Dr Thomas Pierce (1622-1691) in a sermon) does not hold "as to the express terms of every proposition that is matter of faith, but only as to the sense and substance". As an example, Cressy cites the *homoousios*:

> It is not necessary that *ab initio* God the Son should be declared in express terms consubstantial with the Father, which was first put into the Christians' Creed by the Council of Nicea; but only that that doctrine can be shown *ab initio*, which is identified in sense with this.

In other words, the *depositum* left the Church by the Apostles, which *Exomologesis* calls "uniform and complete", was so only as to substance. Further precisions accrued to it later, which affect the form and manner in which the deposit has been handed on, its doctrines formulated and preached, its discipline enforced or altered according to circumstances. Challenging Chillingworth, Cressy asks if "the doctrine of faith concerning the Blessed Trinity is as evidently and intelligibly stated in Scripture as in the first Council of Nicaea". This permits him to affirm the need for something to supply to the deficiencies and obscurities of Scripture, and, by implication, the necessity of some sort of development during which this Tradition will take shape:

---

[47] *Roman Catholic Doctrines no novelties*, 1663, pp. 28-29.

This one consideration, that the necessary mysteries of faith are not so evidently set down in any one place of Scripture, but that other places may be found which may afford ground even to an understanding man to raise objections, will make any man conclude that, either there are no mysteries necessary to be believed, or that something besides Scripture must be made use of to clear all difficulties.[48]

From the point of view of their certainty, traditions, as natural phenomena of the transmission of information, fall into diverse degrees of certitude. Cressy places universal traditions highest of all, for the chances of a universal plot to teach an untruth are very slight. Less universal traditions, particularly the records of events that could have been known only in in a small corner of the world, are of inferior certainty.[49] Cressy's reasoning at this point becomes highly intriguing in view of its recurrent Newmanian slant. After studying the kind of certainty offered by "secular traditions", it examined the "certainty of universal Tradition proposed by the Church considered antecedently to her authority".[50] In this, Cressy does in 1647 what John Henry Newman will do two centuries later in his *Essay on the Development of Christian Doctrine* (1845): Newman will determine *a priori* the conditions to be fulfilled by legitimate development, and then find that this development has taken place in the Roman Catholic Church under supernatural guidance. This comes close to Cressy's method, where Church Tradition is approached from the standpoint of its human reliability and antecedent probability, before the notion of a divine guidance over her guardianship has been brought in.

The highest certainty, to which no secular example approaches, affects what Cressy calls "doctrines or customs shining in the general practice of the Church and withall more or less clearly expressed in Scripture": in this category, which enjoys the highest degree of certainty that "Tradition is capable of"[51] he places "the whole substance and frame of Christian Religion".

Then, in descending order, Cressy lists the tradition of ancient rites and liturgies; the tradition of the books of Holy Scripture, at least "in gross" and leaving aside the problem of the "true reading of particular texts, as appears by the infinite variety of readings in manuscript"[52]; the tradition of very speculative doctrines which

---

[48] *Exomologesis*, p. 397-398.
[49] l.c., pp. 293-294.
[50] l.c., p. 316.
[51] l.c., pp. 311-312.
[52] l.c., p. 309.

could "hardly be expressed in the practise of the Church". Cressy mentions, as for the past, the condemnation of Millenarism as of questionable status regarding the certainty of the Tradition about the last ages of the world, and, as for the present, the opinions about grace and free will, or about the Immaculate Conception.[53]

In the theologizing that led to his conversion, Cressy assessed the human certainty of the traditions proposed by the Church, and thereby her reliableness as a "simple proponent" [54]: "Tradition in general is in itself credible, and some Traditions certain, and above all others that ever were or, I believe, can possibly be, the Tradition of the Church. . . is the most certain".[55] It comes nearest to "experimental immediate knowledge". This led Cressy to a complementary study of the Church's divine authority as she proposes these traditions to faith. We may leave him at this point of his spiritual journey in order to find out what consequences, if any, his emphasis on Tradition entailed as regards the corresponding problem of the Scriptures and their sufficiency for the Christian faith.

Serenus Cressy's approach to the Scriptures is, for his time, relatively critical. He believes that the value of each book of the New Testament depends upon the circumstances and purpose of its writing: "We ought to consider the books of history apart from others of doctrine and prophecy, as being distinguishable both in their occasion and end".[56] The Gospels narrate several happenings of the Savior's life, some of his miracles and "a sum of the principal points of his doctrine". Now at the time of their composition, the memory of these, "excepting perhaps only the several miracles, prophecies, etc." was already sufficiently preserved "in substance in practical Tradition".[57] The writing of the Gospels simply added to this traditional knowledge a store of more detailed information, which implied no substantial complement yet was gratefully received by all those who, because they loved the Lord, sought to be acquainted with his life and doctrine as accurately as possible. Nevertheless, this cannot imply the universal sufficiency of the Gospels: "No general Tradition has come to us that all that is necessary for all persons of all degrees,

---

[53] l.c., pp. 304-307.
[54] l.c., p. 322.
[55] l.c., p. 317.
[56] l.c., p. 203.
[57] l.c., p. 203-4.

whether single or in society, to bring them to heaven is contained expressly in these Gospels". Which is not to say that the Gospels, or, for that matter, given excerpts from them, may not be, in some situations, quite sufficient for salvation. Imagining an extreme case, Cressy admits:

> No doubt to some persons in some sudden desperate circumstances there is in the Gospels to be found enough, yea more than enough of mere necessity, yea in any one of them, yea in two or three verses of any one of them.[58]

There may indeed be persons for whom, in certain circumstances, "not only the Scripture, or the Creed, or one Gospel, but perhaps this one verse in a Gospel, 'This is eternal life to know thee, the one true God, and Jesus Christ whom thou hast sent,' may be instruction sufficient to salvation", although more instruction would be necessary to others "proportionally to other circumstances".[59] Thus the question admits of no simple, universal answer. Sufficiency is not, for Cressy, an absolute: it relates to, and depends on, circumstances of persons, times and places. In this case, it is indeed quite proper for Catholics to confess the sufficiency of Scripture, or of any part of it, for salvation, as long as this is understood proportionally to circumstances.

Such an understanding of sufficiency, far from ruling out authoritative tradition, calls for it. For the value of the various parts of the New Testament is relative not only to their readers, but also to the circumstances of their composition. The Apocalypse, for instance, "is a mere obscure prophecy and can contribute little or nothing to the instruction or discipline of the Church".[60] The Acts "will prove but a very imperfect model" for the Church, far more imperfect than she appears in patristic literature.[61] The Epistles make no claim to containing "an abridgement of the whole body of Christian faith for the whole Church", written as they were for particular congregations in relation to concrete local problems. Furthermore, especially in St Paul's case, they were "written in a style so obscure, such intricacy of arguing, with such digressions interwoven, the logical analysis is so extremely difficult, that the gift of understanding was in those days a necessary attendant of the Apostle's preaching". As a

---

[58] l.c., pp. 205-206.
[59] l.c., p. 217.
[60] l.c., p. 206.
[61] l.c., p. 207.

test of this, we may ask one hundred persons "to resolve the order and method of St. Paul's arguing" and, according to Cressy, "there would not three of them agree for three verses together".[62]

Admittedly, one could wonder what this tends to show: in all this, Cressy refers only to the literal sense of the New Testament, to problems of exegesis which are often of a difficult solution, all the more so as the reader of the Bible is seldom a competent exegete when the multiplication of vernacular translations has placed the Scriptures in everybody's hands. The question of sufficiency could also be raised concerning the spiritual reading of the Bible in the Church, in reference to the spiritual senses traditionally recognised in the letter of Scripture. Cressy is so aware of this that he points out that many Fathers have found much more in the Scriptures than is apparent in its ordinary sense. But Cressy is embarrassed by this, and he tries to imagine what intellectual process made it possible:

> It came to pass that many Fathers, being assured of the truth and authentiqueness of such Traditions, and willing to assert them out of Scripture also, have interpreted many texts as containing such doctrines which either did not at all afford such a sense, or at least not necessarily, though perhaps the outward sound of the words might put a man in mind of such doctrines...

Cressy's analysis of the spiritual interpretation of the Bible leads to the paradoxical conclusion that its use by the Fathers proves nothing about the sufficiency of Scripture, but says a lot about the strength of Tradition: "The less force such texts of Scripture have to evince such doctrines, the greater and stronger proof have such Traditions, seeing the Fathers, prepossessed with a belief of them from the public practise of the Church, accounted them so apparent they saw them even where they were not at all".[63] For Cressy's modern mind, the intricate hermeneutics practised by the Fathers are of little account in themselves; yet they highlight the fact that the transmission of doctrine may have passed through unsatisfactory channels. We are not bound to agree with patristic interpretation; yet the doctrine thus read into Scripture remains. Cressy sums it up in this formula:

> Though perhaps their commentaries there may be questioned, the doctrines in the commentaries ought to be embraced.[64]

---

[62] l.c., pp. 207-208.
[63] l.c., p. 199'
[64] l.c., p. 200.

In brief, Cressy carefully maintains both the normalcy of a critical approach to Scripture, and yet the legitimacy of reading all traditionary doctrines out of the Bible after the fashion of the Church Fathers, as long as these two processes of thought and methods of reading are not confused.

In other words, the sufficiency of Scripture for salvation is perfectly acceptable, provided we have in mind a relative sufficiency. In order to make the matter abundantly clear, Paulinus Cressy lists several meanings of the expression "necessary to salvation"; there is necessity of means or of precept; necessity of explicit or implicit belief; necessity to apply or simply not to contradict a doctrine. Necessity can also be absolute or conditional; and what can be necessary to one person may not be so to others, etc.[65] When therefore we say that Scripture sufficiently contains all points necessary to salvation, we make a very ambiguous statement, which is true in one sense and false in another. At the time of his enquiries prior to his conversion, Cressy found it meaningless to face the problem in the abstract. He had to start with the existential question: Is Scripture sufficient in relation to me? From there he enlarged his problematic and considered the question in relation to "all Christians in general and to the exigence of Churches well ordered and settled", leaving aside the possibility of the sufficiency of Scripture "to one or more persons ignorant, destitute of means of knowledge and in some particular unavoidable exigence". As already seen, even one verse may well be sufficient for such a person; yet Cressy felt that it could not be enough for himself and still less for all the Churches. "No antiquity ever delivered this conclusion in so large a sense". On the contrary, "generally all antiquity protested against it":

> I found that no reason could require that writings evidently intended for special uses, and confuting three or four heresies, should be made use of or however should be accounted sufficiently and expressly convinctive against opinions not named in them and not then thought upon by the authors, as if they had been entire systems of Christianity.[66]

Cressy therefore concludes that, taken in its absolute sense, the sufficiency of Scripture for salvation is unacceptable. Yet "in several respects it may and ought to be assented to by any Catholic",[67] namely in the case of someone "in a desperate estate"; or when

---

[65] l.c., pp. 210-212.
[66] l.c., pp. 221-222.
[67] l.c., p. 216.

Scripture is taken "as joined with the Church's authority"; or still "if the same conclusion be so understood that the words of Scripture may be, I do not say, supplied but even interpreted by the Tradition of the ancient Church and authority of the present".[68] Outside of the desperate case in which God's providence overlooks the poverty of the means of information about salvation and graciously accepts as standing for the whole of Christianity one man's imperfect assent to the Scriptures or parts of them, Scripture sufficiently contains all doctrines necessary to salvation only if it is joined to, or interpreted by, the Church.

Cressy's testimony is of superior interest, in that it both accurately pinpoints then current problems and anticipates later, and now better known, questions and positions. A definite step has been made toward the theology of development, which will retain the attention of John Henry Newman, whose very rationale is adumbrated in Cressy's analysis of Tradition. Yet to raise problems often leaves questions unanswered; and Cressy's immediate concerns did not orient his thought toward untying the knots that still bulked large in his reflection on Tradition.

Cressy also adopted an advanced position in regard to Scripture. True it is, most Catholic controversialists were brought by their polemics to stress the difficulties of Scripture, its deficiencies in relation to us, the need for another Judge than the written word. But few went as far as Cressy toward a critical approach to the value of Scripture understood in its literal sense in the light of the circumstances of its composition and the purpose of its human authors. This stress, however, welcome as it is, was made at a cost: the sense of Scripture as God's word spoken this very day to contemporary readers has little or no place in Cressy's problematic. His religious universe is too neat to make room for spiritual interpretations, which he explains by the Fathers' enthusiasm for Tradition, in whose light they read into Scripture things that were not literally in it. The Fathers misread the sense of Scripture, and their misreading may stand as a testimony to Tradition, though not as a guide to interpret the written Word. The hitch is that such a view of the devoted patristic and medieval tillage of the spiritual senses of Scripture explains away a great deal of exegetical Tradition and traditional exegesis.

---

[68] l.c., pp. 217-218.

Several of Hugh Paulinus Cressy's concerns reappear under the pen of another notable convert of the Commonwealth period, Thomas Bailey (d. 1657?), the son of an Anglican Bishop of Bangor and himself a clergyman in Holy Orders. After being gaoled at Newgate prison for his royalist stand, Bailey escaped to Holland, where he was received into the Catholic Church. He spent most of his later life in Italy, where he seems to have died in impoverished circumstances. In his case as in Cressy's, the events of 1644-45 directly led to his leaving the Church of England: the scandal of the Presbyterian take-over of the Church struck him as incompatible with his faith. Thereafter he could not remain in a Church that was, as far as he could tell, abandoned of God: "When my Church was down, I viewed the foundation, and found the foundation of my Church to be laid in fallibility".[69] While one does sympathise with the sense of shock undoubtedly suffered by Bailey and many others when the episcopal Church of England seemed to sink, one cannot help wondering about the value of this consideration in 1660, six years after these lines were printed. Yet, whatever Thomas Bailey would have thought, had he lived to see the Restoration, he felt, at the time, that the hand of God was writing on the wall; and this served for him as an incentive to seek for the true Church. The result of his meditation took the form, several years after his reconciliation, of a volume which he called: *An End to Controversy between the Roman Catholic and the Protestant Religions Justified* (1654).

Bailey's primary stress is laid very differently than that of Cressy. Whereas Cressy accentuates Tradition in the first place and views Scripture relatively to it, Thomas Bailey's theology is focused on the word of God: all doctrine is contained in, and taught by, the word. But God's word is essentially spoken and not, as Protestants believe, written. The dignity of Scripture derives from its being the Word of God; and Bailey does not weary of singing its praises. Yet whenever he embarks on one of his frequent encomiums of the Scriptures, he always associates the "voice" to the "word": the Scriptures are not a dead letter lying in a book, but a living sound erupting from the hearts of the faithful through the Church's voice. "We have received", Bailey says, "the quickening Spirit. . . Shall the Law which God has put into the minds of men and writ in their hearts, the fiery tongues which sat upon the heads of the Apostles, stand at the bar of words

---

[69] *An End to Controversy between the Catholic and the Protestant religions justified*, Douai, 1654, p. 40.

and syllables for any one to pick and choose what sense he pleases out of such letters? Or has the Spirit left his station and residence within the hearts and upon the heads of his selected ones, to be comprehended only within dead volumes, printed letters, paper or parchment book?" [70]

That the Fathers meant the Scriptures to be a spoken word is obvious, for "they were never called by the ancients *Scriptura* but *loquela Dei*, not the writings, but the word, of God".[71] In conjunction with the Church which gives it life and makes it the word by speaking it, Scripture is perfect:

> We grant with Irenaeus and Vincentius the Canon of Holy Scripture to be perfect, a perfect light to our feet, a lantern to our paths, a perfect rule of faith, provided, as they provide, that the line of prophetical and apostolical interpretation be levelled according to the square of ecclesiastical and Catholic sense. . .[72]

Bailey himself makes a rather quaint use of scriptural similes germane to the spiritual interpretations which Cressy disliked, to drive this point home. If his language is not so precise as that of Cressy, it is by far the more imaginative, as witness this string of interlocking biblical allusions:

> The Scripture is a large field, full sown with the precious wheat of the Gospel by the hands of the good husbandman, and a sea that has good fish, though bad for some, enough for every man that will cast his net therein; but tradition (like the lad from whom the five barley loaves and the two fishes were received that fed so many) must be the *depositum* that must work so great assurance of a truth, not only that Jesus is that Prophet that should come into the world, but assure us also as, concerning him, how those prophecies are to be truly understood. Although the Scripture be the Word, and the Word is God and Christ himself, yet tradition must be the woman of Samaria, for whose saying's sake the Samaritans must first believe; though when this woman of Samaria (this tradition) has once called, summoned and brought us to this Word (this Christ) and taught us who it is, and what he has said, then for the Word's own sake ye must believe, not for the woman's words: you may hear him then yourselves; but she must bring you to him.[73]

Bailey is obviously less chary than Serenus Cressy when it comes to the symbolic use of the Bible. His own thought is full of biblical

[70] l.c., p. 52.
[71] l.c., p. 52; see p. 112.
[72] l.c., p. 101.
[73] l.c., pp. 94-95.

metaphors. To some extent, this is simply saying that Cressy's style is more flowery and likes images and allusions, scriptural or not. Yet this also implies that Scripture itself, for him, is not a book to be read in detached objectivity, but a message to be grasped through the eyes and ears, the heart and the mind of the Church. It is the biblical teaching that,

> though Scripture be the Word of God, yet the Church is the Spouse of Christ; though the Scripture is the Spouse's deed of jointure, yet the Church is the Spouse herself; though the Scripture is the truth herself, yet the Church is the ground of the truth. Though the Scripture be the Law, yet the Church is the Kingdom of Christ; this Kingdom must be governed by that Law, but that Law must be interpreted by the representatives of that Kingdom. Christ is the door, the Scripture is the lock, the Church is the key of Paradise.[74]

These are beautiful, if unprecise, expressions of the essential coinherence of Scripture and the Church. Yet if Bailey's pen could soar, his mind could also pinpoint problems with accuracy. For Scripture in relation to us is ambiguous: it is the Word when spoken by the Church; yet it is also a set of writings that any one can pick up and translate according to his fancy. "Who says", Bailey asks, pointing out one horn of the dilemma, "the Scriptures are uncertain and fallible, as they are the dictates of the Holy Ghost?" Then, turning to the other horn, he adds: "Yet who says they are not fallible and uncertain, as they are translations, transcripts and impressions?" [75]

On the one hand, the Scriptures "are a divine and infallible rule of faith, that is to say, infallible and sufficient in respect of themselves". This is the dominant position, in which Scripture is heard as the Word of God actually spoken. On the other hand, Scripture is also a written text made of "translations, transcripts and impressions". As such, it is "not infallibly sufficient in respect of us, because not immediately instructing us therein, of itself, but by certain means required on our behalf, which are fallible, as, skill in tongues... weighing of circumstances... confering of places... prayer..." [76] In relation to these, Scripture is fallible, it needs interpretation and requires scholarly competence. One may indeed say that "the letter of Scripture, or (to use the Protestants' own manner and phrase of speaking) that God speaking by that letter, may improperly be called

---

[74] l.c., p. 55.
[75] l.c., p. 112.
[76] l.c., pp. 129-130.

the voice of our supreme Judge". Nonetheless, Scripture is not "such a voice and sentence of God" as can publicly settle all differences and controversies as soon as these arise.[77] The voice belongs to the Church. Bailey therefore adds to the method of literal interpretation that he has briefly outlined two other methods, or, better, two degrees in the interpretation of Scripture by the Church, one of which is adequate in ordinary cases devoid of special difficulty, while the other must be appealed to in extraordinary cases:

> Two ways the Scriptures are to be understood, the one ordinary, the other extraordinary: ordinary by Tradition, as to matters that are plain and necessary; extraordinary by the Church, where the Holy Ghost perpetually reigns according unto Christ his promise made in her behalf: by the first, the common people may understand; by the second, the Church her men they must direct.[78]

In the first case, the Church simply draws on what has been inscribed in the hearts of the faithful, on her "living epistles", on "impressions upon hearts".[79] In the second, she calls selected men to a Council, where the strife is "debated and determined".[80] In both instances "Scripture is the light of the world";[81] for, as Bailey says, speaking for the Roman Catholic Church, "We hold that the universal and general definitions of the Church are and always ought to be levelled and directed according to the unerrable precinct of Holy Writ".[82] Yet one must always watch, lest the light of the world "be hid under the bushel of any private brain" instead of shining from "the candlestick of God's Church".[83]

Bailey waxes eloquent when he extols the wonders of Scripture and pictures the beauties of Tradition. The Scriptures are "the fountains of life, the manna from heaven, the sea of wisdom, the armory of the Holy Ghost, the promptuary of God... the will and testament of Jesus Christ... the light of the world... the *suprema lex*...". Tradition is "the principal means that was to be used for a right understanding of the divine verity, as the common road unto the Catholic Church and the highway to heaven, the footsteps of the flock of Christ, the tents that were pitched by his own shepherds,

---

[77] l.c., p. 130.
[78] l.c., p. 115.
[79] l.c., p. 84.
[80] l.c., p. 115.
[81] l.c., p. 111.
[82] l.c., p. 130.
[83] l.c., p. 111.

the direct, beaten and unerring path of Isaiah, the touchstone of truth, the pilot's staff, the broad seal of the Kingdom of Christ, which, once broken, anything is religion and everything is lawful".[84]

Thomas Bailey, who is undoubtedly a poet, even if his images are mostly culled from Scripture, and even though, as seems to be the case, he had already found them in Sylvestor Norris's *Antidote*,[85] is also a gifted theologian. Precisely at this point, speaking of the services rendered to each other by Scripture and the Church, he does not rest satisfied with metaphorical expressions of the unity of the Word and the Spouse; but he brings in two additional considerations which, although at first sight they point in different directions, actually converge.

Bailey is aware of standing in the stream of a long Tradition which has expressed the correlation of Scripture and Church in terms of written and unwritten word: if Scripture is the written word, the Church also possesses the word unwritten, enshrined in the hearts of the faithful. This Tradition found fuel in the recent or older emphasis on the word "partly written and partly unwritten". Bailey in turn picks up this vocabulary in a statement which he tries to make as clear as he can:

> Concerning the Traditions of the Church, this is the doctrine of the Roman Church, viz: that the word of God is partly written and partly unwritten; whereof the one part is called Holy Scripture, sacred writings, commonly the Old or New Testaments, or the Bible; the other part is called apostolical or Church Tradition, which from hand to hand was continued in the Church, the pillar and ground of truth, preserved in her bosom, and delivered by her mouth, as occasion should require, to all posterity: out of whose mouth it is prophesied that truth shall never depart, and against which Church it is promised by our Savior that the gates of hell shall never prevail.[86]

Bailey proves this duality from Scripture and from the Fathers, marshalling all the classical texts from Ignatius of Antioch to Augustine. Elsewhere he provides a list of doctrinal points which, in his opinion, cannot derive from the literal sense of Scripture and must have been drawn from the treasury of the unwritten word: baptism of infants, the *filioque*, the perpetual virginity of Mary, the begetting of the Son by the Father, the *homoousios*, the change of the Sabbath

---

[84] l.c., p. 83.
[85] See supra, ch. 2.
[86] l.c., p. 361.

to the Lord's day, the belief that Scripture is the word of God.[87]
This list is all but identical with that of Sylvester Norris (Norris
puts "Easter on Sunday" instead of "the Sabbath changed to Sunday"). But what a difference in the treatment of this common theme
by these two men! The lists are commonplace, whatever interpretation one should make of them in the patristic authors cited. Yet
Bailey's handling of them introduces a new and very striking element:
his "partly. . . partly. . ." reveals an insight into the problem, already
touched upon by Cressy, of doctrinal development. For the unwritten
"part" manifests itself from time to time in the Church's pronounce-
ments, when the need is felt, because of new controversies, "to
find out the truth".[88]

Thomas Bailey's concern with the past and its total heritage of
written and unwritten doctrine interlocks with his anticipation of the
future and the ongoing march of the Church's awareness of Revelation. Both these orientations of his thought appear jointly in the
following text, which sums up Bailey's view of the use to which
Scripture ought to be put, yet points out the necessity for a more
dynamic stance than reading Scripture to handle the problems and
controversies of post-scriptural history:

> If you would know the wonders of the creation and the progress of
> mankind, read the Pentateuch of Moses; if you would know how
> the ancient People of God were governed, read the Judicials; if how
> the Church, the Ceremonials; how yourselves, the moral Law; if you
> would read divine Histories, read the book of Judges, Samuel, Chroni-
> cles, Esdras and Macchabees; if you would find a salve for every sore
> of mind, read the Psalms of David; if how to possess your soul in
> patience, the book of Job; if how the coming of Christ was promised,
> the Prophets; if how accomplished, the Gospels; if how the Apostles
> carried on their work, the Acts; if what a good pastor ought to have
> over his flock, the Epistles; if you would *caput inter nubila condere*,
> plunge yourselves into divine mysteries and deep things that be
> of God, read the Apocalpyse; but *absit*, let us not make those fixed
> constellations judges of all occurences which we meet by the way of
> controversy, but let us leave those things unto the Church, whose
> property it is to find out the truth, like that peculiar star which showed
> the wise men, not only which city, which inn, but also which stable
> to that inn, the child that was new born and ever given was to be found,
> when all the stars of heaven could never do it.[89]

---

[87] l.c., pp. 88-89.
[88] l.c., p. 136.
[89] l.c., pp. 135-136.

The Scriptures are, like the stars of heaven, "fixed constellations" while the Church, like the star of the nativity, is a moving light, equipped to beam out on whatever new, unexpected questions arise in the course of her history. This provides a good commentary on Bailey's concise principle: "All Scripture is profitable, but all is not sufficient".[90] It is not sufficient insofar as it lacks the agility and the universal relevance that alone a living body has. The Scripture which *suffices* is not "folded up in characters or letters, figured with ink, painted or impressed on paper", but "ingrafted and preserved in conservatives that are more noble, viz., the heart of man, the mouth of the Church, the lips of her priests, the fiery tongues of the Apostles".[91] Thus enshrined in living hearts, the word may be expressed as befits all circumstances, adapted to all the hesitancies of each day and the controversies of each century. The Holy Ghost is thus acting in the heart of the Church to enlarge her knowledge of the Word, so that Bailey may ask, in a rhetorical question which sows the seed of a whole theology of development:

> Shall the infinite knowledge of the Holy Ghost, which shall increase in us more and more the later days, daily teaching and instructing the Church, be restrained and limited to volumes written so long ago?" [92]

In Bailey's theology, the Holy Spirit continually teaches the Church, enlivening the word in her to make it relevant to all historical happenings, and thereby increasing her knowledge of revealed truth. Admittedly, this remains sketchy. Yet the shadow of Newman looms large here again. Bailey gropes for a solution that gives more space to the Spirit and his discontinuous intervention, similar to the sudden appearance of the Christmas star, than to the continuity of organic growth which will receive Newman's attention. No doubt, we would like to know more about the increase in us of the infinite knowledge of the Holy Ghost. But if Thomas Bailey cannot satisfy us, this is because we see the problem much more clearly than he did. He has the merit, at least, of raising it more openly than his predecessors, and of putting it in even better light than was done by his great contemporary Serenus Cressy.

---

[90] l.c., p. 99.
[91] l.c., p. 92.
[92] l.c., p. 86.

CHAPTER SIX

CHRISTOPHER DAVENPORT

The chief depository of Anglican doctrine in the 17th century was the Thirty-nine Articles, which had not yet been relegated to the shelf of antiquated statements. Although they regularly came under fire from the Puritan side as leaning toward papacy by way of prelacy and as insufficiently purifying the Church from non-scriptural accretions, the Articles were accepted and enforced as the standard of doctrine for the *Ecclesia anglicana* both before and after the Puritan Commonwealth. Most Catholic controversialists alluded to them in their works, although, surprisingly enough, very few studied them systematically. Two examinations of the Articles, however, were published within a few years' time in the 1630's, though their intentions and conclusions were quite opposed, the one being totally negative in its judgement on the orthodoxy of the Articles, the other striving, with a tendency to bend over backward which it readily admitted,[1] to find the Articles compatible with the Catholic faith.

It is difficult to know which essay came first. Richard Broughton published his in 1632; and Christopher Davenport's was printed as an appendix to another work in 1634, although it is not excluded that it was brought to light and led a life of its own before the treatise on Nature and Grace to which it was eventually appended. At any rate, we shall consider Richard Broughton's volume first, for the author's career as a theologian ended with this book, whereas Christopher Davenport was only starting on long and fruitful labors that brought him into dialogue and conflict with other theologians of the period.

Richard Broughton (d.1635), a secular priest who returned to England after his studies at the English College at Rheims, where he was ordained in 1593, was mainly a historian and is chiefly known for

---

[1] Davenport was well aware of this, as he showed in the conclusion of his essay: *Insudavi, ut vides, pie lector, reconciliare articulos confessionis anglicae determinationibus Ecclesiae catholicae* ... (The quotes refer to the text of *Paraphrastica Expositio* as published by F. G. Lee, 1865. Quote, p. 116.)

his *Ecclesiastical History of Great Britain* (1633). However, he tried his hand at theology in the book which may well have the originality of being the first thorough study by a Catholic of the Thirty-nine Articles of the Church of England.[2] *The Judgment of the Apostles and of those of the first age, in all points of doctrine questioned between the Catholics and the Protestants of England, as they are set down in the 39 Articles of their religion* appeared in 1632, an anonymous work like so many others, signed by "an old student in divinity". The method of argumentation, as outlined in the title, is obviously inspired, like much of Recusant theological literature, by John Jewel's challenge: to prove that the Fathers of the first centuries disagree with the Thirty-nine Articles amounts to taking up the challenge in the boldest way, assailing the Church of England in its stronghold and removing its vaunted reliance on the Fathers. Broughton's frame of reference is more historical than theological, which is not surprising from a historian. And, unlike Christopher Davenport's conciliatory approach to the Articles, Broughton's judgement is, from first to last, critical, although it finds nothing opposed to the doctrine of the Catholic Church in the first five articles. However, and this point is of the first importance for us, his fundamental criticism is aimed at Article 6, which runs thus:

> Holy Scripture contains all things necessary to salvation, so that whatsoever is not read therein nor may be proved thereby is not to be required of any man, that it should be believed as an article of faith, or be thought requisite or necessary to salvation. By the name of Holy Scripture we do understand those canonical books of the Old and New Testament, of whose authority was never any doubt in the Church.

Time and time again Broughton harps on one point, which is obviously basic to his theological judgement on Anglicanism: the value of all the Articles depends on that of the sixth. For the purpose of the sixth is to establish the foundation of all Anglican doctrines: "This their Article is in their proceedings as the groundwork and foundation whereupon their Religion is wholly framed and builded".[3] Broughton will later argue that little time need be spent on the

---

[2] The Thirty-Nine Articles were adopted, in their Latin text, by the Convocation of Canterbury in 1562. They were imposed on the clergy by Parliament in 1571. We may note that the Recusants are not the only ones who neglected to study the Articles; there is no general study of their history and their doctrines.

[3] *The Judgment of the Apostles*, 1632, p. 3.

others, once the basic article has been disproved: "Having thus absolutely and at large confuted and overthrown by the apostolic age the last article, the erroneous ground of all Protestant religion, we may be more brief in the rest, being all at the least generally confuted and overthrown in their false foundation so destroyed".[4] And once more he will say, concerning Article 19: "In this article nothing needs other answer or confutation than is made before in their article of Scriptures and traditions, where the pretended sole necessity of the written Scriptures, heretically insinuated, is most plainly confuted both by the apostolic doctrine and practise of this age and otherwise".[5] Thus all the articles are substantially reduced to one, and all Anglican or anti-Anglican polemics are equally reduced to the question, which is both central and fundamental, of Scripture as the ground of faith. In Broughton's opinion, Article 6 and, together with it, the doctrine it embodies, are hopeless: the Article is "so weak, feeble, tottering, ruinous, arid, deceitful, that not any one true, certain and infallible point of doctrine (as every Article in true religion is) can be framed upon it, or from it deduced, by the express grant of this article itself and of all English Protestants, professed and sworn maintainers of it".[6] If the supporters of this Article recognize that no infallible doctrine can be based upon it, it should be obvious that they pursue another concern than absolute certainty, and that they have in mind other qualities than the infallibility of the formulas of belief. But Broughton, at this stage of the controversies, thinks he can make fuel of the admssion to show the absurdity of the Thirty-nine Articles and the religion for which they stand. This is no longer satisfactory, but it was, in his circumstances, good polemics.

Broughton stands on firmer ground when he finds that the 6th Article contains a contradiction. It states, in the first place, that "Holy Scripture contains all things necessary to salvation", thus making Scripture the ultimate touchstone of faith and voiding any standard the Church may propose besides the Scriptures. Yet it adds, in the second place, that "in the name of Holy Scriptures we do understand those canonical books of the Old and New Testament, of whose authority was never any doubt in the Church". Our critic comments on these lines in this way:

---

[4] l.c., p. 53.
[5] l.c., p. 100.
[6] l.c., p. 3.

They plainly make the judgement of the Church to be the highest tribunal in spiritual questions, even of the Scriptures themselves. And thus their best and chief writers, published by authority, do gloss and expound this article.

In this we are assured, he adds further on, "That the Church, and Tradition unwritten, is supreme Judge of all questions in religion, even of the Scriptures themselves".[7] Had Broughton pushed this point, he would have been led to explain that the contradiction takes the form of a vicious circle, to which it would have been easy to reply with the logical explanations provided by Edward Maihew or James Sharpe in answer to a similar indictment. Broughton, however, jumps fast from one point to another, and, in this case, switches his ground from theological to historical argumentation, a field where he feels obviously more at home.

To claim the sufficiency of the Scriptures as the only and total rule of faith is simply not compatible with the history of the early Church. For time was needed to shape the canon of the New Testament and, were we to take the Article at face-value, there would have been no standard of faith in that transition period. "It further proves", he says, "how feeble and weak the rest of this Protestant article of the sufficiency and allowance of only Scripture and disabling Traditions is, for if so many canonical books of Scripture in both Testaments were doubted of, until so great a time above 300 years in the law of Christ were passed, and religion generally and in all questions necessary to salvation planted and received, how were or possibly could all these necessary things be read in Scripture or proved thereby (which is the rule of this article) when so many books were not then received for certain and undoubted Holy Scriptures?"[8] By the same token, this takes no account of the well known fact that the Gospel was brought to many nations that were unable to read the Scriptures. "The world", explains Broughton after St Irenaeus, "was not converted to Christ, nor his doctrine and religion received and established, by Scriptures, but unwritten tradition".[9] Which goes to show, as the Church Fathers fully acknowledged it, both the "necessity of Traditions, and their equality with Scriptures".[10] Broughton's reasoning here is unimpeachable and its concern for the formation of the Canon of the New Testament is unusually modern.

---

[7] l.c., p. 22.
[8] l.c., p. 14.
[9] l.c., p. 18.
[10] l.c., p. 20.

In support of most of his statements, Broughton is able to quote Anglican authors, which might be taken to mean that the opposition is not so sharp as he thinks between their religion and his, although he rather concludes from it that Anglican thinking is self-contradictory. In particular, English Protestants willingly confess the "worth and credit of the revealer and deliverer or proposer of holy mysteries supernatural", which is the holy Church.[11] As faith draws its certainty from the value of the revealer and proposer, it makes no difference whether what is proposed to faith comes in writing or not: mysteries and revelations "are the same and as certain in traditions not written, such as Catholics maintain, as in the written Scriptures", as long as not all unwritten traditions are received in faith, but only such as come from Christ and his apostles. The authority that guarantees this descent from Christ is the "true primitive Church".

The chief apostolic Tradition is the Creed, which Broughton, historian though he was, believed to have derived directly from the Apostles, according to a legend long taken for a true record of facts. "And this Creed", Broughton explains, "delivered by word and tradition only by the Apostles before the New Testament written, this Scripture could not possibly be a rule or direction unto it; but rather otherwise, for every rule has priority to the things ruled, and the things ruled posterity to their rule".[12] Broughton even maintains that both the Apostles "and the ancient Fathers by common consent of the whole Church of Christ" [13] witness to the apostolic origin of the Creed, antecedently to the writing of Scripture

Moreover, both the Creeds of Nicaea and of Athanasius were accepted before there was total agreement on the Canon,[14] which plainly shows that they were judged by the standard of Tradition rather than by that of Scripture alone. This also shows, to Broughton's mind, how "frivolous" is Article 8, which accepts the three traditional Creeds on the ground that "they may be proved by most certain warrants of holy Scripture", thus clearly contradicting the historical function of the Creeds, which were standards of faith before the New Testament became one.

Still speaking as a historian, though not always a judicious one,

---

[11] l.c., p. 21.
[12] l.c., p. 24.
[13] l.c., p. 28.
[14] l.c., p. 53.

our critic shows that certain doctrines, which Protestants do not find in Scripture, were taught in the early Church before the formation of the Canon: whence, giving the Protestant contention an unexpected twist, he concludes that, by Protestant testimony, the primitive Church "by so great and living then witness, held and professed them by tradition".[15] Among these he mentions liturgical feasts and the "form and manner" [16] of the Eucharistic sacrifice and of other sacramental practices.

Broughton touches again on these questions in his brief comments on Articles 19 and 21, which deal with the Church's authority. And again, he notes [17] how absurd it is to define the Church as "a congregation of faithful men, in which the pure Word of God is preached and the Sacraments be duly administered" and, in the next breath, to warn that this Church may not "ordain anything contrary to God's word written". To hold the true Church capable of such an aberration is "very idle and anti-Christian".[18]

It remains to identify this Church "which was when these heresies began, even Catholic and universal in all places, and had been so in all times before, has been so ever since, and still so continues and flourishes". None of the Protestant congregations is this Church: for these "cannot be possibly Catholic for place, and as impossibly for time", the two dimensions of Catholicity, which mark out the "Roman Church and religion".[19]

In his indictment of the Articles, Richard Broughton has anticipated much of the dissatisfaction of later times, which has now left the Articles at the periphery of Anglican thought. In his time, however, they were still of permanent importance, and his attempt to cope directly with them showed a desire to take the issue at its hottest. As with James Sharpe, although in another way, the problems in controversy have been reduced to their bare essentials. At the basis of all dissensions there lies the question of the ultimate ground of faith and doctrine, that is, of Scripture and Tradition. One may regret that Broughton, who has perceived the central problem, has handled it as a historian rather than as a theologian. As a historian, however, although he has made mistakes that would be

---

[15] l.c., p. 42.
[16] l.c., pp. 44-45.
[17] l.c., p. 100.
[18] l.c., p. 107.
[19] l.c., p. 108.

unpardonable today, he has, long before Oscar Cullmann, shown insight into the relevance of the formation of the Canon for a theology of Tradition: the time needed to constitute the Canon of the New Testament disproves the claim that, in the primitive Church, the written Scripture was the final court of appeal for doctrine. Broughton further believes, as well he might, that the same conclusion obtains today, although he goes, in this, beyond the historical evidence of the first centuries: the ecclesiological principles of Catholicism, which he briefly hints at in demanding that the Church's Catholicity extend both to time and to space, would require investigation beyond the limited scope of his work.

Christopher Davenport (1598-1680), in religion Franciscus a Sancta Clara, and, in the names which he occasionally adopted to hide his traces, Lathroppe, Francis Hunt or, from his native town, Francis Coventry, became Catholic at Oxford [20] and trekked over to Douai in 1615, while a relative, John, oriented himself toward Puritanism.[21] John eventually migrated to New England and became one of the first Puritan ministers at New Haven, Connecticut. Christopher, meanwhile, entered the Order of St. Francis at Ypres, lived, studied and taught in Franciscan friaries at Salamanca and Douai before returning to England, where he quickly became chaplain to Queen Henrietta Maria. From that time on, Davenport frequented the highest authorities in England, both at Court and in the Established Church. Even during the Commonwealth he did not entirely go underground, since he presented Oliver Cromwell, in 1655, with an *Explanation of Catholic Belief* which, he hoped, might induce the Protector to decree the tolerance of Catholic faith and practise. At the Restoration, Davenport became chaplain to Queen Catherine of Bragancia.

Davenport's essay on the Thirty-nine Articles is a short Latin work called *Paraphrastica Expositio Articulorum Confessionis Anglicanae*, which makes the mistake of assimilating the Articles to a Confession in the sense of Lutheran and Calvinist Protestantism. This gives, to some extent, the tone of the work as a non-historical

---

[20] On Davenport, see John Dockery, *Christopher Davenport, Friar and Diplomat*, London, 1960; Maurice Nédoncelle, *Trois Aspects du problème anglo-catholique au XVIIe siècle*, Paris, 1951, with a comparison of *Expositio* with Newman's Tract *XC* (1841), pp. 113-131.

[21] cf. Dockery, l.c., pp. 11-14.

paraphrase or commentary which takes the text as it stands, without attempting to explain the historical context that could elucidate its meaning by discovering the intentions and purposes of the framers of the Articles. Davenport's method consists in seeking for parallels or approximations in Catholic theological literature, both patristic and recent. Whenever he can find a resemblance between an article and some saying of an undoubtedly Catholic author, Davenport proposes a mild interpretation of the Anglican text, which makes it as Catholic as the wording of it can possibly allow. We are, in this irenic detection of hidden Catholic meanings, poles apart from Richard Broughton's conscious exercise in criticism.

Like Broughton, Davenport finds nothing the matter with the first five Articles, which "merely explain the Apostles' Creed".[22] The first part of Article 6, on which Broughton focuses his attention and which he takes as the main ground for his devastating judgement on all the Articles, Davenport dismisses, postponing discussion of the scriptural principle until Articles 20 ("Of the Church's authority"), 21 ("Of the authority of General Councils") and 34 ("Of ecclesiastical traditions"). The second part of Article 6 lists the books of the Old and New Testament, making a sharp distinction between the strictly canonical books and the others which, "on Jerome's authority, are ordered to be used in the Churches for the instruction of manners, but not to be read for the support of doctrine".[23] Here our irenic paraphraser is unusually harsh: this is a "singular opinion, near to heresy",[24] which however he does not dare condemn entirely because it has a long history behind it and because Cajetan himself hesitated on the status of the deutero-canonical books. Since the Councils of Florence and Trent, however, the Anglican Article would be unacceptable as a Catholic opinion.

Come Article 20, after suggesting mild interpretations of most of the intermediate articles, Davenport has returned to his determination to find Anglican official doctrine as orthodox as possible, even to the point of over-stretching or over-restricting the meaning of their terms. The article is thus worded in the Latin version which Davenport used:

---

[22] *Paraphrastica Expositio*, p. 3.
[23] Davenport's quotation is a summary of the text of the Article: "And the other books, as Jerome says, the church does read; for example, of life and instruction of manners, but yet does it not apply them to establish any doctrine . .".
[24] l.c., p. 30.

Ecclesia potestatem habet decernendi ritus et ceremonias et dirimendi con-troversias in fide. Ecclesiae non licet quicquam instituere, quod verbo Dei adversetur, nec unum Scripturae locum sic exponere potest, ut alteri contradicat. Quare licet Ecclesia sit divinorum testis et conservatrix, attamen ut adversus eos nihil decernere, ita praeter illos nihil credendum de necessitate salutis debet obtrudere.

The standard English form of the text is this:

"The Church hath power to decree rites or ceremonies, and author-ity in controversies of faith; and yet it is not lawful for the Church to ordain anything that is contrary to God's Word written; neither may it so expound one place of Scripture that it be repugnant to another. Wherefore, although the Church be a witness and keeper of Holy Writ, yet, as it ought not to decree anything against the same, so besides the same ought it not to enforce any thing to be believed for necessity of salvation".

Davenport judges the first element (on the Church's power and authority) to be clear and Catholic. The following notation, against ordaining anything opposed to God's word and interpreting Scrip-ture against Scripture, is no less good, "for, according to all the ancients, Scripture is the sure rule of truth". That the Church is "the witness and keeper of Sacred Scripture" perfectly agrees with St. Paul and St. Augustine.

Showing a slight hesitancy on the last words of Article 20, Daven-port has nonetheless recourse to his minimizing reading of the text. When we are told that "besides (*praeter*) Scripture nothing should be enforced as of necessity for salvation", we should understand *praeter* as referring to "what is contained in the Scripture neither actually nor virtually, what is there neither in so many words nor may be deducted therefrom by way of consequence, but what cannot be proven from Scripture, as is said in Article 6".[25] This is also, for Davenport, St. Augustine's doctrine. Further explaining what he means, Davenport adds, as a sort of afterthought, that he has in mind a deduction, not only according to the analogy of faith (*non solum ut consequentiae fidei*), but even according to merely rational logic (*sed etiam evidenti lumine naturae*).

This explanation is recognisably weak. For Davenport refers to the first part of Article 6 to support his interpretation, whereas he has not explained this section of Article 6. We are therefore to assume

---

[25] l.c., pp. 31-32.

that Article 6 is orthodox and that, partly on this account, Article 20 must be so too.

Davenport's understanding of deduction from Scripture is, however, broader than the text of the Article directly implies. For he remarks that the Scriptures themselves teach what is not written as well as what is written (*non de iis solum instruere quae scripta sunt, sed de iis etiam quae non sunt scripta*). The Church may present to faith unwritten doctrines which can be proven from the Scriptures (*Hujusmodi ergo Ecclesia potest proponere credenda, et ex Scripturis probari possunt*). This is, in Davenport's formulation, the Catholic position: and it is not contradicted by Article 20.

Only the last words of Article 21 relate to our problem: the decisions of General Councils concerning the prerequisites of salvation "have neither strength nor authority unless they can be shown to derive from the Sacred Scriptures" (*neque robur habent neque authoritatem nisi ostendi possint e sacris litteris esse desumpta*).[26] In keeping with his commentary on the preceding article, Davenport finds this in harmony with all ancient and most modern Catholic authors: the Councils cannot create new doctrines, or make a true proposition to become heretical; they can only "draw the truth out of the obscure passages of Scripture and out of the Apostles' sayings" (*Solum ex abditioribus Scripturae locis et apostolorum dictis veritatem eruere*). References to Suarez, Vincent of Lerins, Melchior Cano, Duns Scot, Molina, Turrecremata, Valentia, Thomas Aquinas, Conink and St. Cyprian support this. Davenport makes no attempt, in keeping with his interest in verbal and superficial rather than real and fundamental agreement, to find out if the Catholic Tradition and the Anglican Articles mean the same thing when they require all conciliar doctrines to be based on the Holy Scriptures.

This shortcoming of Davenport's irenic investigation, which weakens his study of the Articles, appears again in reference to Article 34, on ecclesiastical traditions:

> *Traditiones atque ceremonias easdem non omnino necessarium est ubique aut prorsus consimiles: nam et variae semper fuerunt, et mutari possunt pro regionum, temporum et morum diversitate, modo nihil contra verbum Dei instituatur. Traditiones et ceremonias ecclesiasticas quae cum verbo Dei non pugnant et sunt authoritate publica institutae et probatae, quisquis privato consilio volens et data opera publica violaverit, is, ut qui peccat in publicum ordinem Ecclesiae, quique laedit authoritatem magistratus, et qui infirmorum*

---

[26] l.c., p. 36.

fratrum conscientias vulnerat, publice, ut ceteri timeant, arguendus est. Qualibet Ecclesia particularis authoritatem habet instituendi, mutandi aut abrogandi ceremonias aut ritus ecclesiasticos, humana tantum authoritate institutos: modo omnia ad edificationem fiant.

"It is not necessary that traditions and ceremonies be in all places one, or utterly like; for at all times they have been diverse, and may be changed according to the diversity of countries, times and men's manners, so that nothing be ordained against God's word. Whoever through his private judgement willingly and purposely doth openly break the traditions and ceremonies of the Church which be not repugnant to the Word of God, and be ordained and approved by common authority, ought to be rebuked openly, that others may fear to do the like, as he that offendeth against the common order of the Church, and hurteth the authority of the magistrate, and woundeth the conscience of the weak brethren.

Every particular or national Church hath authority to ordain, change and abolish ceremonies or rites of the Church ordained only by man's authority, so that all things be done to edifying".

Davenport's commentary is short: the traditions in question are not doctrinal but disciplinary, and may therefore, according to all Catholic authors, be changed by lawful authority for a good reason taken from the public order of the Church, according to circumstances of time and place, "which no Christian has ever said of the doctrine certainly handed down through the Apostles". Accordingly, "this whole Article seems to me most true and agreeable to the Church's practise".[27] Irenic though he be, Davenport is also interested in stating the full Catholic doctrine, whether or not the Articles are compatible with it. To this end he adds a consideration which is somewhat unrelated to the wording of the Article: Denys states that some doctrinal points have been "handed down by the Apostles to those who came afterwards not in writing but orally" (*Fuisse vero aliqua doctrinalia per apostolos non scripto sed verbo posteris tradita eleganter declarat Dionysius*). Davenport quotes Denys and Augustine. But, strangely enough, he neither gives an opinion of his own on this point, nor says whether all Catholics agree with Denys. He ends his commentary by noting that the last lines of the Article, on the legitimacy of different local traditions, carry everybody's agreement.

---

[27] l.c., p. 82.

Had Christopher Davenport published no more than his *Para-phrastica Expositio*, he would hardly deserve a place in the history of theology, although he would fit in a gallery of ecumenical oddities. To the credit of the Holy Office, the book was never condemned in Rome although the Spanish Inquisition, evidently humorless, banned it in Madrid. It is nonetheless a pity that his name remains known largely on account of what he knew to be an essay in paradox.[28] As we shall now see, there is much more to Christopher Davenport than the *Paraphrastica Expositio* would suggest.

In 1648 Christopher Davenport published his major theological work, *Systema fidei, seu Tractatus de concilio universali*.[29] The explanations following the title assert that, among many other things achieved in this book, "the divine authority of the Scriptures is declared" and "the Council of Trent is vindicated". It is in many respects a re-markable volume, covering a wide range of topics very thoroughly. Despite his irenic intentions and his attempt to catholicize the Thirty-nine Articles, Davenport was not inclined to mitigate Catholic doctrine.

His investigation of the authority of councils begins with a study of the concept of infallibility (chaps. 1-2). Next, the theory that definitions result from new revelations is rejected (chap. 3). The bases of faith are defined, and divided into *fundamenta* and *fundamen-talia*: doctrines explicitly contained in Scripture and apostolic tradi-tions are *fundamenta*, while those that necessarily follow from them are *fundamentalia* (chaps. 4-5). After a short chapter on whether philosophical doctrines may be defined (chap. 6), Davenport devotes chapters 7 to 13 to Scripture and tradition. Chapters 14 to 34 explain the nature and authority of councils. The rest of the volume, to chapter 48, deals with specific doctrines of faith.

A brief look at any section of the book shows the author arguing from two principles which he nearly always invokes together as

---

[28] See note 1. Even Maurice Nédoncelle's excellent book (see n. 20) speaks only of *Paraphrastica Expositio* under the misleading title of "The Work of Christopher Davenport".

[29] The complete title should be read: ... *ubi tam ex principiis scholasticis quam monumentis veterum, praesertim magni orbis magistri Augustini, quidditas et potestas concilii, cum singulis vel apicibus de hac re desideratis enucleantur; divina authoritas Scrip-turarum et traditionum declaratur; fidei structura delineatur; ubi innumera antiqua examinantur; distinctio fundamentalium et non fundamentalium in rebus ad fidem spec-tantibus discutitur; abstrusiora quaedam ex naturae penetralibus exponuntur, quibus anima humana immortalis asseritur: Sacrum Tridentinum vindicatur* (Liège, 1648).

though they were one: "ex Sacris Scripturis et Traditionibus" (p. 140), "ex Sacra Scriptura et Patribus" (p. 141), "ex Scripturis vel traditis" (p. 176), "cum veritate scripta vel tradita" (p. 187), "scripto vel Traditione" (p. 359), "tam ex Scripturis quam ex Patribus" (p. 428), etc. At first sight, Christopher Davenport therefore echoes the language of the Council of Trent: the Gospel is contained "in libris scriptis et sine scripto traditionibus". And since he further claims in his title to vindicate the Council of Trent, let us first see how he quotes and interprets it in the matter of Scripture and the traditions.

The Tridentine Decree of April, 1546, on Scripture and the traditions is summed up by Davenport, who, like most of his colleagues, sees no essential difference between "quoting the very words" of the Council, as he says he does, and summarizing or paraphrasing them, as he actually does.

> The very words of Trent I will quote, whose first decree is thus summarized: Having in view the preservation of the purity of the gospel, which the prophets promised, which Christ Himself promulgated, and which finally the apostles, the source of all saving truth and moral discipline, preached, and at the same time perceiving that this truth and discipline is contained in the written books and the unwritten traditions which, having been received by the apostles from the mouth of Christ Himself and dictated by the Holy Spirit, were transmitted to the Church as though by hand, the Council, according to the orthodox fathers' example, receives all the books of the Old and the New Testament and also the traditions regarding faith as well as morals, which come from Christ's mouth or were dictated by the Holy Spirit and have been preserved in the Church by continuous succession, with an equal attitude of piety and reverence.—Later the fathers added: that this was done so that all would understand which bases the Council would chiefly use to confirm dogmas and restore morals in the Church.[30]

This is, on the whole, a faithful summary, which keeps close to the text it shortens. Yet the modern reader is struck by one major difference. In the Council of Trent as we read it today, the gospel (*evangelium*) is the source (*fontem*) of all saving truth and moral discipline (*omnis et salutaris veritatis et morum disciplinae*). In Davenport's epitome, however, the apostles constitute the source of all saving truth and moral discipline: *apostoli denique salutaris omnis veritatis morumque disciplinae fons*. Looking at the Tridentine text, we may

---

[30] *Systema Fidei*, ch. 14., n. 5, pp. 154-155.

easily see that both readings are grammatically correct, although there is little doubt, in the light of the history of the Council of Trent, that Davenport's reading is mistaken. It is the gospel which, for the Council, is the source of all saving truth.

Yet Davenport's misreading suggests a remark. Many theologians of the Counter Reformation and not a few still in our time apply the word *fons*, not to the gospel, but to the two vehicles where, according to the Council of Trent, it may be found, namely, the Scriptures and the traditions. There thus appears a theology of "two sources of faith". Modern authors have wondered how the passage from "gospel: one source" to "Scripture and Tradition: two sources" occurred. The transition is indeed difficult to conceive if *fontem*, in the decree of Trent, is a predicate of *evangelium*. By the same token, it is easy to pass from the concept of "one source", identified with the apostles, to that of "two sources", the two apostolic ways of teaching, Scripture and Tradition. It is, therefore, possible and perhaps likely that at the basis of the dualistic notion of two sources of faith there lay a reading of the Council of Trent different from ours, the difference bearing not only, or even mainly, on the meaning of *et*, the copula joining the Scriptures and the traditions, but also or even primarily on the sense of *fontem*, which would qualify *apostolos* rather than *evangelium*.

Admittedly, the text of Trent is quoted literally elsewhere: *perspiciens hanc veritatem et disciplinam contineri in libris scriptis et sine scripto traditionibus, quae ipsius Christi ore ab apostolis acceptae, aut ab ipsis apostolis, Spiritu Sancto dictante, quasi per manus traditae, ad nos usque pervenerunt, etc.*[31] This citation is used to show that the Council of Trent conceived the *adaequatum fidei fontem* to involve *utraque*, the Scriptures and the traditions. *Fons*, here, may refer either to the apostles or to the gospel. Just before the quotation it refers to *verbum Dei*, which does not solve our problem, since the Word of God, which may be identified with the gospel, reaches us also through the apostles. The meaning of *fons* in this passage remains, therefore, ambiguous.

One implication of the Tridentine decree is that the Church does not base its definitions on new revelations:

> And thus the Council of Trent, in its first decree, clearly wanted, against the followers of this third opinion, no other bases to be used to confirm dogmas and restore morals in the Church besides the

---

[31] l.c., ch. 11, n. 13, p. 109.

ascertained Scriptures and the true traditions of the ancients. It does not recognize new revelations. . . . No other basis is, therefore, to be sought; but one must have recourse to the apostles alone, one must return to the old Church. She has indeed in herself all the necessary traditions of faith received from the apostles, some of which were even committed to writing; and there one must remain.[32]

Without quoting the decree here, Davenport concludes from it that only the Scriptures and the ancient traditions may ground definitions, new revelations being totally excluded. To the apostles we must go, to the old Church, the custodian of all apostolic traditions, some of which were written.

This way of speaking may suggest that Scripture contains only a small part of the apostolic traditions. In another chapter, nevertheless, Davenport studies the opposite opinion: *An solae Scripturae sufficiant pro fundamentis fidei?*

On this occasion, referring again to the Tridentine decree, he spends considerable time explaining the position of those who believe the Scriptures alone to be the bases of faith: "It seems, however, to some that the Tridentine fathers suggested this way when they exhorted not to teach or condemn easily if the point in question does not appear with certainty from the Scriptures and the testimonies of the Fathers".[33] The text alluded to is the same as in the above passages, and again Davenport does not so much quote as give the meaning. He then raises the exact question about which much ink has flowed since it was asked in 1949 by Edmond Ortigues: What is the meaning of *et* in the expression "Scriptures and traditions"?[34]

In their opinion, this copula indicates, and not weakly, that nothing should be taught about faith which is not with certainty in the Scriptures according to the old Fathers' explanations. . . . It is, therefore, manifest, in that opinion, that traditions do not rule with certainty unless they convey to us the sense of the Scriptures successively transmitted by the Fathers.[35]

Davenport names and quotes supporters of this opinion and older authors who seem to favor it: Catharinus, Ockham, Henry a Zoemeren, St. Thomas, Cajetan, Egidius, Vincent of Lerins, Dominic

---

[32] l.c., ch. 3, n. 7, p. 17.
[33] l.c., ch. 7, n. 11, p. 65.
[34] "Ecritures et traditions apostoliques au Concile de Trente" (*Recherches de Science Religieuse*, 1949, p. 271-299).
[35] l.c., ch. 7, n. 11, p. 65.

Soto, etc.[36] He then cites another passage from the decree of 1546
which may support the same view: "If someone does not receive as
sacred and canonical the integral books with all their parts, as it is
customary to read them in the Catholic Church, or with knowledge
and deliberation despises the above-mentioned traditions, let him
be anathema".[37] The argument is, he explains, that the different
expressions, *pro sacris et canonicis non susceperit*, used for Scripture,
and *contempserit*, for the traditions, imply two distinct attitudes,
resulting from the differing status of Scripture and tradition.

What this understanding of Scripture and tradition implies is
explained at length in chapter 7. Davenport is clearly at pains to show
that such a theology does not minimize tradition. *Sufficientia Scripturae* is given a Catholic sense by those who "have considered fundamental only what is expressly contained in the Sacred Letters or
is legitimately deduced therefrom".[38] In the same line, "the traditions are placed within the gospel"; [39] "and in this sense", Davenport adds, "even the traditions and what follows from them are
included".[40]

Many authors also restrict the meaning of *solum*. They believe, with
St. Thomas and Duns Scotus, that "*only* implicitly or remotely all
is in the Scriptures".[41] Or, like William of Ockham, they "at least
admit such traditions as deal with and convey the meaning of Scripture".[42] The Fathers who refuted heretics with the Scriptures did so
in the sense of St. Athanasius: "The Nicene Fathers received the
meaning of Scripture from the Fathers' hands, and they thus showed
that it was tradition".[43] Occasionally, against heretics who knew no
other rule, they used Scripture only. "It is patent that to various
diseases they applied various remedies, now with the Scriptures
alone, now with the traditions alone". Davenport concludes: "When
they proceed adequately, they require both".[44] Noting that St.

[36] Henry a Zoemeren (1420-1472), professor at Louvain, commentator of
Ockham; Gilles de Rome (d. 1316), Augustinian, became archbishop of Bourges
in 1295; Catarin (1484-1553) and Dominique Soto (1495-1560) both of them
Dominicans, were among the theologians of the Council of Trent.
[37] l.c., ch. 7, n. 11, pp. 66-67.
[38] l.c., ch. 7, n. 1, p. 46.
[39] l.c., ch. 7, n. 1, p. 47.
[40] l.c., ch. 7, n. 2, p. 50.
[41] l.c., ch. 7, n. 1, p. 43.
[42] l.c., ch. 7, n. 1, p. 49.
[43] l.c., ch. 7, n. 1, p. 55.
[44] l.c., ch. 7, n. 4, p. 56.

Augustine teaches "the all-sufficiency of Scripture, at least for what is necessary to salvation," Davenport adds his interpretation: "This is true formally or reductively, or, as the School says, implicitly or explicitly".[45] For St. Athanasius also, "the integral faith is not in the Scriptures. . . but only, as it were, its premiss".[46]

Tradition is not minimized by the sufficiency of Scripture; but its place and function is simply to "open the legitimate and true meaning of Scripture".[47] There is no difficulty in accepting together the necessity of the traditions and the sufficiency of Scripture: "And therefore it remains that the Scriptures are sufficient and the traditions necessary. . . . . And in this sense the holy Fathers approve the traditions and think that there is not one faith for the traditions and another for the Scriptures, but the same faith, which is more explicit in the former". Traditions are "explanatory of faith".[48] The mistake lies in arguing from the sufficiency of Scripture to reject tradition. For the two are one: "The traditions that convey the meaning of Scripture are testified to by the Scriptures themselves, as they also testify to the Scriptures".[49]

Christopher Davenport knows that some will dismiss such a position: "*Video aliquibus in latitudine data arridere.*" Yet he wants "faithfully to present and explain it". As for him, his doctrine is well known: "What I think I have declared abundantly, and I shall declare it six hundred times if circumstances require. For I hold that all the traditions universally received must be received according to the rank they obtain in the Church".[50] Clearly, Davenport does not endorse the opinion which he has reported, and he is at times embarrassed by some of the formulae he has examined. Yet he does not reject this position, and he has obviously been impressed by the number and weight of the authorities that may be adduced in support of it. Besides those that have already been mentioned, we find, among those he quotes, explains, and discusses, St. Basil, St. Augustine, St. Jerome, St. Cyprian, St. Albert the Great, St. Bonaventure, Duns Scotus, Bradwardine, Peter Soto, Dominic Lopez, and many others.[51]

---

[45] l.c., ch. 7, n. 5, p. 56.
[46] l.c., ch. 7, n. 6, p. 57.
[47] l.c., ch. 7, n. 8, p. 60.
[48] l.c., ch. 7, n. 9, p. 61.
[49] l.c., ch. 7, n. 11, p. 66.
[50] l.c., ch. 7, n. 11, p. 67.
[51] Thomas Bradwardine (1290-1349) was a professor at Oxford; Pedro Soto (d. 1563) at Salamanca; I have not been able to identify Dominicus Lopez.

Davenport certainly believes that the doctrine he has described is a valid Catholic position. It is, therefore, not correct to consider the interpretation of the Council of Trent proposed in our days by Josef Geiselmann and others to be a recent, if not an aberrant, phenomenon: it was already fully developed in the middle of the seventeenth century. The text of *Systema fidei* makes it impossible to attribute the dualistic concept of two sources of faith to "all the theologians for four centuries", and to believe that the Council of Trent was universally interpreted in the sense of the dualistic conception until "a few years ago".[52]

When Davenport spoke of *locutio illa copulativa*, he was already questioning the meaning of the Tridentine decree, or at least reporting a question about it, even if this was not his own question. Yet, if the question has been asked again by modern historians, the answer mentioned in *Systema fidei* is not the one that has been advocated in our days. The Tridentine fathers modified their schema on Scriptures and the traditions by replacing *partim partim* with *et*. Geiselmann sees this as a refusal to be committed to any theory on the relationship of Scripture and tradition, while in itself it means "strictly nothing".[53] The opinion reported by Christopher Davenport goes further. Far from meaning nothing, *et* implies that "nothing should be taught about faith which is not with certainty in the Scriptures according to the old Fathers' explanations".[54] *Et* is not disjunctive but conjunctive. Scripture and the traditions are tied together in such a way that all doctrines are found in Scripture interpreted by the traditions. The *et* of the Council of Trent has an explanatory sense. It unites Scripture and the traditions like a text and its meaning. This comes nearer to the explanation of the Tridentine decree suggested in *Holy Writ or Holy Church*[55] than to the neutralization of *et* proposed by Geiselmann.

At the same time, another point needs to be corrected. Josef Geiselmann has wondered who first interpreted the copula placed

---

[52] Charles Boyer, "Traditions apostoliques non écrites" (*Doctor Communis*, 1962, pp. 5-21; quotes pp. 7 et 5.)

[53] Josef Geiselmann, "Das Konzil von Trient . . .", l.c., p. 163; see also, *Die Heilige Schrift und die Tradition*, pp. 154-164.

[54] l.c., ch. 7, n. 11, p. 65: *Locutio illa copulativa non frigide subindicat, in sententia eorum, nihil debere de fide statui, quod non certo haberetur in Scripturis secundum veterum Patrum explicationes . . . Manifestum provide est, in hac opinione, traditiones non esse certas regulas, proeter illas quae sensum Scripturarum a Patribus successive traditum ad nos deferunt.*

[55] *Holy Writ or Holy Church*, ch. 12.

at Trent between the Scriptures and the traditions in the interpretive rather than the additive sense. The problem is to determine who started the gradual supersession of the dualistic interpretation of Trent. Among Catholics, Geiselmann finds Johann Sailer[56] in the early nineteenth century, to have had the greatest influence. He also remarks that the Anglican William Palmer, of Worcester College, Oxford, gave an interpretive explanation of the Tridentine formula even before this had had time to spread among Catholics. Yet Palmer presents this without discussing other views, as though it already were an accepted explanation in his time. It is, therefore, likely that he was using older sources, and presumably Catholic ones. That such sources existed as early as the middle of the seventeenth century is obvious after reading Christopher Davenport. If this is so, we might as well say that the dualistic doctrine of two partial sources of faith, which is thought to have been typical of the Counter-Reformation, was never fully accepted.[57] Although dominant, the additive concept of tradition did not do away with the interpretive concept; and Trent was understood in the interpretive rather than the additive sense in the middle of the Counter-Reformation period, even though it was by a minority.

In this case, the question of who first understood Trent in that sense need not be asked: there had always been some who read the Council that way.

Davenport's own doctrine on Scripture and Tradition, as distinct from the ones he faithfully reports, appears from his great care to accept all the points of view of the Fathers and to balance them delicately. "I speak thus, and I would give references to nearly all the ancients in favor of the sole precedency and sufficiency of the Scriptures for salvation, if their other writings did not provide abundant evidence of their belief in the necessity of the traditions".[58] The Church Fathers teach both. They view Tradition mainly as the transmission of the meaning of Scripture: "Ecclesiastical traditions in the

---

[56] Cf Geiselmann, *Die mündliche Überlieferung . . .*, p. 184-187; Johannes Beumer, *Die mündliche Überlieferung als Glaubensquelle*, pp. 113-114.

[57] This is somewhat confirmed by Geiselmann, who sees Georgius Cassander (1513-1566) as the first theologian who adopted the interpretative conception of tradition that will be found much later in the school of Tübingen. Thus it was an early post-Tridentine position. See *Die lebendige Überlieferung . . .*, p. 159, n. 3a.

[58] l.c., ch. 8, n. 3, p. 72.

sense of Vincent of Lerins stand in the line of the interpretation of
the Scriptures".[59] These are the two basic kinds: "traditions grounded
in the Scriptures, or reporting the sense of the Scriptures as transmitted by the apostles, in whom Christ spoke". Between them and
Scripture there is no essential difference: "The other traditions, which
carry the necessary sense of Scripture to posterity, are authenticated
from and with the Scriptures themselves, and were always of faith
according to the ancients".[60] In this way Davenport believes in the
sufficiency of Scripture, yet he also teaches the *principalitas traditionum*.[61]

Davenport's main concern is to receive both Scripture and Tradition and to maintain their unity. This is "the style of all the Catholic
authors I have seen, although some often grant more to the Scriptures,
others more to the traditions. When, however, they explain the
adequate source of faith, they involve both".[62] Significantly, Davenport uses the word *fons* in the singular, in keeping with the language
of the Council of Trent, which he quotes at this point, even though
he does not make clear who or what the source is: the gospel, as at
Trent, the apostles, as in the above version of Trent, or the unity
itself of Scripture and Tradition. Yet the "only rule", for him, "consists of both".[63] Once this was granted, it mattered little to Davenport if one insisted on the sufficiency of Scripture and understood
the traditions to be simply interpretative, or in hardened language
one maintained: "Some points are of faith that are not in Scripture,
but are obtained by divine traditions or by a definition of the
Church".[64] He was not concerned with the exact relationship of
tradition to Scripture, but with the unity of both in the oneness of
the Word of God: "In the written or transmitted Word of God all
doctrines to be believed are explained".

From one point of view, therefore, there is only one rule of faith,
the Word of God. From another, there are three ways of knowing
the Word of God: "Here, indeed, one must remain principally, and
in these three, the Scriptures, the traditions, and the councils' definitions, the boundaries of our faith are placed". The first two constitute
the bases of faith, as Davenport explained at the beginning of his

---

[59] l.c., ch. 7, n. 4, p. 76.
[60] l.c., ch. 7, n. 4, p. 77.
[61] l.c., ch. 9, n. 4, p. 85.
[62] l.c., ch. 11, n. 13, p. 109.
[63] l.c., ch. 11, n. 13, p. 108.
[64] l.c., ch. 11, n. 13, p. 109.

volume; the third forms the fundamentals, deriving from the bases with certainty and proclaimed by the Church in council.

Shall we say that Christopher Davenport has thus finally endorsed the dualistic or additive concept of partial sources of faith? His position is more subtle than that. "The Church or the councils are not supposed to want to give other answers than what can be obtained from the Sacred Scriptures where it [*sic*] is clear or it interprets itself".[65] All statements of doctrine made by the Church are, in her mind, scriptural, analogical, shall we say, to what Scripture formulates clearly. In case this connection should not appear, recourse must be had to "the constant testimony of solid antiquity", so that nothing be asserted with certainty "unless it came from the hand or writings of the old apostles".[66] If something is obscure in Scripture and in the Fathers, let it remain so: "The points that have been indeterminately or obscurely formulated, and are not formally or virtually made explicit, orally or in writings, by the apostles, should remain the way they are".[67]

Christopher Davenport would wish to freeze the clarity of Christian doctrine at the point reached in Scripture and among the early Fathers. Yet past conciliar decisions may have sanctioned teachings that do not seem to have been mentioned at all by the Fathers. Here, Davenport briefly touches on the vexed problem of development, yet, apparently blind to its complexities, he sees no basic difficulty in it. For if such a phenomenon has indeed taken place, faith in the divine guidance over the Church should carry conviction and quieten doubts: "In this case I say that tradition, preserved by the apostles' voice, not written, is to be drawn from the consensus of the Churches".[68] In other words, later unanimity sufficiently witnesses to the validity of a doctrine, whether or not this may be tested by the writings of the Fathers.

Davenport thus recognizes the possibility of apostolic traditions orally transmitted until a Council should define them. He also looks further ahead; for these traditions, in the perspective which he has opened, could simply have appeared at a given time in the post-apostolic period. Yet this underlies the infallibility of the Church more than it asserts the existence of totally extrascriptural traditions

[65] l.c., ch. 19, n. 1, p. 194.
[66] l.c., ch. 19, n. 2, p. 195.
[67] l.c., ch. 19, n. 5, p. 198.
[68] l.c., ch. 19, n. 5, p. 199.

or suggests the intricacies of doctrinal development. At any rate it does not contradict, in Davenport's mind, what he has already stated: the Church never intends to teach anything other than what may be concluded from Scripture where Scripture is clear.

The position of Davenport is clarified, and somewhat toned down, in a short "Dialogue of Scripture and Tradition and how to know them", included in a later publication, *An Enchiridion of Faith* (1655). Although this is a long volume, its treatment of the controversies between Catholics and Protestants is much simpler than in *Systema Fidei*. It takes the form of a conversation, in English this time, between "Disciple" and "Master". As the book is obviously destined to the general public, Davenport avoids side-issues and tries to go straight to the heart of the matter and to answer each question succinctly.

The principle of scriptural sufficiency is maintained, together with the need for authentic interpretation: "The Scriptures are profitable to all and are sufficient in themselves, though not always in order to everyone for our safe-conduct to heaven, inasmuch as they are liable to diverse senses".[69] The remedy to this shortcoming of Scripture's efficiency lies in the transmission of its true sense by the Church's tradition: one must "adhere to the interpretations conveyed by hand to hand from age to age universally by the Christian Orthodox doctors to this present Church, which oral conveyance we call Tradition". In Davenport's approach these traditions include more than a transmission of meaning and they are not to be esteemed only for their intellectual value. Since the traditions hand the Gospel down the ages, they are also truly the Gospel. In Davenport's far-reaching words, "They are the living Gospel of faith which is in-fused into the hearts of the faithful throughout the universal Church: that is, by carrying the sense, they convey the life of the Gospel through the whole Church".[70]

Tradition, residing in the hearts of the faithful by the operation of the Holy Spirit, is necessarily universal in time as well as in space. It carries nothing "which is not the word of God, that is, which from the beginning was not revealed, and since continually conveyed and kept in the Church". Yet the rule of Vincent of Lerins, which Davenport quotes on this occasion, need not be understood

---

[69] *An Enchiridion of Faith*, p. 11.
[70] l.c., p. 12.

literally. The *Quod ab omnibus, quod ubique, quod semper*, implies "the universality of persons, of place and of time"; yet "these titles of Catholicism", as Davenport phrases it, may at times be latent. Davenport speaks here of an "exception", where we would prefer to say a "precision":

> This exception being admitted: everyone of our particular tenets was always by the universality of Christians in all places (so far as Christian monuments are extant to attest them) acknowledged either in formal terms, or virtually included in such which were in terms written or delivered.[71]

In other words, not all was always transmitted in explicit formulation. Both Scripture and Tradition include doctrines that have been, one time or another, only implicitly contained in their deposit. This is obviously the wedge which ought to introduce the notion of doctrinal development into the principle of the universality of the faith. Davenport admits that some past Doctors have been dubious about points that are now affirmed as of Catholic faith. But there is no obligation for everyone to affirm always everything, and there have been particular persons with their own opinions, "who cannot be thought to interrupt the universality of the Church".[72] Thus, a Council may have anathematized opinions that were formerly considered permissible. Whatever decision has thus been reached commits the entire Church, otherwise "the Tradition itself would fail in order to those who follow us".[73] Indeed it may have been the ultimate purpose of a doctrinal crisis to enable the Church to arrive at the truth:

> If any point now condemned as heretical by the Council of Trent were before held diversely betwixt the faithful, it were ground enough for the certain verity of it. . . that it now be held as truth by the universal Church.[74]

One should therefore introduce a distinction among the Church's traditions. In *Systema Fidei* Davenport classified Catholic doctrines as *fundamenta* and *fundamentalia*: doctrines explicitly formulated in Scripture and Tradition are *fundamenta*, others implicitly contained in them, are *fundamentalia*. Davenport makes a similar distinction here, although his vocabulary is no longer the same:

---

[71] l.c., pp. 12-13.
[72] l.c., p. 13.
[73] l.c., p. 14.
[74] l.c., p. 15.

Hence you see that there are two sorts of universal traditions. One which passes so clear that amongst Orthodox or Catholic Christians it has not suffered any rub or dispute. Points thus conveyed are like the stars *primae magnitudinis*; if any man be ignorant of them, having lived where there is public profession of Christianity, it can hardly be otherwise than *pravae dispositionis*, that is, with malice: such are the Articles of the Creed, the Sacrifice of the Mass, etc. The other, which has admitted some little umbrages in particular men's various opinations or altercations, are such which St. Augustine speaks of, *Epist. 99*, treating of Christ's descent into hell and of Adam's redemption thence. . . Yet the whole Catholic Church being afterwards asked by her Councils, when there was necessity, has declared against these private opinions that she always reserved it in her repository or treasure-house (as St. Irenaeus calls it) as her faith. These are points *secundae magnitudinis*, of an inferior light than the former, and therefore admitted some cloudiness in particular persons' understanding; and herein good Catholics may have ignorance *purae negationis*, that is, a faultless nesciency, or not knowing them until sufficiently declared by the Church. . . .[75]

Davenport's conception is both bold and hesitant. For while he is willing to list many points of faith among the stars of the second order, he is not prepared to admit that these may have been, at any time, in a completely hidden state, leaving the Church entirely in the dark concerning them. What, for him, was missing when scholars controverted the doctrine of the Immaculate Conception, to take an instance which he mentions, was only a satisfactory investigation of Tradition. The doctrine to be defined later was always present and—this is where Davenport departs from subsequent theories of development—could have been seen at any time by sufficient study. Thus Santa Clara tries to hold the two horns of the dilemma together. On the one hand, he willingly recognizes progress in the Church's statements of faith:

Some things therefore, though indeed of faith, yet are not perfectly declared by constant consent of the Church, till afterwards upon occasion of difficulty; others from the beginning were admitted and thence clearly conveyed to us.[76]

On the other hand, Davenport continues with this paradox:

But in each of these, any present age, if authentically examined, would render us secure, else it is not conceivable how it could descent by tradition. . . . Nobody can better tell us what the Church received

---

[75] l.c., pp. 15-16.
[76] l.c., pp. 16-17.

from the Apostles than the Church herself which received them. If she therefore shall once or in any age fail to know what she has received, all fails.

Davenport has now glimpsed the fundamental problem of Catholic Christianity: Do the definitions made during the Church's history clarify points of doctrine that were always present in the hearts of the faithful and *could have been discerned previously* by a more thorough inquiry? Or do they instance an objective growth in what is believed, so that Tradition does not only preserve and explain the always given, but also enlarges it? He clearly sided with the former conception. Yet the question remained; and it was raised again in his century.

CHAPTER SEVEN

THE LEGACY OF WILLIAM RUSHWORTH

Among the authors of his time that Christopher Davenport mentions in *Systema Fidei*, one, who is never named, recurs several times among those who hold the position, which Davenport criticizes, most favorable to the scriptural principle. No name is given; but Davenport refers to him as *amicus meus*, and, more often, *dialogista noster*. This personage should now be introduced.

In 1640 there was published in Paris an anonymous volume entitled, *The Dialogues of William Richworth, or the Judgement of Common Sense in the Choice of Religion*. Although no name of author appeared on the title-page, the preface, signed with the initials T. W., attributes the authorship to William Richworth himself: the work appeared posthumously. Richworth (or Rushworth) is known to us: of Lincolnshire origin, he had been ordained at Douai in 1615, became Prefect of the College, returned to England in 1618, and worked there until he died in 1637. He used two aliases, being known at Douai as Charles Ross and signing Robinson a learned correspondence about mathematics. Richworth was apparently interested in all kinds of scientific and curious areas of knowledge, including theology. Whether he was a theologian of value or not, we do not know outside of *The Dialogues of William Richworth*.

But, and here the matter becomes more involved, a second edition appeared in Paris in 1654 (a reprint had already been made in 1648, with no changes in the material): this edition had a minor difference in the title, spelling the name Rushworth, and many small alterations, corrections and additions to the text. It was, according to the title-page, "corrected and enlarged by Thomas White, gentleman"! These changes are not substantial, yet they amount to a careful editing of the previous text, including stylistic modifications, doctrinal shifts of emphasis, and the addition of a fourth dialogue to the three of 1640. Furthermore, another book was published in the same year 1654, *An Apology for Rushworth's Dialogues*, signed, this time, by Thomas White. This apology acknowledges White's authorship of *Rushworth's Dialogues*, yet only for the edition of 1654, "which alone has felt throughout this author's last hand".[1] This would suggest that White was not only responsible for the final editing of the text of the *Dialogues*, but also somehow involved in their origin. This could be easily explained if the *Dialogues* had been live conversations between two persons before becoming literary dialogues. "Uncle" and "Nephew" of the book may originally have been Rushworth and White, an older man with experience and with personal reflections about theological issues, and a younger man, freshly out of the schools or perhaps still in them. After "Uncle's" death, "Nephew" publishes a report on the dialogues they had, which, later, in view of criticisms levelled at the first volume, he edits and publishes again in a different form, caring enough about the issues to write also a defense of the *Dialogues*. Precisely, 1648 is the date of Christopher Davenport's *Systema Fidei*, in which the position of *dialogista noster, amicus meus*, the author of what Davenport calls *Dialogus de religionis electione* while acknowledged to be Catholic, is criticized, Davenport refusing to be identified with its doctrine.

Thomas White (1593-1673) is well known as one of the most controversial figures among English Catholics of the seventeenth century. After his schooling at St. Omer and Valladolid, White studied for the priesthood at Douai, where he was known under the name of Blackloe. After his ordination in 1617 he taught at Douai for a while, then travelled extensively, being found successively in England in 1623, Paris in 1624, Rome in 1625, then again at Douai, in Lisbon as President of the English College in 1633, in England, back at Douai in 1650, and finally in England, where he stayed, living in London, for the last twenty odd years of his life. Besides Blackloe, he used other aliases: Anglus, Candidus, Albus, Bianchi, Vitius. . .

Thomas White was involved in the unfortunate ecclesiastical polemics of his time, and led what was called the Blackloist party of English Catholics, which advocated the expulsion of the Society of Jesus from England. He was a prolific writer, but all his works date from after 1640, when his life acquired some stability. Some of his works are theologically important and manifest a mind that is both sharp and traditional. His advocacy of a Platonic philosophical and theological position, in his work *Institutionum sacrarum Peripateticis inaedificatarum. . .pars theoretica* (vol. I, 1646; vol. II, 1652), and his

---

[1] Thomas White, *Apology for Rushworth's Dialogues*, "advertisement".

views on purgatory (*The Middle State of Souls*, Latin ed., 1653; English, 1659) provoked the hostility of the Bishop of Chalcedon, Richard Smith, and the censures of the Faculty of the English College at Douai. Several propositions excerpted from his works were condemned by the Holy Office in 1655 and 1657. After the Faculty of the English College had censured a few more statements from the *Institutionum*, White successfully cleared himself of the suspicion of scepticism (*Apologia pro doctrina sua adversus calumniatores*, 1661).

If we compare the *curriculum vitae* of William Rushworth and that of Thomas White as they are known to us, the only times when the two men may have been together and therefore able to hold the conversations recorded in the *Dialogues*, were before Rushworth's resignation as Prefect of the College in August 1618 and his subsequent return to England, or during White's short sojourns in England in 1623 and in the 30's. It is therefore likely that the book of the *Dialogues* was published, and perhaps written, long after the conversations took place. In this case, the authorship of the book belongs to the recorder more than to the main speaker.

That White, rather than Rushworth, is the actual author can also be concluded from Christopher Davenport's careful way of alluding to him in his *Systema Fidei*: *amicus meus, dialogista noster*, would apply to a living person, whom, in the circumstances of penal times, one prefers not to name, rather than to a deceased one who could not be hurt in any way by being, like other recent theologians, mentioned by name.

Thomas White is conscious of the originality of Rushworth's *Dialogues*: their doctrine, he writes in the epistle dedicatory of the *Apology*, "takes a path not much beaten by our modern controvertists".[2] They use "the antique weapons of Dialogues," which "want neither ornament nor particular efficacy", though White's *Apology* will change this "into the modern mode of direct discourse".[3] The dialogue takes place between "Uncle" and "Nephew", Uncle answering the puzzled questions of Nephew in regard to controversies of religion. The unbeaten path mentioned by White is that which some of Uncle's answers follow. It will appear from the doctrine of Scripture and tradition contained in these volumes.

The starting point for Rushworth—White's investigation is

---

[2] l.c., Epistle dedicatory.
[3] l.c., p. 2.

sharply formulated by Nephew: Why "we Catholics, who bear so great reverence and veneration to the Holy Scripture, receive more of it than others, write infinite volumes of commentaries upon it (as Paul's Churchyard can witness) and are so exact to improve ourselves (I mean our learned men) in the knowledge of it, should, nevertheless, when we come to join in the main point, that is, to the decision of controversies in religion, seem to fly off and recur to other judges, though we acknowledge it to be Christ's word and law?" [4] Nephew is understandably puzzled by this apparently double-faced attitude. Uncle acknowledges the problem as it may appear to the observer: "I see by experience that the one part seeks by all means to destroy the authority of God's Church, and the other seems to lessen the power of Scripture for the deciding of controversies".[5] A significant difference is made between the part that "seeks to destroy" and the one that only "seems to lessen". One can already sense what Rushworth's answer will attempt to show: while one part does seek to destroy the authority of the Church, the other's lessening of the authority of Scripture is only a mistaken appearance. One can also feel this in the remote consequences that Rushworth foresees: since "we think by Scripture alone, left without the guard of the Church, nothing or at least not enough for the salvation of mankind can be sufficiently proved", it follows that, in our view, "to stand by Scripture only, as they do", may be "but a plausible way to atheism", so that the ultimate question will be "whether we must rely upon a Church or be atheists". In order to escape this dire consequence, one must show that Scripture does resolve points of controversy. And if this can be made manifest, the Catholic side must give way: "we were worse than beasts if we should refuse to be judged thereby".[6] Rushworth is prepared to stake all on the outcome of his investigation.

The inquiry begins with Scripture, since Protestants claim to know all the faith with Scripture alone. How does one read Scripture? Rushworth distinguishes two ways, scholarly and plain. But only the plain way is relevant to the question of understanding Scripture. For Scripture is not given to scholars: all the people of God must be able to understand Scripture if this is indeed the con-

---

[4] *Rushworth's Dialogues*, 1640, pp. 221-222.
[5] l.c., p. 223.
[6] l.c., p. 224.

veyer of revelation. The question of the scientific reading of Scripture is, therefore, irrelevant to our problem.

> There are two manners of understanding Scripture, the one a kind of
> large manner, taking it in gross and a great deal together as we take
> a discourse of play which pleasingly passes away without great demur
> or particular weighing of every word; the other more curious and
> exact looking into every little property which may breed diversity.
> And I suppose you would tell me that this second belongs only to
> scholars, but that the former guides our life and governs our actions
> .... I must needs confess that what good effect soever is the end for
> which Scripture was ordained, if it be anything belonging to man's
> life and conversation, it must be compassed by this gross, common
> and ordinary course of reading and understanding.[7]

The plain manner of understanding Scripture is described many
times in the three volumes of Thomas White. It is for him the only
religious way, the only one that matters for the knowledge of Scripture
and revelation. It is also, paradoxically enough, the more certain.

> This common manner of using Scripture is more secure than the
> minute and precise balancing of every phrase and syllable. For neither
> the variety of translations, nor errors of copies, nor difficulties of
> languages, nor mutability of words, nor multiplicity of the occasions
> and intentions of the authors, nor the abundance of things written,
> nor different framings of the books—all which are causes of un-
> certainty in a rigorous examination—have any such power to break
> the common and ordinary sense of the writer in general, as we every
> day find by experience.[8]

Thus White proceeds analogically from our daily experience of
reading and writing. The meaning of an author is not ascertained by
exact philological inquiry into each of the words he uses, but the
sense is grasped by our mind seeing a sentence, a chapter, or a book
as a whole. In such a way the Church Fathers read and expounded
Scripture, and there is no reason now to depart from their method:

> You shall have them cite many places, some proper, some allegorical,
> some common, all some times avoidable if they be taken separately
> but the whole discourse more or less forcible according to the natural
> parts of heavenly light more or less communicated to one than to
> another, yet still in the proportion of orators who speak to the multi-
> tude and not to Socrates or Crysippus.[9]

---

[7] l.c., pp. 329-330.
[8] *Rushworth's Dialogues*, 1654, pp. 126-127.
[9] *Rushworth's Dialogues*, 1640, p. 339.

Given these two possible ways of interpreting Scripture, it is in relation to the second that the controversy between Catholics and Protestants must be resolved, unless we wish to be lost in "a labyrinth of voluntary and unendable disputations".[10] Protestants challenge us on the basis of the first way of reading Scripture. They want us to show "every point of our faith in particular" in Holy Writ.[11] Catholics should eschew this pitfall: "To what end, unless for gallantry and to show wit, should they undertake to prove their tenets by Scripture? For this were to strengthen their opponent in his own ground and principle, that all proof is to be drawn from the Bible".[12] Yet how far the plain reading of Scripture can take us in the direction of the full Catholic faith remains a legitimate question.

Here lies the originality of the *Dialogues*. Thomas White does not simply deny or refute the possibility of proving all points of faith from Scripture alone. Once he has distinguished a scientific and an ordinary way of reading Scripture, he maintains that the second supports the Catholic faith. Such is the assertion made in the *Dialogues*: "The other means or way to make one a Catholic"—corresponding to "showing every point of our faith in particular" from Scripture—"is by some common principle; as if by reading of Scripture we find nothing contrary to the Catholic tenet or practise which our adversary calls in question, or also if we find it commended there in general or the authors and observers of it praised. And in this way I doubt not but a sensible and discreet reading of Scripture at large may and will make any true student of it a perfect believing Catholic, so he proceeds with indifference and with a mind rather to know Scripture than to look for this or that point in it".[13] This passage was reproduced with minor modifications in the edition of 1654. The reading that Rushworth envisions here is indeed that of Scripture alone, without the help of tradition. This is made clear elsewhere: "I think that the Catholic cause may not only be maintained by Scripture, but also that it has the better standing precisely to Scripture alone" [14]—a statement which was still reinforced in the text of 1654: "For I think Catholic religion may not only be proved by Scripture, but that, standing exactly and precisely to the written

---

[10] l.c., p. 354.
[11] l.c., p. 332.
[12] *Rushworth's Dialogues*, 1654, p. 129.
[13] *Rushworth's Dialogues*, 1640, pp. 334-335.
[14] l.c., p. 350.

Word, Catholicism is far more maintainable than Protestancy". This was followed by a word of caution: "I confess that this kind of disputing is not fit for many auditors, but only persons of moderation and understanding".[15] Although the second formulation avoids the Protestant expression "Scripture alone", it is actually more forceful: the vague subject "Catholic cause" has become the much more exact "Catholic religion" and "Catholicism".

Thomas White's *Apology for Rushworth's Dialogues* carefully explains these passages, supports them, and professes to give their standing and strength in Catholic opinion. The text is long but deserves to be fully quoted:

> Thirdly, we confess the Bible contains all parts of Catholic doctrine, in this sense that all Catholic doctrine may be found there, by places and arguments be deducted thence; nay more, be topically or oratorically proved out of it; so that, if an able preacher be in a pulpit, where he speaks without contradiction, with a full and free scope, he may, merely discoursing out of Scripture, carry any point of Catholic doctrine before the generality of his auditory, and convince at the present such a part of them as either are but indifferently speculative or have not taken pains in the question.
>
> Fourthly, I affirm that if any point be brought to an eristical decision before judges, where the parties on both sides are obstinately bent to defend their own positions by all the art they can imagine; so the question be not, which part is true, but only which is more or less conformable to Scripture, the Catholic position may be victoriously evidenced, by arguments purely drawn from thence, compared and valued according to true criticism, without the aid of Fathers, explications or any other extrinsecal helps. Thus far I esteem all good Catholics do *de facto* hold.[16]

In this important page White affirms two distinct points. In the first place, an oratorical use of the Bible in preaching can fully establish the Catholic faith to the satisfaction of the average listener. Evidently, such a recourse to Scripture does not stand on the literal sense alone. It is, as White says, "topical or oratorical." It corresponds to the essential purpose of Scripture, which is "to inform our lives by an ordinary reading of it, or by preaching, singing, and such like uses".[17]

In the second place, even at the tribunal of the letter alone, with the use of all the tools of criticism, the Catholic faith can be established with sufficient evidence to be accepted by an impartial judge. This

---

[15] *Rushworth's Dialogues*, 1654, p. 131.
[16] *Apology . . .*, pp. 141-142.
[17] *Rushworth's Dialogues*, 1640, p. 352.

is not to say that all judges would accept the evidence. For White rejects the equivalence of his position with another, against which, as he says, he "engages the Catholic negative", namely, that "the Scripture be a sufficient storehouse to furnish either side with texts, unavoidable and convincing beyond any shadow of reply, in the judgement of sworn and expert judges who are well practised what *convincing* signifies, and how much the various acceptions of words and mutability of meanings import in the construction of sentences".[18] Recourse to Scripture alone in favor of the Catholic faith does not, in White's opinion, make all shadow of reply impossible, for there is always the possibility of quibbling on the meaning of terms. It is, nevertheless, strong enough to counterbalance the Protestant appeal to *Scriptura sola* by making the Catholic interpretation of Scripture reasonably plausible. In other words, it does not fully establish the "truth" of Catholicism; but it supports its "conformity" with Scripture. Should one object that this is not a proper use of Scripture and that to bring the Catholic faith to courts, there to be judged with the help of nothing but the Bible, is tantamount to throwing it into jeopardy, White could colorfully reply, as he does in another context: "Such arguments are the abortive issue of immature brains, not able to distinguish the force of a cannon shot from a fairy's squib or a boy's pot-gun".[19]

Thomas White's conception of the sufficiency of Scripture to explain the Catholic faith is, in his mind, entirely compatible with Catholic doctrine on traditions. His clearest definition of tradition is contained in the *Apology*: "Tradition we call the delivery of Christ's doctrine from hand to hand in that part of the world which, with propriety, is called Christian".[20] The *Dialogues* define it in similar ways: an opinion which "passes for a thing delivered by hand to hand from Christ".[21] "A Tradition, or a point of faith delivered by tradition, is a point universally preached and delivered by the Apostles and imprinted in the hearts of the Christian world, and by a universal belief and practise continued unto our days, whereof our warrant is no other than that we find the present Church in quiet possession of it, and whereof no beginning is known".[22] "The Tradition we speak

---

[18] *Apology* . . ., p. 142.
[19] *Rushworth's Dialogues*, 1640, p. 173.
[20] *Apology* . . ., p. 7.
[21] *Rushworth's Dialogues*, 1640, p. 173.
[22] l.c., pp. 554-555.

of is the public preaching and teaching and practise exercised in the Church, settled by the Apostles through the world".[23] Since tradition is this universal transmission of doctrines and practices from the Apostles down to us, White distinguishes between written and verbal tradition. Written tradition is the Scripture itself, in which Tradition is expressed in a set form of words that can no longer change. Verbal tradition is the transmission of ideas, which may be expressed with different words and terms in diverse countries and circumstances: "The meaning of verbal, here intended, is only as contradistinguished to written Tradition; which, being in set words, whose interpretation is continually subject to dispute, is therefore opposed to oral or mental, where the sense is known, and all the question is about the words and expressions".[24] There are thus two forms of tradition: the one is in set, written words, the meaning of which is open to debate; the other is in unquestioned ideas, the expression of which remains subject to discussion and can always be improved upon. Whereas Protestants stick only to the former, Catholics rely on the latter and therefore always know what their faith is: "Those who rely on Scripture are in perpetual quarrels about the sense, whereas to Catholics the sense of their Faith is certain, though the words be sometimes in question".[25]

The Catholic reading of Scripture results from the convergence of the known Tradition with the written word, and conversely, the errors of heretics derive from their separation of Scripture from Tradition.

> Whoever have at any time, under the pretense of reformation, opposed her authority, such have constantly raised up their altar against Tradition upon the dead letter of the Scriptures: which, as the Catholic Church highly reverences, when they are animated by the interpretation of Tradition, so, by too much experience, she knows they become a killing letter, when abused, against the Catholic sense, in the mouths of the devil and his ministers.[26]

In these conditions it becomes important to know where the strength and value of Tradition comes from. How does one know that a belief is indeed the tradition handed down by the apostles? The contention of the Reformers, that many traditions of the Catholic

---

[23] *Apology* . . ., p. 126.
[24] *Rushworth's Dialogues*, 1640, p. 91.
[25] l.c., p. 92.
[26] l.c., p. 136.

Church were in fact traditions of men falsely attributed to the apostles, must be taken seriously if tradition is made, as it now is, the touchstone of the reading of Scripture.

White's solution falls back upon the traditional notion of the presence of the Gospel at the heart of the Church: "You rely upon the testimony of the whole Christian Church, you rely upon the force of nature, borne to continue from father to child, you rely upon the promises of Jesus Christ of continuing his Church unto the end of the world, and upon the efficacy of the Holy Ghost sent to perform it, by whom Christ's law was written in Christians' hearts and so to be continued to the day of doom".[27] What imports here is the testimony of the present Church in its totality, not the academic conviction of a few scholars. "For our faith being in some sort naturally grafted in the hearts of Christians, learned men may now and then mistake some points of it, as well as the causes and effects of their own nature itself".[28] Its strength resides in the unanimity of the interior Christian sense in spite of differences in national cultures, "the root and strength of Tradition being grounded upon this, that such a belief is fixed in peoples' hearts of several nations".[29] A study of the Fathers reveals "the public doctrine of the ages in which they lived";[30] this is what gives the Fathers their value. But one could reach the same conclusions by simply seeking out the public doctrine of the Church today. It is not "because such a number of Doctors held it" [31] that a teaching belongs to the irrefragable tradition of the Catholic Church, but rather because such is the feeling and the sense of the faithful today as in the past: "It is held as a main distinction betwixt the laws of the Jews and of the Christians, that those of the Jew were to be written in stone and paper, and those of the Christian in the hearts of men by Tradition".[32]

Tradition being the unanimous testimony of Christian hearts, those who separate Scripture from tradition erect a divisive element into a universal rule of faith, focusing all belief upon the particularity of the Hebrew and Greek Scriptures while they have foregone the universality of the Christian witness. Thus Thomas White reaches the following conclusion:

---

[27] l.c., pp. 555-556.
[28] l.c., p. 560.
[29] l.c., p. 573.
[30] *Rushworth's Dialogues*, 1654, p. 72.
[31] l.c., p. 72.
[32] *Apology . . .*, p. 163.

I would entreat you to make a little reflection and compare the knowledge we have by these means, to that which Scripture affords, if handled
in a litigious way, as in controversies is necessary; and you shall
find Tradition is grounded on that which all men agree in, which is
common to all ages, all nations, all conditions; but the knowledge
we have by Scripture is grounded on that which is different in every
nation. Hence springs another diversity between them; that the one
is planted in nature and in what God created in man; the other in
what men themselves framed, and that not by design or art but by
custom and chance. Out of which again it follows that the one is
capable of necessity, as all natural things are, the other not; the one is
fixed on universals, the other vagabond in particulars.[33]

In White's mind, this entails no renunciation to what has been
called the "scandal of particularity"; nor does it follow that Scripture
is less certain than tradition. It implies rather that "if the one were to
bring in verdict upon the other, it would be much more forcible and
evident to conclude, this book is Scripture, because conformable to
the doctrine taught and preached, than that this doctrine is apostolical,
because conformable to the Book".[34] But in the Catholic mind no
such verdict is necessary. For all is tradition: "In common, relating
generally to the body and substance of Catholic doctrine, there is no
doubt among Catholics but their reliance is upon Tradition, this
being the main profession of great and small, learned and unlearned,
that Christian Religion is and has been continued in our Church,
since the days of Our Saviour, the very same faith the Apostles
taught all nations, and upon that score they receive it".[35] White
carries this principle to the point of contradicting "our Schoolmen",
"very many" of whom "maintain that Tradition is necessary only
for some points not clearly expressed in Scripture".[36] If this is what
they say, it is not what they do, for "there is a wide distance betwixt
these two questions, what a man relies on for his assent or faith,
and what he says he thinks he relies on".[37] White refers explicitly
to Bellarmine. The Fathers knew better than that, for a Father
"being nearer to the Fountain, could less doubt that the stream, of
which he saw no other rise, reached home to the Springhead".[38]

White's concept of tradition as that which has been with Christians,

---

[33] *Rushworth's Dialogues*, 1654, pp. 219-220.
[34] l.c., p. 78.
[35] *Apology* p. 41.
[36] l.c., p. 38.
[37] l.c., p. 39.
[38] l.c., p. 43.

inscribed in their hearts, from the beginning, in the form of ideas that could be expressed in different sets of words, does not rule out a development of Tradition. But the development in question progresses only in extension, as when a formerly local tradition becomes universal. "We acknowledge some points of faith to have come in later than others, and give the cause of it, that the Tradition, whereon such points rely, was, at the beginning, a particular one, but so that at the time when it became universal, it had a testimony even beyond exception, by which it gained such a general acknowledgement".[39] A development in depth, therefore, White would not accept in matters of faith. If such a progress seems to have taken place, its scope remains within theological knowledge and does not affect faith itself: "I shall not deny the Church may come to know somewhat which haply before she never reflected on. But then those new truths belong to the science we call theology, not to faith; and even for those, the Church relies on Tradition, as far as they themselves emerge from doctrines delivered by Tradition".

The true place of Scripture, according to the theology of Rushworth-White, is therefore in Tradition. It is one tradition that has passed from particularity to universality. At the beginning a writing was known as apostolical by the local Church to which it was addressed. Only little by little did it reach the entire Church. On the contrary, the doctrine of Christ was delivered to all the apostles equally, and by them to the Churches to which they preached. Scripture remains particular: it is a local formulation of the universal doctrine. To oppose it would be absurd; but it would be equally erroneous to read the particular as though the light of the universal could not shine upon it:

> Christ having delivered by the hands of his Apostles two things to his Church, his doctrine, as the necessary and substantial element thereof, and his Scriptures, *ad abundantiam*, it was convenient the strength of Tradition for one should far exceed its strength for the other; yet so that even the weaker should not fail to be assured and certain.[40]

The two editions of *Rushworth's Dialogues* and their *Apology* constitute one whole, somehow set apart from White's more philosophical and speculative works. Yet the conceptual framework in which he wrote them remained his. As we have been able to notice,

---

[39] l.c., p. 37.
[40] l.c., p. 46.

the differences between the 1640 edition of the *Dialogues*, criticised in a friendly way by Davenport, and the "corrected and enlarged" edition of 1654, are minor and do not affect the fundamental notions and the trend of thought of the *Dialogues*. That White stood his ground is also clear from another book, published in 1659, *Controversy Logicke*, which, in a series of "reflections" and "shuffles" (with Protestants), purports to examine some of the problems raised in the controversies among Christians. The Fifth, Sixth and Seventh Reflections are particularly relevant:

5th: How Christian religion has been propagated and conserved.
6th: That the Scriptures, duly read, will bring a man to the truth of religion.
7th: That the reading of the Fathers will bring a man to the truth of religion, and that natural reason will greatly advance a man thereunto.

As explained here, Tradition is the transmission of doctrine and of whatever patrimony needs to be transmitted, from father to son. It implies a relationship of authority and trust: the father's authority to teach and the son's trust in his father. That the Christian faith was originally given in this way by Christ cannot be gainsaid. In the same way it was transmitted by the Apostles and their successors: "It is evident that the general propagation of the Christian faith was by vocal preaching and by vocal tradition, from father to son, of the doctrine first planted among them by the Apostles".[41] And the method that was good at the beginning remains necessary in later times:

> No doubt but the method of the first institution is in a manner ideal to the following continuation, which is but a kind of continuation of the beginning. And so, we might justly conclude without any further pains, that the conservation of religion ought to be likewise effected by original delivery, that is to say, by tradition.[42]

This appears still more obvious if we ponder over the fact that the Christian faith has to be transmitted, not to individual scholars who enjoy time, leisure, and the capacity to look up things for themselves, but rather to a people. And White deems it essential to the concept of a people as the collective unit of the human beings of one country,

---

[41] *Controversy Logicke*, p. 43.
[42] l.c., p. 43-44.

that knowledge comes to it by way of authority, from father to son:
"In whatever sense this word (people) is taken, it appears manifestly
that Tradition is the necessary and only means to establish faith in
the people... It is evident that the people... must rely upon an
authority for knowing what is the true religion and what is not".[43]
Scripture cannot do this, for as far as the people is concerned, it
contains too many ambiguous passages. "Now", White continues,
still drawing on his concept of Tradition and his notion of a people,
"if the meaning of ambiguous words will not serve to settle the
belief of Christian doctrine in the hearts of mankind, it is clear that
nothing but Tradition can perform that work, since there remains
nothing else that can pretend thereto: and consequently, nothing
but Tradition can be the means to plant and continue religion in the
world".[44]

Perhaps reminiscing on the way he himself had preserved and
transmitted Rushworth's precious conversations, White sees the
whole process of transmitting doctrine on the pattern of a memorial
which not only remembers, but keeps things alive:

> To Antiquity hangs Tradition, that is, the receiving of doctrine and
> customs from the ancient Church. The which Catholics place in this,
> that it is derived from the Apostles to us by the continual and imme-
> diate delivery of one age to another: the sons continuing their fathers,
> both belief and conversation in Christian life, and treading the same
> paths of salvation.[45]

It is inherent in such a concept that Tradition cannot lie. In another
book, *A Catechism of Christian Doctrine* (2nd ed., 1659) White asks,
with a note of impatience: "Do you not see that the Church is the
congregation of Christians which is dispersed through the whole
world, and therefore cannot come together to frame a lie?" And he
concludes: "If then they consent together that such a thing was
delivered to them for the doctrine of Christ, it cannot choose but be
so. And this is that which Divines call Tradition".[46]

White remarks that, taunted by Catholic logic, some Protestants
have come to admit a certain type of Tradition: they recognize that
"they received their doctrine by the tradition of the Bible made unto
them by the Churches continuing since the Apostles' time". But

---

[43] l.c., p. 45-46.
[44] l.c., p. 48.
[45] l.c., p. 228.
[46] *A Catechism of Christian Doctrine*, 2nd ed., 1659, pp. 96-97.

this is, for White, an equivocation: Tradition implies much more than "the delivery of a mute book or killing letter". Other Protestants, perceiving the weakness of this, have gone further and acknowledged Tradition as "the testimony of the Fathers of all ages", thus holding it to be a depository of documentary evidence from the past. But this is not sufficient: it even "diverts the question, turning the proof of religion (which is plain and easy to every ordinary understanding) into a business of learning and long study, in which, though they be worsted, yet the people cannot see it nor descry their falsehood". Having thus disposed of the documentary concept of Tradition which, at that very time, was gaining ground among continental Catholics, White affirms that nothing less than Tradition as "the delivery of doctrine, that is, of sense and meaning" will do.[47]

As for Scripture, White's position has not varied from what it was in *Rushworth's Dialogues*. On the one hand, the Scriptures must be interpreted "by the law written in the heart of that which has always adhered to the doctrine that from time to time they have received from their predecessors"; [48] that is, a Catholic, who shares the heart of the Church and the law inscribed in it, "knows the doctrine of Christ, that is to say, the sense of Scripture, independently from the words of the Scripture".[49] It follows that, in all substantial points, his interpretation of Scripture, made in the light of his faith, "cannot teach or interpret amiss".[50] On the other hand, even apart from knowledge of Tradition, "if the Scripture be read in such sort as it ought to be, it will of itself bring the man who reads it to the true religion". And to read Scripture in the proper way, White believes that five conditions have to be fulfilled: one must read with sincere intention, sound understanding, long and attentively, and the determination to practise what one will read. The third condition, which we have omitted in this list, is the most unusual: "That he meddle with no commenter or interpreter that is more cunning than himself, nor rely for the mind and sense of the Scripture but what the Scripture itself affords him". This contention, which was already formulated in *Rushworth's Dialogues*, had provided the basis for the early claim of White's Catholic adversary, Richard Smith, Bishop of Chalcedon, to demonstrate no less than two hundred and sixty

---

[47] *Controversy Logicke*, pp. 228-229.
[48] l.c., p. 50.
[49] l.c., p. 62.
[50] l.c., p. 50.

points of Catholic doctrine with the help of Scripture alone.[51] Once again, the question is not one of scientific exegesis. "I easily believe", White admits, "that many a pert bachelor will be ready to tell us that he can find ways to salve all these places of Scripture, and many more if they were urged. But that concerns me not". What attracts his attention is the plight of the unequipped reader confronted with "the outward face of Scripture". He wonders "to what belief it will lead an honest heart left to its own strength". For this reason, the main condition for reading Scripture should be "that they who, by Scripture, aim at coming to the truth, should admit of no interpreter".[52] At this level, White entertains no doubt that Scripture alone leads its unprejudiced and unlearned reader to the Catholic Church and that it teaches Catholic doctrine: "It will be sufficient to satisfy him fully that the outside and letter of Scripture is clearly on the side of antiquity and of the Catholic Church".[53]

Thomas White's concept of Scripture and Tradition is remarkable for many reasons. In the first place, White's approach sounds surprisingly modern. One of the problems he faces squarely is exactly the one to which attention has been drawn in recent years: Is all revealed doctrine in Scripture? His answer is a definite yes, qualified from the standpoint of how Scripture is read. Here, two ways may be distinguished. One may read Scripture in the light of Tradition, with the purpose of illustrating faith rather than calling texts to prove it. This is the way of the preacher, for whom Scripture is not a storehouse of quotes for arguments: it is written for edification and should be used for that purpose, and it acquires its full value in the light of the Church's doctrine rather than through scientific exegesis. One may also, as Richard Smith had already shown, approach Scripture without doctrinal prejudices either way, in complete readiness, disposed to follow its injunctions and to apply it in one's life. Thus taken at face-value, naively, Scripture also speaks for Catholic doctrine and the Catholic way of life: even here, at the level of ignorant people, Scripture conveys the authentic Revelation in its substance.

In the second place, White's conceptions are a perfect example of what is commonly considered to be a pre-Reformation theology.

---

[51] See infra, ch. 4.
[52] l.c., p. 61.
[53] l.c., p. 59.

Yet he wrote in the middle of the Counter-Reformation and belonged to a section of the Church caught in a polemical situation in which he himself was actively engaged. That the Counter-Reformation universally taught the doctrine of two partial sources of faith is a myth.

In the third place, one cannot help feeling that White not only anticipated our problems but also already answered them. He does leave us still unsatisfied on the matter of the development of doctrine, to which he does not give the importance which the post-Newman era sees in it. But on the relationships of Scripture and tradition, his position is patently that which Geiselmann has described as disappearing after the Council of Trent and reviving in the School of Tübingen: it was very much alive in the second quarter of the seventeenth century. From the viewpoint of the history of theology, this is notable enough. But one should also look at the matter from the standpoint of the best way to approach Scripture and Tradition. It is now a moot question whether we are not today recovering as something new an old view which we had forgotten: our problems may have been solved already in the seventeenth century. With this possibility in mind, this inquiry acquires a certain piquancy.

In the fourth place, White to some extent anticipated also the problematic of the traditionalist school in the nineteenth century. His comparison of the process of tradition to the communication of knowledge and principles by father to son, his qualification of tradition as a universal element contradistinguished from the particularity of writing, belong to the understanding of tradition as a universal human phenomenon, which the philosophy of the traditionalists will develop two centuries later and which will find its way into theology in the Lammenaisian school of thought, in Lacordaire's Conferences of Notre Dame, and in the writings of Joseph de Maistre. This school has little influence today, partly on account of its exaggerated claims for tradition as a phenomenon of culture, partly because of the condemnation of Lammenais by Pope Gregory XVI in 1832.[54] But this should not blind us to the fact that more recent Old Testament and New Testament exegesis has found traces in the Bible of such a tradition as was described by these men of the nineteenth century. Thus Thomas White appears, in the seventeenth century, as a genial anticipator of future trends.

---

[54] Encyclicals *Mirari vos*, August 15, 1832, and *Singulari nos*, June 25, 1834; see D.-S., nn. 2730-2732.

The theology of Rushworth-White, if it was expressed with particular force by Thomas White, was by no means an aberrant phenomenon in the English seventeenth century. As we can tell from the works of Smith and Davenport, White was not isolated from his predecessors and contemporaries. It is particularly fascinating to see his understanding of the sufficiency of Scripture for salvation defended, against the criticisms of the Anglican Henry Hammond, by John Belson (d. after 1688) in *Tradidi vobis, or The Traditionary Conveyance of Faith Cleared, in the Rational Way, against the Exceptions of a Learned Opponent* (London, 1662). Belson is most clear and vocal in his explanation of what the *Dialogues* mean to say, and he forcefully supports the same positions.

According to the *Dialogues* there is a sense, acceptable to Catholics, in which all revealed truth is in Scripture. "You know the *Dialogues* hold Catholicism may be victoriously evidenced to be more conformable to Scripture than Protestancy by argument purely drawn from the text, without extrinsical helps".[55] They maintain "that a discreet and diligent perusal of Scripture will make a man a perfect Catholic, but not with that steady firmness as to be able to evince his religion before a critical judge, against a wrangling and crafty adversary".[56] This is also John Belson's doctrine, which he expresses in several ways. "That Scripture has couched in it most, if not all, truths essential to Christianity in diverse expressions, I conceive to be true".[57] If the question concerns the possibility of salvation by individual readers of Scripture, Belson sees no need to start a quarrel: "This paragraph conjectures a man may be saved by Scripture alone, and since it does no more, I might, if I would, make a drawn match of it, by opposing my 'No' to your 'I'. But sincerity and diligence being virtues which God may much favor, and since a weak vessel will bring a man to his haven, who sails in a perpetual calm, I cannot see what it prejudices me to admit what you say to be true".[58] Belson does not present this as simply Thomas White's or his own theology, but as the doctrine of the Catholic Church: "We deny not but all may be contained in Scripture some way or other, particularly or under general heads".[59]

---

[55] *Tradidi vobis*, p. 75.
[56] l.c., p. 47; see p. 34.
[57] l.c., p. 29.
[58] l.c., pp. 38-39.
[59] l.c., p. 154.

The moot question between Catholics and Protestants does not, therefore, refer to the contents of the Scriptures; for Catholics also, Scripture contains all revelation. It asks rather in what way revelation is contained in the Bible. Thus the last-quoted passage continues: (We deny) "that all is so contained as is necessary for the salvation of mankind; to which effect we conceive certainty and to that evidence requisite, neither of which are within the compass of naked words left without any guard to the violent and contrary storms of criticism".[60] Belson formulates exactly the pending question several times. " 'Tis true also that the reader, duly qualified, may by due reading Scripture come to truth; but that this truth will be enough to serve all the exigencies of all mankind in all circumstances, or that what satisfied his sincerity and diligence will be able to satisfy all manner of peevishness and obstinacy, are two positions which I see you have not, and think you cannot prove".[61] That one man or even many men can be saved through Scripture alone "is nothing to our question, whether it be sufficient for the conduct of all dispositions found in mankind, through all circumstances the Church will be in from the Resurrection to the day of Judgement".[62] The problem, then, is not whether Scripture contains revelation, but whether it is the ultimate means of salvation for all mankind. While Protestants teach the latter, Catholics only admit the former. Thus Belson replies to Hammond: "Your conclusion... does not in any way prejudice the tenet I am maintaining; to contain sufficient truths and to be a sufficient means to salvation (which may possibly be true on respect of some persons and circumstances) being quite another thing than to decide all quarrels carried on by factiously litigious persons, and this in all times and cases".[63] The salvation of mankind, not the writing down of revelation, is in question: "That faith has been so transmitted by Tradition that it has not been written, is not Mr. White's tenet, but that that writing, at least the writings we have, is not able so to transmit it as is necessary for the salvation of mankind, without Tradition".[64] As Belson is thus suggesting, Catholics and Protestants have been arguing at cross-purposes. Both of them teach that all revelation is contained in some way in Scripture. But, for Protestants, this gives

---

[60] l.c., pp. 154-155.
[61] l.c., p. 61.
[62] l.c., p. 103.
[63] l.c., p. 108.
[64] l.c., p. 297.

mankind a sufficient knowledge of revelation, whereas for Catholics reading Scripture alone, without tradition, provides no sufficiens knowledge of revelation for mankind in general, whatever particular exceptions may be admitted in rare circumstances.

Scripture is "a determinate number of words",[65] and tradition "a determinate sense",[66] which may be expressed in fewer or in more numerous words according to the needs of the audience. Therefore, Scripture will be "the very same" as tradition, once the truths it contains "are indisputably acknowledged and practised both with constancy and high esteem by a multitude".[67] But Scripture, being written once for all, does not explain itself, while tradition, being constantly spoken and preached, comments on itself at whatever length is necessary. Admittedly, Scripture must have been fully adequate to its readers' needs when it was written; but this no longer obtains for its readers today. " 'Tis true that Scripture was intended to be intelligible to those to whom it was written, but not to after ages without other means".[68] Today the only way to be certain of the meaning is to stand in the line of tradition. Belson sums up his argument in a passage that deserves full quoting on account of its clarity and forcefulness:

> You assert: We deny *Scripture* to be the *rule of faith*; every of which words deserves its particular reflexion. For first, by *Scripture* is meant either words or sense; that is, the words containing a sense, so as that another may be found in the same words; or else a sense expressed accidentally by such words and which might have been expressed by others. By a *rule*, since 'tis our belief must be regulated, and our belief is of things, not sounds, is understood either a determinate sense or a certain means to arrive at it. We say then that Scripture, taken the first way, cannot be a rule, nothing being more evident than that words, merely as such, are neither sense nor means to arrive at a determinate one, since the same words may comprehend many senses. Take *Scripture* the second way, and the question is quite changed; none denies the sense of it to be the word of God by which all our belief and actions are to be regulated; our dispute then in that case is not whether it be a rule, but how 'tis known: whether by the bare words in which 'tis couched (which we deny, because other senses are couched in the very same words) or by the Church's authority of interpreting it by Tradition, which you conceive unnecessary. To Scripture interpreted by Tradition, or the sense of Scripture

---

[65] l.c., p. 25.
[66] l.c., p. 27.
[67] l.c., p. 19.
[68] l.c., pp. 24-35.

acknowledged by Tradition, we submit all our thoughts and actions, but deny the title of a rule can belong to Scripture taken for mere words, unsensed, that is, characters; and conceive the sense of Scripture cannot be sufficiently discovered by the bare scanning of the words, which after all, being capable of many senses, leave it undetermined which is the true one.[69]

Scripture, therefore, in the eyes of Catholics, is inseparable from tradition, which conveys its sense. In a way, as explained by Belson after White, Scripture occupies a dominant place within tradition. For the expressions of faith "should be uniform" and "the best way in order to it is to make use, as much as may be, of those which the Holy Ghost in Scripture has before made use of".[70]

This does not make Scripture absolutely sufficient, for the expressions used in it presuppose, among those who read them, a faith which rests upon tradition. "The positions then are both true, that the Scripture is the best rule to govern our expressions by, and yet not sufficient to regulate our belief".[71] The Catholic doctrine is that "Tradition is the best interpreter of Scripture". It is "the security of whatever writing faith is contained in: if it be Scripture, we know the sense by Tradition; if a Father, he is of authority in as much as what he writes is consonant to Tradition, if anything be found to disagree, this not having any weight".[72]

The word "tradition" is not, however, free of all ambiguity. The sort of tradition that Belson understands to be Christian must be carefully distinguished from another, which he associates with Jews. In so doing, Belson eliminates esoteric concepts of tradition, as an oral transmission taking place in secret, known only to a few: "Tradition with us signifies a public delivery to a multitude, so as what was so delivered was settled in their understanding and rooted in their hearts by a constant visible practice. Their [the Jews'] Tradition was a close underhand conveyance from a few to a few, neither so many nor so honest as to be secure from mistakes, both accidental and wilful, and yet the cheat, if any happened, remaining by the secrecy undiscovered, so that nothing more apt to make void the law of God than such a Tradition as this".[73] Because it is thus open and public, tradition always involves the whole Church. It cannot be

---

[69] l.c., pp. 115-117.
[70] l.c., p. 137.
[71] l.c., p. 209.
[72] l.c., p. 297.
[73] l.c., p. 79.

the tradition of a few men mistakenly taken as universally binding. It cannot be imposed by a minority on a majority, for it is always universal. It dwells in the hearts of all believers. Notably enough, Belson finds a close parallel between the written decrees of councils and the written Scripture: both are set in so many words, and both need interpretation. Yet there is a major difference: Scripture does not provide its own interpretation, whereas bishops in a council have time to explain the meaning of the words they have used. Thus Belson answers his adversary:

> The parity you next urge between Scripture and Councils I should think of great force, if there were nothing but the bare letter in both. But in the former the word is the only interpreter of the sense; in the latter the word is interpreted by the sense; in the first, the sense is to be accommodated to the word; in the second, the word to the sense... When the words are agreed on, they [the bishops] perfectly know what they mean by them.... This they certify by their practise when they are out of Council, and so leave to their posterity not only a rule but a method to preserve it from being wrested by the craft and the perverseness of their adversaries. Now in Scripture the case is quite different: there are none to tell you the sense of the word in question, neither can the word help you, for 'tis of it you doubt.... The printed determinations therefore of Councils barely are not our Rule, but the printed determinations understood and practised; and were Scripture so qualified, I know not what conditions it would want necessary to a Rule.[74]

It logically follows—and this is the position of John Belson—that Scripture is such a rule, if the total life and faith of the Church are taken to be the practice by which the written word is understood. Scripture is then interpreted by tradition; it is not a bare letter, but a letter with a meaning.

---

[74] l.c., p. 44.

CHAPTER EIGHT

THE INFALLIBILITY OF TRADITION

Christopher Davenport and Thomas White held our attention in the last two chapters as men who rank higher than most of their colleagues in Recusant theology. The quality, rather than the size, of their output marks them out as theologians who, however unsystematic or unscholastic they were in their method and in the form of their theological reflection, did better than simply refute or disprove the positions of their adversaries: they developed a theology of their own. This was already the case, though with less color, with some of the authors who worked earlier in the century: Matthew Kellison, Edward Maihew, Sylvester Norris, Richard Smith, were original in the good sense of the term, that is, their theology transmitted but also carried forward the past. They were, like all Catholic authors, tradition-bound; yet they also furthered the tradition by contributing their special point of view to the debated question to which they paid special attention, that of Scripture and Tradition.

Henry Holden (1596-1665), alias Johnson, belongs in the same category. There is something unique about his theological approach to our question that gives it a special place in the story. Admittedly, other reasons too would militate in favor of Holden's privileged standing. Unlike most other English priests trained at Douai, he never seems to have returned to England for pastoral activity. After 1622 we find him, a Doctor of the Sorbonne, in Paris, where he lived in association with the theological circles of the Capital until his death. Whatever pastoral work he engaged in was carried on, rather interestingly, in the parish of St. Nicolas du Chardonnet, which was, in the middle of the seventeenth century, one of the centers of spiritual reformation for the clergy of the city.[1] If more was known about this aspect of Holden's activity, we conceivably might have to place him among the highlights of the French clergy as much as among the English exiles.

Like Thomas White, Holden met with his share of troubles with Catholic authors, although the objections to his theology seem to

---

[1] See Schoenker, *Histoire du Séminaire de St-Nicolas du Chardonnet (1612-1908), d'après des documents inédits*, Paris, 1909.

have developed after his death rather than during his lifetime. His conception of the inspiration of the Bible, which Holden tended to restrict, as Newman will try to do it later, to religious statements, his explanation of the certainty of faith, his classification of four kinds of Catholic truths commanding diverse degrees of assent and obedience drew the criticism of later theologians, who objected to their apparent novelty. There certainly were weak points in Holden's theology; but at least he was a theologian in an age surfeited with polemicists, and his main offense, that he often struck out on his own, should have been to his glory. His major work, *Analysis Divinae Fidei* (Latin text, 1652; English, 1658), is less concerned with the refutation of Protestants than with the constructive elaboration of a theology of faith. Of the two parts of the work, the second is the better known, be it only because it was incorporated in Migne's *Theologiae Cursus* (vol. VI): this is a summary treatment of some of the questions in controversy raised by the debates with Protestant thought. The first part, however, provides the theological framework for Holden's attempt to cope with the Reformation. Omitted from Migne's library of theological tractates because of the controversial opinions that give Holden a place among the creative authors of his time, it is indispensable for understanding his approach to Scripture and Tradition.

This first part constitutes a treatise on faith and Revelation. Holden successively studies the general structure of faith (ch. 1), the special structure of divine faith (ch. 2), the means to discern what has been revealed (ch. 3), the object of revelation (ch. 4), Scripture as a medium of revelation (ch. 5), the function of private reason in relation to revelation (ch. 6), the private inspirations of the Holy Spirit in relation to revelation (ch. 7), the tradition of what has been revealed (ch. 8), the General Councils and the Supreme Pontiff in relation to revelation (ch. 9).

As appears from this list of chapters, Holden starts from an analysis of faith, examines the object of faith (what is revealed), and goes on to survey the media of Revelation and its transmission. In the light of this, his second part will try to clarify the question of exactly what has been revealed and must be believed, concerning the Apostles' Creed (ch. 2), the Scriptures, the Councils, the Supreme Pontiff (ch. 3), the sacraments (ch. 4), original sin (ch. 5), purgatory (ch. 6), prayer to the saints (ch. 7). Holden will then briefly examine several "articles of an inferior order" (ch. 8), and a few "natural truths" (ch. 9).

We need not examine all the aspects of Holden's theology of faith; but the salient point should help us grasp Holden's basic approach to Tradition. Because he starts from "faith in general", as "an assent of the understanding, which we give to anything that is told us, grounded upon the testimony or authority of him who tells it",[2] Holden identifies two characteristics of faith at all its levels, natural or supernatural: faith relies on "the judgment or opinion of the believer, whereby he thinks the reporter tells truth", and it always remains obscure. It thus requires a judgment of credibility about the witness or medium of what is to be believed, while the object of belief remains shrouded in an intrinsic inevidence. Holden is thus led to define the certainty of faith, not according to its object, which, remaining in darkness, cannot compel assent, but according to the believer's relationship with, and trust in, the medium of knowledge (in the case of a natural testimony) or of Revelation (in the case of the Christian faith). This in turn demands that, in faith, certainty be disassociated from truth: there may be subjectively certain belief in something which is objectively false. In the one case, we have true faith, in the other fanaticism. "It is quite a different thing for an assent of the understanding to be completely and absolutely certain, and for it to be true".[3] The certainty of faith is not the certainty of its objective truth, but of the medium of its transmission. As Holden forcefully states it,

> The first fundamental stone upon which the building of faith is grounded, is the believer's knowledge of the value and worth of the testimony for whose sake he does give his assent, and of the security or means by which the same testimony is applied and conveyed unto him.[4]

When this is applied to Christian faith, it becomes obvious that, if this faith must be called supernatural insofar as the act of faith is prompted by God's testimony and bears on divine mysteries,[5] its certainty is no more than natural; it can be no higher than the certainty of the means through which divine Revelation reaches us:

---

[2] I quote the English text from *The Analysis of Divine Faith*, translated by W. G., Paris, 1658; quotation, p. 2.

[3] l.c., p. 12.

[4] l.c., p. 15.

[5] l.c., p. 24.

For although belief, precisely as belief, be resolved into authority, and therefore divine belief into divine authority, which of itself is apt to beget all possible certainty, yet because the certainty of our assents of faith, and even of our divine faith, does in its substance essentially depend on the certainty and infallibility of the means by which the authority is conveyed to our understanding, it is impossible that our faith should have a greater certainty than the certainty which that means can give it, which, as we shall hereafter show, cannot be properly called supernatural.[6]

The certainty of divine faith is that of the means by which we know it. In other words, it can be no higher than the credibility of the means of transmission of faith: the judgment of faith is identical, from the standpoint of its certainty, with the judgment of credibility: "It is impossible that any man's assent of faith, no, not even of divine faith, should have a greater truth and rational certainty than has the same man's assent unto the means by which the object of his faith is applied and conveyed unto his understanding".[7] Holden, accordingly, rules out other conceptions of the certainty of faith, which cannot be grounded directly on individual enlightenment by the Holy Spirit. The latter idea Holden calls "common" and he expresses his amazement (*soepius miratus sum*) at it. For it seems to him to be undistinguishable from the theory of the private spirit, and therefore liable to all the objections made against it by Catholic theology: "To ground the certainty and infallibility of our Catholic faith upon this supernatural, internal and invisible notion or influence, and to derive its last resolution into such a singular instant, seems to me most absurd and ridiculous".[8]

The basic question, for Holden, therefore concerns the transmission of Revelation down to us. Because we are human, all we know must be communicated to us mainly through our sense-organs.[9] The certainty of the assent of faith boils therefore down to the certainty of the transmission of faith. In order to compel assent, the transmission of Revelation needs to be effected by means that are visible to all, including the illiterate and the infants [10]; and in themselves able to convey the highest possible certainty.[11]

[6] l.c., pp. 24-25.
[7] l.c., pp. 29-30.
[8] l.c., p. 32.
[9] *Analysis Divinae Fidei*, in Joseph Braun: *Bibliotheca Regularum Fidei*, tomus II, Bonn, 1844, p. 22.
[10] l.c., pp. 22-25.
[11] l.c., pp. 25-26.

Before describing the medium of transmission of Revelation, Holden devotes one chapter to the object of revelation in general. Here again he departs from commonly trodden paths and distinguishes between four kinds of "Catholic truths". "Divine and Catholic truths" [12] alone are explicitly revealed and command an assent of divine faith; *veritates quae dici possunt pure catholicae* [13], are described as follows: "such truths as we may call purely Catholic. . . which have been always undoubtedly received by the full consent of the universal Church, and which, although they be not properly divine nor revealed truths, yet do they rely and are strongly built upon universal tradition". In the first category, Holden places the articles of the Creed. The second embraces the historical data of Scripture which record points of fact irrelevant to divine institution or to the Church's life, and other historical facts which Holden calls "of an inferior order" because they are not recorded in Scripture, like the coming to St. Peter to Rome or the apostolic institution of Lent. A third category covers "those truths which we may properly call purely canonical", that is, formal definitions made by General Councils or Supreme Pontiffs, "which the universal church does not acknowledge to have received immediately and expressly either by divine Revelation or universal tradition". These are decisions destined to answer heretics or to put an end to theological controversies. Finally, Holden mentions "theological truths", very few in number, held by theologians, as "universally acknowledged or manifestly deduced by evident consequences out of the principles of faith, and out of those truths which we have put into the first and second order".[14] Only truths of the first category are dogmas of faith. Those of the second category, not being revealed, are not objects of faith; they are nevertheless true and most certain, for they are held by universal Christian Tradition. All the faithful must assent to them. Truths of the third category have no more certainty and authority than are assigned them by the decrees which formulate them. Truths of the fourth category are still more remote from faith itself, since they depend on the reliability of human reason for a logical analysis of Revelation.

This brings us directly to Henry Holden's theories on Scripture and Tradition. For Holden classifies most of Scripture as pertaining

---

[12] *The Analysis of Divine Faith*, p. 46.
[13] l.c., p. 47.
[14] l.c., pp. 48-49.

to the second category, the Apostles' Creed belonging to the first; and he ascribes the value of this second category to the universality of Tradition on which it is based. This underlines, in his word, "how much it concerns them (= Catholics) and all Christians, to establish and settle the evident certainty and manifest infallibility of universal tradition".[15]

Holden's approach to the problem of Scripture in the context of his analysis of faith is focused on the question raised in the title of chapter 5: "Whether the holy Scripture can of itself be the means whereby revealed truths are to be conveyed and delivered to the whole Church".[16] The problem is to discover the adequate medium of Revelation: Is it Scripture?

Holden divides this chapter in two lessons: a descriptive one ("What is the Holy Scripture, and what is it for the Scriptures to be canonical?"), and one which leads to a negative conclusion ("The Holy Scripture alone cannot be a convenient means to convey all the revealed tenets of our Catholic faith to the whole body of the Catholic Church").[17] There is little to remark about the first lesson, besides the anticipated conclusion which Holden already formulates and in which he incorporates two contrasted standpoints about Scripture:

> It does likewise follow of what has been said (which we shall make yet more clear in the following lesson) that though it were true that all the revealed tenets and dogmas of the Catholic faith are at least implicitly contained in the Holy Scripture, yet can we not then rightly infer that the Scripture alone were a convenient and naturally proportionate means to communicate and convey all the divine tenets and dogmas of our Catholic faith unto the whole society of the universal Church.
>
> Lastly, it is to be observed that the Fathers and Doctors of the Church, refuting the heresies of their times in every age did principally make use of the Holy Scripture to prove the truth of the Catholic faith, both because their adversaries would acknowledge no other authority, (which is the property of all heretics) as also because out of the Scripture alone, understood in its natural sense, all the articles of our Catholic faith may be truly evinced.

Holden accordingly believes that all Catholic dogmas are implicit in the Scriptures and may be drawn therefrom, even when Scripture

---

[15] l.c., pp. 50-00.
[16] l.c., p. 59.
[17] l.c., pp. 64-75.

is taken in its natural or literal sense. The Latin text, admittedly, is more cautious here than the English text, adding a *penitus* which slightly qualifies *omnes*, whereas the English says, without restriction, "all the articles". Yet Holden also thinks that this by no means makes of Scripture an adequate medium of Revelation for the entire membership of the Church.

These two points are explained in the second lesson of the chapter. No sooner has the principle been accepted that Jesus taught a number of doctrines which must be continually kept "with a continual succession from age to age to the end of the world", than Scripture, taken in its materiality, as "the bare outside of the material letters and words", appears inadequate for such a continuous transmission.[18] The material letter must have a meaning, which eventually should convey the teachings of Christ. This provides Holden with his main argument: supposing that nobody, today or in the past, was competent, either by his function or by his scholarship, to interpret the Scriptures, it would still remain that a scriptural interpretation is certainly true if it coincides with the consensus of the Church Fathers or with that of the present Church.[19] On the contrary, should there be no such consensus, the meaning of Scripture would not be available to the great bulk of the Christian people. Protestants have proposed insufficient standards of interpretation: To regard Scripture as the Word of God does not remove the necessity of proving, from the Church's consensus, that it actually is the Word of God; nor is it enough to aver that Scripture "gives testimony to itself that it is the word of God", for, as Holden, keeping in mind his main concern for the availability of Revelation to the entire Church, replies, "Whatever may be the truth in this point, it is certain that few there be who can discover and discern this light".[20]

The history of heresies furnishes us with a counter-test: were the Scriptures the only means to know Revelation, divergences of interpretation in essential matters could not have been allowed to happen by divine Providence. Yet is is obvious that men, believing Scripture to be the Word of God and reading it with their own lights, arrive at totally opposite meanings. As Holden rightly asserts, "this must necessarily follow out of the very nature and condition of words and of human language. . . because words are ordinarily ambiguous and

---

[18] l.c., p. 65.
[19] *Analysis Divinae Fidei*, pp. 42-43.
[20] *The Analysis of Divine Faith*, pp. 68-69.

equivocal, both in themselves and in their circumstances".[21] To this fundamental reason taken from the nature of human language, Holden adds five others, which make it inconceivable that Scripture alone should be the adequate medium of the transmission of Revelation: the hiddenness of the divine mysteries; the many centuries that have passed since Scripture was written; our all but total ignorance of the particular circumstances surrounding the instructions recorded in Scripture, which would offer clues to their exact intentions and purposes; the influence of men's subjective dispositions on their interpretation of what they read; the occasional nature of Scripture and the circumstances of its transmission, which raise a thousand questions. As this gives us a hint as to Holden's awareness of exegetical problems, we may quote this passage:

> In fine therefore it is evident that the books of the Holy Scripture, especially of the New Testament (which is now chiefly in question), having been written as it were accidentally upon several occasions (what a rule of faith, or what a method of instituting a new Law is this?), a thousand and thousand times copied out by unlearned as well as by learned clerks (what a number of faults must there not needs be in these copies!), printed over and over, God knows how many times and in how many places (how different these editions must be with various lections, let any man imagine!), translated into I know not how many tongues by particular and private men (with what security of a faithful expression of the true sense, who dare say?)...[22]

Having disposed of the opinion that Scripture interprets itself sufficiently to convey all Revelation to all Christians in all ages, Holden briefly dismisses the theory of the sufficiency of human reason as obviously leading to complete chaos. In the same chapter 6, however, he treats a question that has exercised the minds of many theologians since his time and that was at the forefront of theological concerns in the first half of our century: What is the power of the human reason to deduct necessary theological conclusions from the data of Revelation? "Whether, at least upon supposition that such or such tenets are revealed articles of divine faith, human ratiocination cannot draw from them such sequels and consequences as may have the like force and same degree of truth as have the articles themselves".[23]

Holden makes a valuable distinction here. If the conclusion is

---

[21] l.c., p. 72.
[22] l.c., pp. 73-74.
[23] l.c., p. 79.

immediate and evident to all the faithful, then we have a truly revealed doctrine, "because the universal consent of all men in any truth immediately belonging to our revealed and supernatural belief is a convenient foundation to build an assent of divine faith upon it".[24] If, on the contrary, this evidence appears only to a number of scholars and doctors of the faith, it does not sufficiently establish articles of faith, even for the man who is convinced of it. For faith is not founded on opinions, however logical and convincing; it is grounded in the consensus of the universal Church. "All true faith and religion is either Catholic and universal, or none at all".[25]

Akin to the theory of the human reason is that of the private spirit, or of private inspiration by the Holy Spirit. This cannot constitute a rule of interpretation because many different kinds of inspirations have been granted men for various purposes and functions, and they require the difficult art of discerning the spirits. Holden lists mystical grace, prophecy, external revelation, internal revelation, none of which is an adequate means of transmitting the Revelation of Christ, for the objections already made to the adequacy of the private reason equally militate against the sufficiency of the private spirit.[26]

In several of our authors, especially in Thomas White, Tradition has been compared to a family patrimony, to an education, handed down from father to son, seen therefore in the perspective of what may be called a father-son relationship. Thus a sort of pedagogical concept of Tradition has been developed which, extended not simply to one family, but to the entire family of nations, becomes a philosophy of culture: Christian Tradition is a religious form of a phenomenon which already accounts for the education of children and for the transmission of human lore among all the peoples of the world. Holden's approach to Tradition is similar to this. He describes tradition in general (ch. 7, lesson 1) before seeing it at work in the context of the Church (lesson 2: the Church; lesson 3: in what the universal tradition of Christian revealed truths consists; lesson 4: on the value of the universal tradition of revealed truths), and finally comparing the two (lesson 5). He defines it in generic terms applicable to many kinds of human traditions:

---

[24] l.c., p. 80.
[25] l.c., 83.
[26] l.c., ch. 7.

> Tradition considered in general is nothing else but a verbal con-
> veyance of communication of any truth, whether written or unwritten,
> with a continual succession of time or years from hand to hand and
> from father to son, and so from age to age.[27]

Implied in this approach is the assumption that, the more universal
a tradition is, the higher certitude it enjoys, for it would be inconceivable that a great number of persons living in different countries
with little commercial and cultural intercourse should be simul-
taneously mistaken on matters of importance. Accordingly, Holden
speaks of "the infallibility of universal Tradition"[28] even in the
secular realm. The tradition of holy things and doctrines is, from one
standpoint, a particular case of the universal phenomenon of Tradition. There nevertheless is a major difference between the secular
tradition of human culture and the transmission of divine Revelation
in the Church. For the former takes place "without any order,
method or discipline, but as it were by accident and by the bye[29],"
whereas the latter was entrusted to the Church of Christ, his "moral
and mystical Body", a "sacred society",[30] which is kept together by
"this connexion and conjunction of these parts and members one
with another—in the divine chain of faith and golden tie of charity".[31]
Since this society has been empowered to transmit Revelation,
Church and Tradition are, from the point of view of the teaching
of Christ's doctrine, co-terminous:

> Whence it appears (which is to be specially noted) that in our Catholic
> language it is all one in effect to say that the Catholic Church is infal-
> lible and that universal tradition is infallible, I mean, inasmuch as
> these two things have reference to the resolution of divine faith.
> For in reality we say the same thing, when we say that the universal
> Tradition of the whole Church is free from error, and when we say
> that the Catholic Church is infallible in the tradition and delivery of
> her divine and supernatural doctrine.[32]

Tradition being a handing down from father to son, from one
generation to the next, Catholic truth is channelled down the ages,
not by Scripture, human reason or the private spirit, but by our
receiving doctrine from our forefathers and our teaching it in turn
to our descendants. This constitutes "the universal Tradition, which

---

[27] l.c., p. 98.
[28] l.c., p. 101.
[29] l.c., pp. 102-103.
[30] l.c., pp. 106-107.
[31] l.c., p. 106.
[32] l.c., p. 108.

we take to be the sole and final rule of our Christian faith in relation to us".[33]

Holden forcefully asserts the unvarying nature of this Catholic Tradition. "It is a thing known to everyone that all Catholics do hold it for a most certain maxim that nothing ought or can be maintained as a revealed and Christian truth, but what we have received from our forefathers, and what has been so delivered from hand to hand and from ear to ear in a continual series of succession from the Apostles".[34] And again: "It were easy to show that this universal Tradition perpetuated in a continual line has ever been held the only rule of faith in relation to us and the only means whereby revealed tenets are to be conveyed to the whole Church and so transmitted from age to age".[35] Tradition must be, in this perspective, the sole means of transmitting the faith: by hypothesis, there cannot be any other. It is *fidei regula*,[36] or, as the English translation states it more exactly, "the rule of our faith in relation to us": [37] "Christ has instituted this means as the sole and only way of receiving and conveying his revealed doctrine".[38] Whatever distinctions ought to be made in the revealed data thus transmitted cannot affect this basic contention of the infallibility of the transmission of Revelation from the beginning. Holden acknowledges differences between divine, apostolic and ecclesiastical traditions, in keeping with his conception of the several kinds of Catholic truths. He also gives due importance to what was one of Serenus Cressy's chief concerns: Tradition is not only a transmission of doctrines, but also a series of events in the life of the Christian people.

> ... all these revealed truths of faith do either immediately and directly consist in action and practise, or at least have a necessary and essential relation to some principal exercise of religion. Whereupon the lives, actions and practises of Christians, acting as Christians, do give a continual testimony of their belief and thereby confirm it; yes, and both infer and in some sort produce the unity of faith among Christians, being all the chief practises of Christian religion and divine worship are found to be everywhere the same.[39]

---

[33] l.c., p. 114.
[34] l.c., p. 115.
[35] l.c., p. 118.
[36] *Analysis Divinae Fidei*, p. 86.
[37] *The Analysis of Divine Faith*, p. 138.
[38] l.c., p. 108.
[39] l.c., pp. 126-127.

The interesting aspect of Holden's clear affirmation of the un-changeability of Catholic Tradition lies in the fact that this did not blind him to the problem of what today would be called development of doctrine. Like some of the other Recusant theologians, Holden raises the question and attempts to solve it in a less negative way than was done by the French thinkers of the same period. Matthew Kellison, Thomas Bailey had already faced this problem. Henry Holden goes further in analysing the components of a possible solution.

On the one hand, the very concept of Tradition excludes varia-tions, even the variations along the same line that would effect an enlargement of the previous datum. The Church, as Holden insists more than once, has no power to make new articles of faith. She cannot teach new dogmas out of new revelations, for she receives no such communications from heaven. Those who believe in such a growth of Revelation are unintelligent and ignorant:

> If we find any that says the number of our revealed articles may be daily increased, we are to think that either it is the inconsiderate opinion of some private Catholic or the false calumny of some ignorant heretic.[40]

Another passage repeats the same point in similar terms. The pastors and rectors of the Church are only, Holden explains, *custodes et testes*; they are not, and no Catholic believes them to be, *articulorum fidei conditores*. It is therefore a tenet of Catholic faith, that

> We all acknowledge there are no new revelations given to the Church in common, or to any man in particular, upon which an article of the Catholic faith can be grounded. To say therefore that the number of revealed articles of our Catholic faith may be increased must either proceed from malice or ignorance.[41]

This, in Holden's mind, is part and parcel of the analogy of faith, by which all the articles hang together to such a point that to displace one of them or to add an extra dogma to the heritage received from the Apostles would so upset the balance that it would destroy the entire structure of faith: "The nature and condition of our Christian discipline and of our Catholic doctrine is much more immutable and further from all change than any other discipline whatsoever; for the order and method of it is to hold fast and as it were bound together

---

[40] l.c., p. 112.
[41] l.c., pp. 154-155.

all its parts, so as if the least portion of it fail, the whole body of it falls presently to the ground. . . It is therefore evident that no tenet can be brought into the Church as a revealed article, without breaking the order and nature of Tradition; which, since we see it is the rule of our faith in relation to us, no man can doubt but that the ruin of our faith must thence necessarily follow".[42]

Outside of Revelation, the Christian Tradition has received and transmitted also truths of another order. For, in Holden's theology, which is on this point at variance with that of most of his contemporaries and with the consensus of our times, the Church may hold and teach by universal Tradition beliefs that have not been revealed. These correspond to Holden's second kind of Catholic truths, which are "purely Catholic" yet not "divine" and revealed. These must be faithfully accepted on account of the authority of the Church's consensus, yet they may never be placed among the articles of faith. Such are, for Holden, "many things", among which he names the sojourn of Peter in Rome and the Assumption of the Virgin Mary:

> There be likewise diverse things which do constantly rely upon universal Tradition (as that St Peter was at Rome, that the Blessed Virgin's body was assumed or taken up into heaven, and the like) which are not revealed, and therefore are excluded out of the number of the articles of our Catholic faith.[43]

In these conditions—and whatever one should think of the distinction of divine and revealed truths from purely Catholic truths—Holden's theology raises the problem of development much more forcefully than that of his predecessors. For it needs to account for the strange fact instanced in these examples of Catholic truths, namely for the universal teaching by the Church of truths that are outside Revelation. Admittedly, as long as these are not introduced into the body of the articles of faith, the delicate balance of which Holden has spoken is not threatened. Nonetheless, a Tradition of non-revealed truths must logically have at its disposal other means of information than Revelation. It has, for Holden, the knowledge of the historical facts of the first ages of the Church, which, whether or not it has been recorded in the Scriptures, is a true knowledge. Its objects are to be believed as facts and as Catholic truths, though not as revealed and necessary to salvation.

This is not yet the problem of development, which, as such,

---

[42] l.c., p. 138.
[43] l.c., p. 162.

bears on a different matter: Can the revealed datum, without being added to, be enlarged? Holden does realize that a further question remains. For he mentions the problem, and evidently acknowledges the legitimacy, of "a more plain and more ample declaration and explication of the articles of our faith".[44] This problem is all the more serious as the very nature of language makes semantic evolution unavoidable and therefore establishes the *a priori* possibility of successive interpretations of the same formulations of faith. Holden sees this clearly:

> No truth, much less any Christian truth, can be ordinarily and naturally transmitted and conveyed from ear to ear and from man to man but by the means of human speech; which cannot likewise be performed but by voice and words. Now all words are either equivocal of themselves or at least may be variously and diversely taken by a multitude of auditors. Whence it is that in all discourse and verbal communication there does generally arise much ambiguity and diversity of intelligence.[45]

Furthermore, not only language, but thought itself follows a natural bent toward varieties of interpretation. There is a "natural disposition of men's minds and understandings, that the same expressed truths are diversely conceived and understood by diverse men; yea, and from the selfsame truth diverse men do infer diverse consequences".[46] While here lies the source of all heresies, hence also arises the necessity for the Councils to state clearly "whatever is directly and expressly divinely revealed or instituted",[47] in order to maintain the two goods of "union and truth".[48] Whether the Councils may go further and promulgate decrees on "the proper signification of some terms, or (on) a more full and ample explication of some revealed truth, or in fine (on) some consequence and sequel deduced out of our revealed truths", is a much more vexed and thorny question.[49]

At this point, Holden introduces the category of implicit-explicit, a *communem et tritam distinctionem*, which theologians have, *more suo*, Holden opines, insufficiently clarified. There are, for him, three possible meanings of this distinction. First, it refers to the clarifying of obscure terms, so that we may clearly (explicitly) believe what

---

[44] l.c., p. 112.
[45] l.c., p. 155-156.
[46] l.c., p. 156.
[47] l.c., p. 157.
[48] l.c., p. 160.
[49] l.c., pp. 159-160.

hitherto we believed obscurely (implicitly). Second, it connotes the deduction of truths out of the revealed datum or of universal Tradition (in Holden's categories, out of Catholic truths of the first and second grade). Third, it implies the possibility of generally assenting to doctrines with which one has no particular and detailed acquaintance. There is no basic difficulty about the first and the third meaning of implicitness: the Catholic faith is implicit in both these senses, and it becomes explicit when terms are explained and doctrines detailed out by Councils. Holden, however, rejects the second kind of explicitation: deduction remains a theological task which may never be raised to the level of faith. Truly, any one of the articles of faith, on account of the cohesiveness of Revelation, implies all the others: "All supernatural truths are in this sort contained implicitly in any one, so that from the perfect comprehension of any one we might come to the knowledge of all the rest".[50] But theologians have in mind something else also, namely rational deductions leading to theological conclusions. They thereby run foul of Holden's fundamental principle on the boundaries of theology:

> I conceive that we have sufficiently demonstrated already that no truth which is only deduced by some particular man's ratiocination out of our articles of faith can ever reach to the absolute certainty and solidity of our divine and Catholic faith.

Should theological conclusions ever be promulgated or defined by the Church, they would acquire greater authority, but no higher degree of certainty than the logical strength of their deduction warrants. Remembering now what he has previously said about deduction from Scripture, Holden suggests that a Council may very well formulate the same old traditional truth in more adequate language, for the truth, like the Scripture, does not reside in words but in their sense: "The Catholic Church does not know and deliver her revealed doctrine by the bare and naked outside of words and material letters, which are different and diverse in every several kingdom, nation and country, but by the sense and signification of words and speech, which is instilled into the hearts of Christians and imprinted in their souls by frequent instruction and discipline".[51] Councils may also endorse logical deductions from Revelation that are of immediate evidence: in this case, what is then declared is truly

---

[50] l.c., p. 163.
[51] l.c., p. 165.

"but the same revealed truth now more clearly explicated, which before was implicitly believed by all, and explicitly believed by the more learned".[52] Both explicitations are legitimate, and constitute, in our terms, proper developments of doctrine.

There remains the question of more remote, less immediately evident deductions, requiring the tools of human ratiocination and philosophy. Once more, Holden falls back on his conviction regarding the place of human reason in matters of faith: a conclusion from Scripture or from the articles of faith which relies on natural logic may never be defined as belonging to Revelation, because it rests, not on the ground of God's original public manifestation and its transmission by universal Tradition, but only on the powers of a few men's intellects. To give it the assent of faith would be tantamount to receiving a new Revelation:

> The Church does not acknowledge any new beams of divine light to shine every day upon her, whereby she can have an infallible certainty, or equal to that which she has of her revealed and universally delivered articles of faith, in relation to such truths as may perhaps be newly discovered, and in some sort made appear by the profound ratiocination of some particular and learned men.

In other words, Holden reaches to the threshold of a notion of development of dogma in the strict sense, and, in keeping with his fundamental idea that the certainty of faith is that of its medium, he rejects theological conclusions as unable to rise above the certainty of human logic and therefore doomed to remain outside the realm of revealed certainty. The implicitly revealed must be evident to all, or it cannot be defined as demanding divine faith. These conclusions may occasionally be defined by the Church in order to prevent schism and to preserve peace. In this case, the Church's decisions should be obediently accepted, but the Church will not and cannot impose them as though they pertained to Revelation.

By making the universality of Tradition the one ultimate recourse of faith, Holden avoids the mental gymnastics of those who try to escape, with the help of Aristotelian logic, the circular reasoning by which Scripture proves Tradition or the Church, and Tradition or the Church in turn proves Scripture. Holden condescendingly calls this "that circular labyrinth", and opines that it rests on "the common

---

[52] l.c., pp. 166-167.

and unexamined opinion of the vulgar".[53] Those who have let
themselves be caught into this snare have been "dancing in a round".
There is no such circle in Holden's theology. An "instinct of the Holy
Spirit", an "interior motion of divine grace" is required for faith
as for all supernatural virtues. Yet the certainty of faith does not
rest on this instinct: "We say therefore that all the infallibility and
unerrability whereof man's nature is capable is most clearly and
evidently to be had by the means of universal Tradition".[54] By this
assertion Holden does not downgrade the Holy Scriptures, but sees
them as texts and words, whose meaning is conveyed by universal
Tradition. They are thus, in their essence, carried by the Tradition.
In the meantime, Holden, has, like White, envisioned Tradition as a
human phenomenon which has its value in itself, even apart from
the consideration of Church Tradition. He has also, and this is not
the least of his merits, gone one step further toward the problem
of theological development, which he has squarely envisioned. His
theology, however, forced him to stop short in his investigation of it,
because he could not conceive of absolute certainty being reached
by way of human means. From this point on, it will be enough for
Holden's objection to vanish—but this Holden did not do—in order
to open the vision of a trans-logical development within the analogy
of faith. But perhaps we should not anticipate: the seventeenth
century perceived the problem of development and its difficulty;
the nineteenth, with Newman, will try to provide the principle of a
solution.

[53] l.c., p. 179.
[54] l.c., p. 181.

CHAPTER NINE

TOWARD A DEVELOPMENT OF DOCTRINE

The writers surveyed in the last few chapters were in some sense creative authors, who not only prolonged previous lines of thought but also introduced new viewpoints and added depth to existing doctrines and assumptions. Yet the seventeenth century, like all centuries for that matter, abounded in less arresting personalities that were no less involved in the theological controversies of the times and that bore a heavy share of the defense of Catholic positions against the inroads of Anglican and Puritan theology. They published surveys of the points of controversy, in which they added whatever barb they could to the usual arguments. They wrote "manuals" and "abridgements" designed to help ordinary people to protect their faith or teach their children. They made tedious, thorough investigations of problems and produced refutations of adversaries which simply lack the luster of greatness.

Yet one would have a wrong view of Recusant literature unless these more pedestrian essays were also taken into consideration. And although it would be superfluous to spend too much time on them, a quick look should be taken at some of these works in order to provide the backcloth on which the more brilliant authors ought to be seen.

Going slightly back in time we may mention the *Miscellania, or a treatise containing 200 controversial animadversions,* published in 1640 by Roger Anderton [1] under the initials N. N. P. This book does not suggest any specific doctrine concerning Scripture or Tradition. Yet its Animadversion 168 raises the important question of what criteria the Church uses to check the validity of Traditions, and states that "the Catholic Church delivers certain rules for the more perfect knowledge of true Traditions".[2] The first rule listed by Anderton is that of universality: "When the Universal Church does embrace any doctrine as a point of faith, the which is not found in the Holy Scripture, it is necessary to say that the said point proceeds from the

---

[1] See ch. 3, n. 34.
[2] *Miscellania*, p. 290.

Tradition of the Apostles". This clearly implies that several doctrines taught by the Church are not in Scripture. In Anderton's mind, however, some of these are equally obscure in the documents of the early Church. His third and fourth rules maintain that even then, a doctrine taught universally is to be assumed to derive from apostolic Tradition. Looking at the issue from a different angle, he enumerates a fifth rule, which assigns to apostolic Tradition the teaching of the Churches that have enjoyed "continual succession from the Apostles", the test being now an institutional one. Yet this investigation cannot neglect to judge the value of a tradition by its content; whence Anderton's second rule:

> When the universal Church does observe any thing which not any but only God had power to institute, and yet which is not found written in the Scripture, the same we are to presume to be delivered from Christ and his Apostles.[3]

That these rules raise more difficulties than they solve does not seem to have struck Roger Anderton. In any case, his animadversions were too brief and concise for him to look at the problem from all the possible angles.

Still more terse is Henry Turberville's summary of the question of Tradition in *An Abridgement of Christian Doctrine* (1649):

> *Question*: Is it enough to believe all that is written in the Bible?
> *Answer*: No, it is not; for we must also believe all apostolical Traditions.
> *Q.*: How do you prove that?
> *A.*: Out of 2 Thess., 2:15.
> *Q.*: What other proof have you?
> *A.*: The Apostles' Creed, which all are bound to believe, although it be not in the Scripture.[4]

Turberville (d. 1678), a priest from Douai who served as Chaplain to Henry Somerset, first Marquis of Worcester, during the Civil War, wrote a slightly more wordy *Manual of Controversies, clearly demonstrating the truth of the Catholic Religion* (1654). The article, "of Apostolic Tradition", seems to have been marked by the influence of *Rushworth's Dialogues*, the second edition of which was published in that same year 1654. Turberville formulates the Catholic doctrine in these few lines:

---

[3] l.c., p. 291.
[4] *An Abridgement* . . ., ed. of 1687, p. 11.

> Our tenet is that the true rule of Christian faith is apostolic Tradition; or a delivery of doctrine from father to son, by hand to hand, from Christ and his apostles, and that nothing ought to be received as faith but what is proved to have been delivered.[5]

The proof of this takes the form of four syllogisms, which stress that Tradition was the primitive method of conveyance of Christ's doctrine, that Tradition is infallible, that the primitive Church cannot conceivably have delivered false Traditions to the men who succeeded it, and that "the whole world" cannot possibly be united in forging one and the same lie. This last argument is worth quoting, as it entails the broad view of Tradition as a human phenomenon that we have already met in some of our authors:

> To make a whole world of wise and disinterested men break so far with their own nature as to conspire in a notorious lie to damn themselves and their posterity (which is the only means remaining to make an apostolic Tradition fallible), such a force of hopes or fears must fall on them at once as may be stronger than nature in them.— But such a force of hopes or fears can never fall on the whole world or Church at once, which is dispersed over all nations.—Therefore it is impossible for the whole world or Church at once to conspire in such a lie and consequently to err in faith.[6]

Turberville's conclusion follows, in which the process of Tradition is traced back to its origin: "It is the assurance of the impossibility, that moves the Church of the present age to resolve her faith and doctrine into the precedent age, and so from age to age, from sons to fathers, up to the mouth of Christ and his apostles teaching it, saying: We believe it, because we have received it".

Turberville also thinks that the appeal to Scripture alone will show that "either many controverted Catholic doctrines are sufficiently contained in Scripture, or many Protestant ones are not".[7] On the whole, however, this cannot make Scripture a sufficient test of doctrine, since several points of faith—and the three Creeds to begin with—are not contained in it. Furthermore, the true sense of Scripture can never be found "without the rule of apostolical Tradition".[8] Indeed, insistent as he is on the value of apostolic Tradition, Turberville falls into the contrary excess of considerably weakening the meaning of Scripture. This is quite clear in the following assertion:

---

[5] *Manual of Controversies* . . ., p. 103.

[6] l.c., p. 108.

[7] l.c., p. 109.

[8] l.c., p. 116.

We prove indeed the Church's infallibility and the credibility of the Scripture by apostolic Tradition, but that is evident of itself and admits no other proof. When we bring Scripture for either, we use it only as secondary testimony or argument *ad hominem*.[9]

Turberville's estimate of the place of Scripture in theological argumentation makes indeed sense if the books of the New Testament are only "short manual notes for Christians within the Church",[10] or "brief memorials" [11] in which some sayings of Christ "are deliverd to us but under certain general heads and brief notes without any order or connexion at all that can appear to any the subtillest wit that is".[12] Vincent Canes (d. 1672) or, in his Franciscan name, John-Baptist, or also Bodwill, describes the Gospels in this less than adequate way in a book that does not pretend to theological status, yet contains valuable material. Canes spent most of his time after 1642 on the English mission. His first book, *The Reclaimed Papist* (1655), undertaken as a therapeutic distraction after the death of two close friends, contains three humorous dialogues in which a Protestant Lady, a Presbyterian Minister and his Independent wife (the "Vicaress") try to convert a Catholic Knight. This was followed in 1661 by a very original and interesting volume, *Fiat Lux*, which was not a work of apologetics, but an invitation to all parties to make peace on the ground that there is "an impossibility of ever bringing our debates to a conclusion, either by light or spirit, reason or Scripture-texts, so long as we stand separated from any superior judicative power unto which all parties will submit".[13] Thus Canes summed up the intent of the book in a subsequent self-defense written in a more polemical vain, *Diaphanta, or Three Attendants upon Fiat Lux* (1665).

That Vincent Canes was pessimistic—or perhaps realistic—about the possibilities of the discussions of his days ever leading to an agreement, and that he at times underestimated the place and importance of Scripture, did not mitigate his regard for the Catholic Tradition. The Church, understood in its organic Catholic sense, is co-terminous with the truth: "The spouse of Christ is blessed and so united with her head that she cannot depart from the truth em-

---

[9] l.c., p. 120.
[10] *The Reclaimed Papist*, p. 91.
[11] l.c., p. 89.
[12] l.c., p. 88.
[13] *Diaphanta . . .*, p. 15.

bowelled within her breast and, as it were, identified in herself".[14]
This betrays a high doctrine of Tradition: Scripture is the Church's
book, written, copied, preserved and interpreted by her, in keeping
with the principle that "the mind and meaning of any writing no
man can understand so well as the author, no man can interpret
aright contrary to the author, no man where it is obscure and un-
couth may peremptorily interpret without the author".[15] The Gospel
has been "writ in the heart and entrails of the Church"; and as
Canes believes,

> to imprint in the Church's breast a law from which she should never
> deviate is in my judgement a greater argument of divinity than any
> written Gospel could afford.[16]

In order to find the true Christian doctrine, one should therefore
read the Church's heart, that is, learn her "larger explicit declaration"
of the faith, and witness the "full and ample practise thereof in her
bosom".[17] This follows upon Christ's will and action, for he "gave
notice that he would use his special prerogative of legislatorship
and write his law in hearts, promising to animate the body of his
Church with his own Spirit which should lead them into all truth".[18]
Out of the Church's heart there stems a permanent Tradition, by
which all Scriptures, all Christian books and all Councils have been
"formed afterwards, directed, swayed, rectified and ordered".[19]
From the point of view of Tradition, all Catholic doctrines are
equally important and binding, coming as they do from one and the
same source: "All points of faith have an equal proportion of truth,
however they may differ in their own material weight". Their intrinsic value may vary, some being closer to the center of faith and
salvation and therefore, implying "more of necessity and obligation
to an explicit belief and practise",[20] yet all rightly claiming the same
exclusion of "positive misbelief". Canes formulates this notion of
fundamental beliefs in this way: "I am not bound to know or practise
all things of the Church's doctrine, but I am bound not to disallow,
condemn or reject any of her traditional Christianity has been equally
handed down from age to age unto us".

---

[14] *The Reclaimed Papist*, p. 215.
[15] l.c., p. 83.
[16] l.c., p. 107.
[17] l.c., p. 91.
[18] l.c., p. 109.
[19] l.c., p. 145.
[20] l.c., p. 146.

Stressing Tradition, Canes by no means wants to forget Scripture. Indeed, both "go hand to hand together as a joint rule of faith".[21] Yet this is qualified "so as that Scripture gives Tradition the right hand as being its elder and judge of itself, as well as co-judge with it of all other doctrines". Thus Scripture is at the same time under or in the Tradition that gave it birth, and united to it as its equal to pass sentence on specific questions. This does not entirely rule out a certain type of language which Canes admits he occasionally uses: "It may chance that in discoursing I may say some time that all the articles of our Catholic faith be taken out of Scripture wherein they be implicitly contained".[22] Yet such a way of speaking is not accurate, for the facts are in reverse. The Scriptures themselves "were drawn by the rule of our traditional doctrine and explicit faith, and not our explicit faith gathered out of them".[23] The whole process of Tradition is more complicated than an explicitation from Scripture, yet Scripture fulfils a positive function in relation to it. Canes briefly describes this process in a passage referring specifically to the Catholic belief in praying for the dead:

> The whole body of Christians then present held it so, their forgoers and fathers delivered it, sacred Scriptures sufficiently insinuated it, Catholic writings and monuments confirmed and commended it unto them.[24]

Canes cannot avoid the objection, made by the Protestants against whom he writes *Diaphanta* (Owen, Pierce, Taylor), that the Church has made "new articles of faith", thereby trespassing over a divine preserve. In the mind of these critics, the Church has not kept, but has adulterated the faith by addition. That the faith "increases" in the Catholic Church, Vincent Canes denies, whereas he points out that it "decreases" in Protestantism. The added articles (he speaks at length of transsubstiatantion and of "consubstantiation", or the consubstantiality of the Father and the Son) are not new except in words. And Catholic religion "is not words; nor are words Catholic religion; but the sense and life and meaning delivered us by help of words for faith, hope and charity to feed upon".[25] New words do not make new articles; and such words belong to the faith, "only in so

---

[21] l.c., p. 147.
[22] l.c., p. 146.
[23] l.c., p. 147.
[24] l.c., p. 150.
[25] *Diaphanta 111*, p. 278.

far as they conveigh the old faith, by this new invented word guarded against the subtleties of heretics then living, who by their circumventing sophistry deluded all other expression concerning the real presence of the Godhead in our Lord's humanity, and of his humanity in the Eucharist".[26] Once the heresy has been vanquished, Canes adds, the word defined is of no longer use and the faithful need not "trouble their heads" about it, "unless haply the same heresies should rise again".[27]

In 1655, an unidentified author who called himself J. P. published at Douai a short (61 pages) volume: *Truth Manifested, or a short discourse clearly showing that we can have no certainty in Christian religion without an infallible Church to adhere to*. This is a far less polemical production than most works of the period. Very little space is devoted to refuting Protestants, and the whole thrust of the book is to establish the truth of Catholic ecclesiology, expressed in ten theses, each of which is carefully explained and defended. In many places the argumentation is so concise as to become cryptic. For instance, J. P. is showing that "in the Church there is a clear successive testimony of the same doctrine",[28] which is his third thesis, and he objects to Protestants that they "firmly believe the Trinity, Redemption, etc." even though these doctrines are "not evident by the words of Scripture" [29] if these are taken without the Church's interpretation. J. P. comes then to the heart of the debate, which he ciphers thus:

> You may say, *both are equivalently in Scripture.* Then not clearly expressed but gathered by deduction. Probable or evident; probable or impertinent; evident or impossible, as experience shows, then also disputable, then not Scripture: how then grounds to condemn a Church? Is there any sense of yours, by which you condemn it, more clear than that was of the Arians? or theirs was of the primitive times, who untaught, depraved the Scriptures to their perdition? [30]

Yet even in such passages as these, J. P.'s line of reasoning comes through. It is conveniently summed up in the last pages of the book. J. P. starts from the fact that Scripture does not sufficiently explain itself to be intelligible without external assistance. This is not detri-

---

[26] l.c., p. 279.
[27] l.c., p. 280.
[28] *Truth Manifested . . .*, p. 12.
[29] l.c., p. 64.
[30] l.c., pp. 15-16.

mental to Scripture, but rather points to its close relatedness to God, who is himself beyond comprehension: "The Scriptures are an image of God's Word and Will, mysterious, obscure and venerable".[31] Owing to this mysteriousness, no single human mind can ever decide with certainty which is the true sense of Scripture among the many that have been proposed. Even "the highest judgement and greatest human authority" can obtain nothing better than a probability; and probability provides no "sufficient foundation of a Christian and divine faith".

The only way to arrive at something more than a probable interpretation of Scripture is to have recourse to "a Church morally one, in one faith and government, with the primitive, which manifestly hands to us Christ's Word written and unwritten". This Church is the Catholic Church.[32]

The main key to J. P.'s demonstration comes from his double approach to the Word, in which we may recognise a frequent theme of Recusant literature: "What has been taught as faith and printed in the hearts of Christians by the careful teaching of Christ's disciples and their true successors is as well the Word of God as the Scripture written, commanded to be delivered, with promise of protection to the teachers thereof".[33] This adds a useful note to the doctrine of "Scripture imprinted in the heart", for J. P. makes it clear that it is in the heart of the faithful under the form of faith. The Word-in-the-heart results from the Tradition, or teaching of Christ's disciples; yet it cannot be simply connumerated with the written Word. For Scripture is also "delivered" or transmitted by the teaching of the disciples, with the result that the Word is born in the heart when man responds to the transmission of the Word of God by assenting to it.

The second key to J. P.'s doctrine lies in his identification of the Church, not only with the organs or institutions of transmission or with the sumtotal of believers, but also with the delivery as such. In a breathtaking telescoping of perspectives usually seen in fragmentation, J. P. states with his usual succinctness which, at this point, verges on eloquence: "The Church is a clear successive testimony of the same doctrine never interrupted".[34] And again: "The present age of the

---

[31] l.c., p. 57.
[32] l.c., pp. 57-68.
[33] l.c., p. 11.
[34] l.c., p. 20.

Church with all former ages make one clear successive and indivisible testimony of the same doctrine delivered".[35] This ecclesiology is undergirded by a broad conception of human unanimity which hints at a philosophy of Tradition: "The eye is not more convincing", J. P. asserts, "to the judgement of a wise man, than the uniform testimony of a well governed community: what doubt then can there be of the testimony of agreeing ages, especially in matters of fact?"[36] No sooner is this idea applied to Christianity than the Church's traditionary nature springs to light: "Every succeeding age of the Church, even to this present, has been undoubtedly uniform to the primitive: then all ages of the Church make one morally indivisible testimony of Christ and his doctrine". From this two consequences follow regarding the nature of Christian Tradition.

In the first place, the Church's unanimity through time endows its teaching with indivisibility and infallibility. The Church makes "one indivisible and infallible testimony of Christ's doctrine written and unwritten. Indivisible, because morally the same. . .; infallible, because confirmed by Christ's miracles, which equally give credit to the same continued Church in all ages".[37] In the second place, such a succeeding Tradition of the same divine teaching cannot be a merely human testimony. The Church today stands in uninterrupted continuity with the apostolic Church and therefore shares the same charisms: "The voice and pen of the apostles and evangelists was a divine testimony, for the clear assistance they had from the Holy Ghost, dignifying and elevating them by a moral union; the same union appears in all succeeding ages, while the continuance of the same indivisible voice is evidently undisprovable".[38]

There is therefore some sense in which the apostolic charism which guided the primitive Church and, in the form of inspiration, led the pen of the New Testament writers, has continued to preside over the Church's teaching through all succeeding ages. This should open an interesting vista on the nature of the Church's Tradition and on the charismatic elements of its life. J. P., however, does not pursue this line of thought and fails to enter through the gate that he has pushed ajar. As he says of all his presentation in the concluding

---

[35] l.c., p. 21.
[36] l.c., p. 27.
[37] l.c., p. 30.
[38] l.c., p. 32.

lines of his book, "The business is of highest discernment".[39] Whoever he is, J. P. has discerned some new light to bring to bear on the matter. He ends his conclusion by inviting critics to tell him what flaws they may find in his volume; he should also have invited friends to follow the lead he had suggested toward an investigation of the pneumatic dimension in the process of transmitting the Word.

For James Mumford or Montford (1606-1666), a Jesuit who joined the English mission in 1650 after spending some twenty-five years in the Netherlands, the *Question of questions, which rightly resolved resolves all our questions in religion* is "who ought to be our Judge in all these our differences". This was actually the title of a volume he published in 1658 under the name of Optatus Ductor, in which, among other things, Mumford intended to show that "no fewer than twenty-four" points of faith necessary to salvation cannot be known with certainty with the help of Scripture alone. The counterpart to this line of argumentation he presented in 1662, with another book signed I. M., *The Catholic Scripturist, or the plea of the Roman Catholics shewing the Scriptures to hold forth the Roman faith in above forty of the chief controversies now under debate*. Mumford thus traced two lines, toward the insufficiency of Scripture alone to bring man to salvation, and toward its relative sufficiency to bring man to the Catholic Church and doctrine. He acknowledged that, for all good Catholics, the problems raised by the Reformers are solved by the simple fact that "they taught contrary to what we had learned",[40] but he reckoned that Protestants need another type of answer to be convinced of error.

Mumford's presentation includes the usual contentions of the Catholic controversialists, which we may bring down to three. Firstly, the high dignity of Scripture, which is called, among other terms of praise, sufficient and infallible, provides an opportunity to treat Catholic scriptural doctrine in a highly positive way, pointing out its divine origin, its quasi-necessity for faith, its importance for spiritual life. Secondly, the insufficiency of Scripture, which does not by itself account for all the requirements of the salvation of all men, is sketched with a more polemical brush, which aims at the Reformers rather than at the inadequacies of the written Word. Thirdly, the remedy to scriptural insufficiency is introduced, in the form of the

---

[39] l.c., p. 60.
[40] *The Catholic Scripturist* . . ., preface.

Catholic Tradition and its dignity, which correlates that of Scripture. The first point is affirmed by Mumford in unequivocal terms:

> We say Scripture was dictated by him (the Holy Ghost) for many most high ends belonging to the knowledge and love of God and belonging to the increase of all virtue and hatred of sin...that... thus walking cheerfully by those comfortable examples and these rare documents and fervent exhortations given us in Scripture to all virtue, we may gain the end for which God made us. Yea we add that Scripture wants not this honor of providing sufficiently for our unity in faith about all points which can ever fall in controversy; not that it ends all these by itself alone, but that it bids us to have recourse in these cases to his Church...[41]

In the more condensed language of *The Catholic Scripturist*, Mumford makes this point at the start of his book: "No Roman Catholic does deny the Scripture to be a sufficient rule to direct us in all controversies, if we take the Scripture rightly interpreted." [42]

The second turn in the argument is illustrated by Mumford's list of "more than forty" doctrines where Scripture alone fails to convince the reader "without you take the Bible as it, by many and very clear texts, sends us for more full instruction to the Church".[43] But Mumford does not only reason a posteriori: he also analyses the difficulties inherent in the idea that Christian doctrine is "plainly set down in Scripture".[44] There is nothing unusual in the six difficulties he lists, except the wording of the third one:

> The third difficulty, cleared plainly by no Scripture, is that these words on which the controversy depends, be infallibly taken in this place in their common and usual sense, or perhaps taken figuratively, or spoken mystically of some other thing. For how is it possible by Scripture only to come to have an infallible knowledge of this, on which the controversy wholly depends? being that this depends merely on the inward free will of God, who perhaps would use only the plain vulgar sense of these words in this place, perhaps would use them only figuratively, or only mystically. To know this secret free will of God, and that infallibly, I must have such a Revelation or such an assistance of the Holy Ghost as you will not allow to the Church represented in a Council, and therefore it cannot prudently be allowable to any private man; neither can any private man shew plain Scripture for his particular pretense to know this secret will of God.[45]

---

[41] *The Question of Questions*, p. 111; see pp. 6-7, 12, 163-164, 173.
[42] *The Catholic Scripturist* . . ., p. 1.
[43] *The Question of Questions*, p. 12.
[44] l.c., pp. 39-43.
[45] l.c., p. 39.

This passage presents a miraculous conception of hermeneutics, in which the sense of the words of the Bible depends on a secret will of God that cannot be known except by Revelation or special charismatic assistance. Refusing to believe that the Spirit guides the Church toward the true sense of the texts, Protestants are left to the device of trying to prove the Bible by itself, one text by another, one translation by another. But, as Mumford colorfully objects, "No circle is rounder and goes more about and about again in the same footsteps, than the circle we are made run-in blindfold, by having no other assurance that the only rule of all our faith is a Bible containing all things necessary to salvation, without error against faith and manners; and having no other assurance of what is necessary to salvation, what not; what is against manners, what not; but by another Bible, of which Bible's truth we have no other assurance than the former. . .".[46]

The third point of the Catholic case is carried by describing Tradition and its sufficiency to bring all men to salvation. Here again we find little that is new. Yet Mumford insists more than others on the test of a true Tradition: one should interrogate the prelates of all the world in order to assess their unanimity. A long and cumulative sentence, which is rather typical of Mumford's very effective style, comes nearest to depicting Tradition as a vital process involving the entire life of the Church in all times and places:

> But Tradition is the only thing which teaches us this, to wit, what the apostles did teach us both by writing and by word of mouth without writing; which this Tradition performs by millions of true believers of the first age, all taken apart (as witnesses use to be to find out how well they all agree in their testimony) and placed in several parts of the world; many vastly distant from one another and yet delivering the same thing to those other millions, who in greater number succeeded them in life, and in delivering the same thing in the same manner to new millions of their posterity, all constantly agreeing in the testification of the very selfsame points, all affirming them to have been delivered publicly in Churches and great assemblies everywhere all their country over; and that so very exceeding often and by so very many and by so very diverse persons of all kind of conditions, that it is more possible for all men in the world to fall into a fit of dancing just for a quarter of an hour at one and the selfsame time without ever agreeing to do so beforehand, than it is possible for all these millions of men in so different places and of so different judgments by nature, and so contrary in their humors, inclinations and proceedings, to conspire thus in one and the same story concerning

---

[46] l.c., p. 103; see pp. 113-114, 353, 364-365, 401.

so many particulars, without that thing had been really and notoriously true, which so many millions taken in so different circumstances, all testified unanimously to be true.[47]

This unanimous transmission of the same faith all over the world by people who are separated from one another by great distances cannot be a purely human, natural phenomenon. In spite of the naturalistic aspects of the above description Mumford firmly maintains the charismatic dimension of Tradition: it is the work of the Spirit, who assists both the individuals and the collectivity of the Church. Yet the same Spirit does not inspire individuals in the same way as he guides the Church. Concerned lest his concept of Tradition should lead to an illuminist view of the Spirit's action, Mumford qualifies it with this striking sentence: "To private persons the Holy Ghost is given as the spirit of sanctification, but to the Church he is given as the spirit of truth guiding her into all truth and so excluding all error from her".[48]

As with J. P., we are thus led to the brink of a pneumatic explanation of Tradition. Unfortunately, Mumford, still like J. P., opens a gate, points out the landscape, and withdraws.

In 1664, Edward Stillingfleet (1635-1699), then rector of Sutton in Bedfordshire, infused new blood into theological controversies with the publication of his major book, *A Rational Account of the Grounds of the Protestant Religion*. This was occasioned by a lengthy criticism of Laud's *Conference with Mr Fisher the Jesuit* (1639), by Thomas Carwell (1600-1664), a Jesuit whose real name was Thorold.[49] Even though Carwell's volume, *Labyrinthus Cantuariensis* (1663), came out too late to be of great topical interest, it was sufficiently biting and compendious to invite refutation. Stillingfleet had already reached fame with his non-polemical *Origines Sacrae, or a Rational Account of the Grounds of Christian Faith as to the truth and divine authority of the Scriptures* (1663). Whereas the first *Rational Account* compares the Scriptures with the documents of profane and ancient history, the second contrasts Catholic and Anglican doctrines on "the grounds of faith" (Part I), examines the accusation of schism (Part II) and

---

[47] l.c., pp. 402-403; see pp. 7, 344-345, 350-351, 388, 394, 396, 400; *The Catholic Scripturist*, pp. 12, 15-16, 2-, 32, 52, 62.

[48] *The Catholic Scripturist*, p. 62.

[49] On the theology of Stillingfleet and "latitudinarianism", see H. R. McAdoo, *The Spirit of Anglicanism*, New York, 1965; G. R. Cragg, *From Puritanism to the Age of Reason, 1600-1700*, Cambridge, 1950.

treats of several "particular controversies" (Part III), especially on the nature of Councils, on the possibility of salvation in the Roman Church and on purgatory. The first part is the most important, as it discusses at length two of the most basic problems raised in the Catholic-Anglican debates: the nature of "fundamentals" of faith (ch. 2-4), the resolution of faith and the infallibility of Tradition (ch. 5-9). Stillingfleet's treatment of these topics is marred by the method of quoting and refuting which is further complicated by Stillingfleet's desire to explain the true doctrine of Archbishop Laud before coming to Carwell's strictures. Theologically it is a well-reasoned book, although Stillingfleet's latitudinarian orientations considerably detract from its value: his *Rational Account* is definitely dated and of little interest today except to historians.

Be that as it may, Stillingfleet's long book naturally provoked a Catholic reaction, so that one may speak of a Stillingfleet controversy, which roughly corresponds to the Chillingworth controversy of the 1630's.

The Stillingfleet controversy occasioned many publications, as the Catholic and Anglican polemicists entered the fray with old or new arguments pro and con the Catholic conception of the grounds of Christian religion. Some wrote a lot of indigestible prose in which their concern lest a few lines of their adversaries' would go unreproved involved them in winding arguments which discourage modern readers. Once in a while, however, a gem shines in the forest of these proofs and counterproofs, by which the reader's efforts are rewarded and the author's work redeemed.

It is on account of such rare finds that Edward Worsley (1605-1676) ought to be remembered. Worsley authored three long polemical pieces. *Truth Will Out* (1665) is directed mainly against Jeremy Taylor's *Dissuasive of Popery* (1664), although Pierce and Stillingfleet come in for a good deal of criticism. *Protestancy Without Principles* (1668) is, as its title suggests, an overall refutation of Protestantism. *Reason and Religion, or the certain rule of faith* (1672) is a very obscure collection of arguments against Protestantism. It touches on the question of the Rule of faith in its chapter XIV by a somewhat odd bias, the main argument against Scripture alone being that Scripture cannot prove Christianity to a Chinese, for a Chinese will naturally prefer the writings of Confucius.[50] A last volume affirms, against its

---

[50] *Reason and Religion* . . ., pp. 139-140.

detractors, *The Infallibility of the Roman Catholic Church* (1673).

Whatever the value of Worsley's excursions into the Chinese problem, and the general obscurity of his style, his statements of Catholic doctrine are often well coined. "All know", he writes, "that the objective verities writ in Holy Scripture and the belief of those verities in a Christian's heart are to be distinguished. By the first, God speaks to us. By the second, we yield our belief to his Word. All know likewise that if my belief be true faith, it must say exactly and express that *in mente* which God speaks in Scripture, neither more nor less. And this is saving faith. . .".[51] In a sense Scripture expresses the entire faith in a generic way, provided we do not require every particular to be accounted for, and on condition that Scripture be interpreted by "no other but the Spirit of truth, the Holy Ghost": [52]

> The general truths contained in Scripture, because they teach us to believe the Catholic Church, Tradition, and other apostolical doctrines, are in this general way able to make us wise to salvation, but none can so much as probably draw from hence that all things in particular, necessary to salvation, are explicitly set down in Scripture.[53]

Worsley's theology constantly harps on "the infallible doctrine of the Catholic Church", on "Scripture explicated by that never erring oracle of truth, the Catholic Church", on the infallibility of "Tradition and the Church's interpretation".[54] But this is so far from serving a static conception of Catholic truth that Worsley formulates more explicitly than anyone yet in his century the problem of development of doctrine. This short text is quite remarkable:

> (The Arians) cried out, Novelties, novelties, as loud as the Doctor (Jeremy Taylor). I answer with St. Gregory *in Ezechiel, homil. XVI, post med.* p. 1164, 6th ed., Antwerp 1615, that *per incrementa temporum crevit scientia spiritualium patrum*: With time faith increases, but how? Not that either the Church or the Pope have power to coin Articles at pleasure, or to force Christians to the acceptance of novelties contrary to Scripture or ancient Tradition; no, but the power given them is to dispense the mysteries of the Word of God, to lay out more clearly verities contained in Scripture (so the Fathers did in the Nicene Council when they defined the Son to be consubstantial with his Father, which word *omoousios* is never read in Scripture), finally, to declare more explicitly what the ancient Tradition of the Church and sense of the Fathers has been; within such a compass the Church

---

[51] *Protestancy without Principles*, p. 154.
[52] l.c., p. 210.
[53] l.c., *Notes on Mr. Poole's Appendix*, p. 44.
[54] l.c., p. 142.

holds itself when after mature deliberation it defines in Council.
Hence both divines and canonists teach that, rigorously speaking,
the Church has no new Articles of faith; but only a more full and
explicit knowledge of that belief which anciently was among primitive
Christians.[55]

It is of course to be regretted that Edward Worsley did not investigate the matter further: this concludes the first chapter of his
book, after which he passes to other questions. Yet, succinct at his
treatment of the topic remains, he has not only indicated the general
problem of "increase of faith", he has moreover pointed his finger
toward at least one solution: faith increases by way of unfolding what
was infolded at the beginning. This is done by way of clarification of
the truth, which is now "laid out more clearly". Yet a rather different
perspective is also suggested: to "dispense the mysteries of the Word
of God" cannot result from a mere logical deduction and must
entail some more profound activity of the Spirit than a guarantee of
proper reasoning. What this can be, however, Worsley left to others
to investigate.

Among the Catholics who responded to Stillingfleet's challenge,
Abraham Woodhead (1609-1678), alias Thomas Harrison, or, as he
signed most of his books, R. H., presents the strange feature of
having been one of the most appreciated controversialists in his
lifetime, and of being one of the least legible today. An Anglican
priest, Fellow of University College, Oxford, Woodhead joined the
Catholic communion after travelling on the Continent, some time
before 1655. He lived henceforth as a layman, was reinstated in his
Fellowship at the Restoration, and was actively engaged in the
intellectual life of the times, remaining close to a number of Anglican
personalities. Like his intimate friend Obediah Walker (1616-1699),
another convert who continued to be one of the lights of Oxford
and became Master of University College in 1676, Woodhead belonged to the small group of Catholics whose activities mediated, at
least at the level of University life, between the Recusancy of most of
their co-believers and the Established Church of England.[56] Walker,
however, was hardly a theologian although he wrote several books
of piety besides his philosophical and scientific studies. Walker
nonetheless committed himself to theological publication as printer

---

[55] *Truth will out*, p. 14.
[56] On Obediah Walker, see Maurice Nédoncelle, l.c., ch. 11.

and publisher, for he owned a press, on which a number of polemical works were printed, and out of which came several posthumous works of Abraham Woodhead.

Woodhead's theological output was considerable, though little need be remembered. Woodhead, however, perceived and clearly stated the problem of Tradition in his best, which was also his first, work: *A Rational Account of the Doctrines of Roman Catholics concerning the Ecclesiastical Guide in controversies of Religion* (1666). The title at least of the book is inspired by Stillingfleet's recent "rational accounts"; yet the scope of the work goes beyond the immediate controversy, and Woodhead speaks of many other Anglican writers, giving due place to Chillingworth, Stillingfleet's great predecessor. Woodhead's style of writing is heavy and incomprehensibly involved, and his polemical method is equally complicated. Yet if we have the patience to plough through his long paragraphs, we can clean valuable insights, some of which bear directly on the problem of Scripture and Tradition, which Woodhead carefully delineates:

> But though, I say, Catholics maintain several credends that are not expressed in Scriptures, necessary to be believed and observed by Christians after the Church's proposal of them as Tradition apostolical, amongst which is the Canon of Scripture; yet they willingly concede that all such points of faith as are simply necessary for attaining salvation, and as ought explicitly by all men to be known in order thereto, either *ratione medii* or *praecepti* (as the doctrines collected in the Creeds, the common precepts of manners and of the more necessary sacraments, etc.) are contained in the Scriptures; contained therein, either in the conclusion itself, or in the principles from whence it is necessarily deduced.[57]

Here, the Church's position in regard to the principle of Scripture alone contains a certain ambiguity: several „credends" are not expressed in Scripture, yet all necessary parts of the Christian faith are included in Scripture, if not as formal statements, at least in their principle. This places Scripture at the core of all dogmatic teaching:

> The main and substantial points of our faith . . . are believed to be apostolical, because they are written in Scripture. . . Therefore the Church from time to time defining any thing concerning such points, defines it out of the Revelations made in Scripture.[58]

It follows that Woodhead must define Tradition in relation to the scriptural source of Christian doctrine:

---

[57] *A Rational Account* . . . (ed. of 1673), p. 137.
[58] l.c., p. 138.

> And the chief Tradition, the necessity and benefit of which is pretend-
> ed by the Church, is not the delivering of any additional doctrines
> descended from the apostles' times *extra Scripturas* i.e., such doctrines
> as have not their foundation at least in Scripture; but is the preserving
> and delivering of the primitive sense and church-explication of that
> which is written in the Scriptures, but many times not there written
> so clearly.

Tradition communicates the sense of Scripture, so that what is not
clear in it is nonetheless known and believed by the faithful. By a
logical progression, this leads Woodhead to formulate the state of
the question as between Catholics and Protestants concerning the
sufficiency of Scripture:

> This then being the Tradition that is chiefly vindicated by the Roman
> Church, it is not the deficiency of Scripture as to all the main and
> prime and universally necessary-to-be-known articles of faith (as if
> there were any necessity that these be supplied and completed with
> other not written traditional doctrines of faith) that Catholics do
> question; but such a non-clearness of Scripture (for several of these
> points) as that they may be misunderstood (which non-clearness of
> them infers a necessity of making use of the Church's tradition for a
> true exposition and sense) is the thing that they assert.

Catholic questions are not focussed on the contents and the limits
of Scripture, but on its clarity as a medium of Revelation: Scripture
does need, not a complement that the Church would draw from other
sources of information, but an interpretation which she provides
out of her spiritual discernment. Should one ask about the material
contents of Scripture, Woodhead would give this answer:

> For, as to the Scriptures containing all the chief and material points of
> a Christian's belief, what article of faith is there, except that concerning
> the canon of Scripture (which Protestants also grant cannot be learned
> out of Scripture) and excepting those practicals wherein, the Church
> only requiring a belief of the lawfulness of them, it is enough if they
> cannot be shown to be against Scripture; I say, what speculative
> article of faith is there, for which Catholics rest merely on unwritten
> Tradition; and do not, for it, allege Scripture; I mean, even that
> Canon of Scripture, which Protestants allow?

In other words, all Catholic doctrines are grounded in Scripture, even
the list of canonical books, which Protestants themselves found on
Tradition. What, then, is the problem? And where do Catholics and
Protestants differ? Abraham Woodhead reduces the issue to its bare
minimum:

I say, then; not this, whether the main or, if you wish, the entire body of the Christian faith as to all points necessary by all to be explicitly believed, be contained there; but this, whether so clearly that the unlearned, using a right diligence, cannot therein mistake, or do not therein need another guide, is the thing here contested.[59]

This long piece of unwieldy prose places Woodhead squarely in the line of the major figures already studied, Franciscus a Sancta Clara and Thomas White. Similar passages could be culled from R. H.'s *Considerations on the Council of Trent* (1671), where Abraham Woodhead sees all Tridentine statements as flowing from Scripture: "I know no definition of the Council of Trent in any matter of faith, that is opposed by Protestants, which is not pretended to be grounded on the divine Scriptures; on these Scriptures either, if it be in speculative points of faith, revealing it; or, if in matter of practise, either commanding or not prohibiting, this latter being enough for an obliging of that assent or belief, which the Council requires, viz., that the thing, not so prohibited, is lawful".[60] Woodhead admittedly knows that Tradition is not always taken in the sense which dominates his own theology, and he makes the required semantic distinctions: "Tradition unwritten in Scripture is either a delivery of something not contained in Scripture, or the exposition or delivery of the true sense of what is contained there".[61] But the weight of authority supports this second notion rather than the first: "The latter sort of which Traditions the Church much more makes use of and vindicates than the former".

Admittedly, this leaves open the problem of the existence of extra-scriptural traditions or, to remain in Woodhead's perspective, of traditions that are more clear and explicit than the corresponding Scripture. A passage takes place from the infolded to the evolved, which is not reduced to a transition from Scripture to Tradition, for Tradition also undergoes a process of unfolding and clarification. Woodhead handles this question briefly in *A Discourse of the Necessity of Church-Guides for directing Christians in necessary faith* (1675), as also in a posthumous volume published by the good offices of Obediah Walker, *A Compendious Discourse on the Eucharist* (1688).

Abraham Woodhead is demonstrating the need for "infallibility in the governours of the Church", and reasoning by analogy. Just

[59] l.c., p. 139.
[60] *Considerations on the Council of Trent*, p. 224.
[61] l.c., p. 223.

as the infallibility of Scripture does not render pointless the assurance and certainty of Tradition, but requires such a Tradition, likewise, the function of Tradition not only does not contradict, but also demands an infallible authority in what we today call the *magisterium*. A number of valuable remarks are made in the course of his development of this point. Thus, Woodhead presents Tradition as a developing process, in which clear doctrines are "extracted" from more obscure ones:

> Though many are, yet all points of faith are not, delivered and transferred to posterity by the forementioned Tradition in their express and explicit terms; but some have only descended in their principles: the necessary deductions from which are by this infallible Church extracted and vindicated from age to age against those dangerous errors that may happen to assault them.[62]

Interestingly enough, the seat of infallibility is said by Woodhead to be the whole Church, and not only its governors. In his language, the whole Church includes the people, whether or not these are aware of infallibility. This comes out well enough in such an involved statement as this:

> And it is here observable that, though in the descent of Tradition the *congregatio fidelium*, when it first delivers to a person the infallibility of the Church and of Scripture, appears not to him as yet absolutely infallible; yet indeed as to delivering necessaries it then and always is so. For this *Congregatio fidelium* in every age that testifies such things, it, or some part of it, is the very same Body that is promised by our Lord his perpetual assistance, and is preserved forever by God's Spirit and Providence from erring in necessaries. [63]

Again, Woodhead sees Scripture, Tradition and Church-authority in one and the same perspective, Tradition making Scripture clear, or expressing distinctly what Scripture formulates ambiguously or contains implicitly, and Church-authority prolonging this drive toward the better known by further clarifying what Tradition still leaves in the dark. In one movement, Scripture leads to Tradition, which leads to Authority; in another, Authority makes Tradition effective, which already made Scripture effective. This lesson is also to be learned from another complicated sentence:

> After this point of Church-infallibility is once established and confirmed by such Tradition, one may hence sooner and easier learn

---

[62] *A Discourse of the Necessity of Church-guides* . . ., p. 89.
[63] l.c., p. 90.

from her plain definitions and proposals thereof, than from Tradition much dispersed abroad, whereby its uniformity is the harder to be discerned; or from the Scriptures, in several points not so perspicuous, and so the more subject to misinterpretations, and where, for the thorough studying the one or the other, the vocations and employments of most Christians admit not a competent vacancy.

"To explain the business a little", as Abraham Woodhead says in his *Compendious Discourse on the Eucharist*, a distinction should be made between an article of faith as *dogma verum*, which is always true and can never change, and an article of faith taken as *dogma necessario credendum*. In the first sense there never are new articles of faith, for what is true today was true yesterday. In the second, "as article of faith is taken for *dogma necessario credendum*, for a divine truth necessary, when known to be so, to be believed and not opposed: so a divine truth may be an article or object of my faith today which was not yesterday".[64] The newness of a definition of faith does not lie in the substance of what is defined, but in the presentation of that substance to our assent. Here we arrive at the problem of the scope of dogmatic definitions, which Woodhead explains in this way:

> When therefore a thing is said to be no *dogma fidei* before, and at such a time to begin to be so, the meaning is this: that it is now a *dogma fidei*, or object of faith necessary to be believed, which it was not before (necessary to be believed), not for the matter thereof—as if the actual knowledge and faith thereof were absolutely necessary to salvation; thus a few points only (some think not all those of the Creed) are necessary; and nothing thus necessary at any time that is not always so—but necessary *ex accidenti*, because we have a sufficient proposal thereof that it is a divine truth.

That is to say, nothing ever becomes necessary to salvation: it always is so. Dogmatic definition does not create a new condition for salvation or increase the substance of faith. By the same token, it does not require a positive faith, reserved to the substance of Revelation, but a negative acceptance, in the sense of not denying it once we know what the Church has defined. For Woodhead continues, making a distinction which has now disappeared from our usual theology:

> Not that the error in or ignorance of such a point, even after such a proposal, does derogate from our having absolutely necessary faith, any more than it did before, nor that, in disbelieving or dissenting from it, we are more defective in the necessarily salvifical principles of divine truth; but that we are defective in our obedience to and

---

[64] *Compendious Discourse* . . ., p. 134.

acceptance of divine truths made known to us by the Church, as some way conducible to Christian edification, to the peace of the Church or to some other good end. Therefore the duty she requires to many of her decisions is not so much an actual knowing of them, as the not denying, opposing, contradicting them, when made known to us.[65]

Applying to Tradition something that Bellarmine says of Scripture, Woodhead sums up the argument by sugesting that these dogmas are to be believed because they are defined, but are not defined because they are to be believed.

These few milestones along the way of a theology of development point toward the possibility of a greater synthesis than Turberville, Canes, J. P., Mumford, Worsley or Woodhead attempted. By the second half of the 17th century in England the problem of development was raised in the context of a growing awareness of the centrality of the question of tradition in the Catholic-Protestant debates. Descriptions of the transmission of doctrine as an already given deposit have the knack of coming to a halt before blatant facts which an increasing consciousness of historical reality makes it impossible to overlook. In spite of Bossuet's longing for a hieratic order, the Catholic theology of the Counter-Reformation was already looking ahead toward John Henry Newman. We may even wonder if it did not already progress a long way toward the solution that Newman tried to provide.

---

[65] l.c., pp. 134-135.

CHAPTER TEN

THE HARVEST OF JOHN SERGEANT

The many trends that have been instanced in our study of English Catholic thought converged, during the second half of the 17th century, toward the work of a man who, in the field of Tradition, carried Recusant theology to its climax. John Sergeant (1622-1707), alias Smith or Holland, became Catholic while a student at Cambridge, apparently under Christopher Davenport's influence. Ordained at the English College in Lisbon, Sergeant returned to England in 1652, and published his major book in 1665: *Sure-footing in Christianity, or Rational Discourses on the Rule of Faith*. Thus entering the fray of the Stillingfleet controversy and operating in the framework of the "rational" concerns imposed on English thought by the growing latitudinarian movement, Sergeant did however better than produce a polemical piece: he rather transcended the immediate situation in order squarely to face the problem of Tradition in itself. Others before him had approached the question from the angle of the theology of faith, thus leaving aside the sterile polemics of former years on "the traditions of men". As to him, he perceived that a theological consideration of Tradition must proceed by severely controlled logical steps, and that the sort of haphazard argumentation that often took place could only prolong debates endlessly. He accordingly tried to define a *method* for the study of Tradition, partly uncovering the latent rules of his forerunners' theological essays, partly devising new or further approaches to the heart of the problem.

Sergeant did not only forge a theological method. He also added a point which has gained considerable importance since his time, even though we may not be more advanced than he was in our mastery of it: he distinctly focused the entire problem of Tradition on the analysis of the act of transmission by which the doctrine of faith passes from one age to another. This, admittedly, was already prominent in the Rushworth-White orientation: Sergeant knew it well, and only considered himself to be a disciple of White. But he was able to reach further in this analysis than his predecessors had done.

This effort was not easy, and Sergeant ran foul of several authors who, misunderstanding his doctrine, accused him of heterodoxy and

14

denounced him as a breeder of the "Blackloist" heresy, the supposed scepticism of Thomas White, which, as depicted by the *vigilanti*, reduced the Christian faith to purely natural principles and Christian ethics to sheer pelagianism. Sergeant defended himself in several Latin pamphlets in 1677 and 1678. He returned to the problem of Tradition ten years later, with his *Five Catholic Letters* (1687 and 1688), in which he summed up his theology and serenely surveyed the controversy that had arisen about it.

"I cannot wonder", Sergeant writes in his "preface to the intelligent reader" at the start of *Sure-footing in Christianity*, "if disputes come slowly to an end when few of them were ever rightly begun".[1] The polemics between Catholics and Protestants have been led without method, haphazard, with many arguments *ad hominem* that could produce no lasting effect. Protestants are responsible for this in the first place, for they, as Sergeant understands their position, can be sure of nothing, having no fundamental self-evident principle to rely upon, but building their faith "on the inevidence or ambiguity of words and (their) way to manage them".[2] If "the Bible alone is the religion of Protestants" (as Chillingworth had written), Protestantism is a religion without certainty, which puts forward no principle "to secure to us books written so long ago". At the root of the confusions of polemics, there lies the Protestant rejection of the only certain principle that one can have, namely, of Tradition. It is "most easy" to show "that they have never a principle of self-evident ground to begin with; that till they settle such a principle all their discourse is frivolous; that their rejecting the Church's living voice or Tradition brings all into doubts, both sayings of Fathers and texts of Scripture".[3]

Unfortunately for the sanity of the disputants and the ending of controversy, Catholic controversalists, out of charity, have also debated without following a sure and logical sequence, without clearly defining their first principle and bringing the matter to a strict conclusion which would be as self-evident as the principle it is drawn from. They have indeed argued from the Fathers and the Councils; they have made fuel of traditional documents; they have asserted their position with eloquence. But this cannot be enough.

---

[1] *Sure-footing in Christianity*, preface, n. 1.
[2] l.c., n. 3.
[3] l.c., n. 4.

Indeed, "many things in Catholic writers of the testimonial strain carry a strong force of conviction with them",[4] but this is not tantamount to scientific certainty. Patristic proofs avail nothing if "the validity of any testimony from Father or Council cannot be weighed, understood or pressed with force upon the adversary". And this is precisely the case when Catholics object traditional statements to Protestants after neglecting to show the necessity of Tradition. "For, if these be but parts of the living voice of the Church essential of their time, that is, of Christian tradition, it will follow that till the force of Tradition be evidenced, theirs will not be clearly known". This type of approach is, on the part of Catholics, charitable and it may have been prudent, yet it is "less suitable both to their own genius as Catholic and to the nature of their cause".[5]

In other words, John Sergeant wants to attempt a more lasting work than that of his forerunners. Although the end of controversy has been envisaged before, it has not arrived. It is now time to state the fundamental methodic principles that will make the end possible by placing Catholic doctrine in the light of its full evidence. One must proceed scientifically. The "direct road to science" is to "begin with first or self-evident principles", establishing the foundation on which to build, after which "the way of science (is) to proceed from one piece of sense to another".[6] It is directly contrary to the Protestant practice, which prefers to "carry the war out of the bounds of science where solid ground is to be found to fix one's foot upon, so to overthrow or be overthrown, and to transfer it to a kind of *spatium imaginarium* of fancy and unsignifying sounds, the proper sphere for chimerical discourses to buzz confusedly and make a noise in, where the Catholic must either let them alone, and then they cry, Victory, or follow them thither, and so hazard to prejudice his own cause by seeming to allow their method of discoursing".

Another type of discussion is called for by the nature of Catholic faith, which Sergeant describes thus:

(The Catholic) builds not upon those airy skirmishes for his faith, nor consequently esteems it conquerable by such attempts; he receives his faith from the present Church witnessing its delivery from the former age; to this anchorage he sticks; he stands on immemorial possession, nor doubts he that Christ's doctrine is his true and proper

---

[4] l.c., n. 6.
[5] l.c., n. 4.
[6] l.c., n. 2.

inheritance, while brought down by the testimony of so many Christian nations.[7]

The Catholic build-up for controversy ought then to consist in establishing the strength of Tradition by rational evidence, "for the certainty of first authority must needs be manifested by pure reason".[8] This done, it will be easy to discover what Tradition teaches. Supernatural faith will believe, yet there will also be a self-evident rational ground in the natural certainty of Tradition.

This natural certainty enables Tradition to play the part of a criterion of faith. That is to say, it is not Tradition for its own sake, or as a process of transmission that most counts; ultimately, the problem in controversy is to ascertain the Rule of faith. Is this, as Protestants assert, Scripture? or, as maintained by Catholics, Tradition? Both sides hold that faith must imply certitude; they disagree on the source of this certainty. A good method ought therefore to analyse the notion of Rule of Faith, laying bare the meaning of the two words "rule" and "faith", on the logical principle that "the meaning of a word includes in itself the nature of thing as signified by that word".[9] There is no need for us to follow Sergeant's reasoning in this analysis. We may simply read his conclusion:

> Summing up then the full account of our discourse hitherto, it amounts to this that out of the genuine meaning of the word Rule, which as used by us denotes an intellectual rule, and much more out of the meaning of the word Faith, it is clearly evinced that the Rule of Faith must have these several conditions: namely, it must be plain and self-evident as to its existence to all, and evidenceable as to its ruling power to enquirers, even the rude vulgar; apt to settle and justify undoubting persons, to satisfy fully the most sceptical dissenters and rational doubters; and to convince the most obstinate and acute adversaries; built upon unmoveable grounds, that is, certain in itself and absolutely ascertainable to us.[10]

Once this has been shown, Sergeant continues to reason things out in order: he will look at the two candidates to the functions of rule of faith, and conclude that Scripture does not meet the required conditions (Discourses 2-4), and that Tradition on the contrary fulfills them (Discourses 5-9). There follow no less than forty-one corollaries, some thirty pages adducing "the consent of authority"

---

[7] l.c., n. 3.
[8] l.c., n. 5.
[9] l.c., *First Discourse*, n. 1, p. 1.
[10] l.c., n. 17, pp. 11-12.

to the substance of Sergeant's doctrine and three polemical appendices directed at Pierce, Whitby and Stillingfleet. In Sergeant's mind, however, the notion of rule of faith does not only dominate methodology. It is in the whole range of faith that the search for a rule is primary. "A Church", Sergeant explains, "is a congregation of the faithful, that is, of such as have faith; which, not being possible to be had without certain means to come unto it, or the rule of faith, it follows that the first thing that must be cleared is the certainty of the rule of faith, antecedently to the notions of faith, faithful or Church".[11] Nor can one establish faith on the Fathers' testimony taken as the ultimate recourse. For "both Council and Fathers presupposes the notion of Church; Church presupposes the notion of faithful; faithful the notion of faith; faith, of the rule of faith; it is most evident then that, in the way of generating faith, the knowledge of the rule of faith is antecedent to the knowledge of all these".[12]

Patently, this approach does not favor a high doctrine of Scripture. The rule of faith is all important, but Scripture is not it. Thus most of what Sergeant has to say about Holy Writ takes on a negative tone: none of the conditions of the rule of faith can be fulfilled by Scripture. In the context, however, it cannot be the whole of Scripture that is involved in such a critique, but its face-value, its appearance, its externals, its letter. Sergeant is well aware of the possibility of looking at Scripture from another vantage-point that reveals more than he will himself show. But it is the burden of his theology that if you have in mind Scripture taken together with its full meaning, you actually bring the whole of Tradition to bear upon it. When on the contrary you speak of Scripture alone, as Protestants do, you logically envisage no more than its letter. Taken with its sense, Scripture is not alone but is read in the framework, under the light, and with the interpretation of Tradition. Faithful to his method, Sergeant wants to sort out problems and to introduce the necessary distinctions. Protestants claim that Scripture alone is the rule of faith: very well, let us look at it strictly in isolation and compare it to the rule of faith, to see if perchance it should fit. Furthermore, Scripture with its sense would imply not only the formal aspect of faith, but also its material contents. Everyone regards Scripture as a material rule, that is, as containing in itself at least a part of the object of belief. In this sense some Catholic authors speak of it as "a partial rule of

---

[11] l.c., *Second Discourse*, n. 10, p. 18.
[12] l.c., n. 11, p. 20.

faith, yet they can mean only materially, not formally, that is, that
some part of faith is signified by Scripture's letter, not that Scripture's
letter alone is sufficient security to signify it to private understandings
so as to beget that most strong and firm assent found in divine
faith".[13]

The question raised by Protestants, however, does not concern the
material, but the formal, rule of faith. Accordingly, John Sergeant
delimits the vast scope of the problem at hand:

> To speak to them in their own language who say Scripture is their rule,
> we must premise this note, that they cannot mean by Scripture the
> sense of it, that is, the things to be known, for those they confess are
> the very points of faith, of which the rule of faith is to ascertain us:
> when they say that Scripture is the rule of faith, they can only mean
> by the word Scripture that Book not yet sensed or interpreted, but as
> yet to be sensed; that is, such and such characters in a book with
> their aptness to signify to them assuredly God's mind, or to ascertain
> them of their faith: for, abstracting from the sense or actual significa-
> tion of those words, there is nothing imaginable left but those charac-
> ters with their aptness to signify it.[14]

In this restricted horizon, Scripture calls for the assistance of two
kinds of agents to elicit its meaning. It needs the help of science to
determine as exactly as possible the true state of the letter, to compare its various parts, to read its grammatical sense, to assess its
historical impact. It also requires the support of the Church's Tradition to determine its true spiritual interpretation and its relevance to
faith and to the kingdom of God. Science cannot suffice: this "wordish
way of grammar and criticism", as Sergeant styles it, is "evident by
principles to be ambiguous and by experience to lead men into
different senses", and can therefore "never satisfy us thoroughly that
the sense we arrive at by this method is infallibly the true one or
Christ's, and so never engages certainly the authority of God's
Word".[15] At this level, Scripture may indeed build up rhetoric but
not theology:

> And hence it is that Scripture thus interpreted is of slight force, and
> at best good only for ecclesiastical rhetoric or sermons, where the
> concern is not much if the preacher misses in this particular passage
> the substance of the point he preaches on, or his text be truly Christ's
> doctrine; nor is Scripture thus interpreted even a competent proof in

---

[13] l.c., *Appendix 11*, p. 185.
[14] l.c., *Second Discourse*, n. 2., p. 13.
[15] l.c., *Consent of Authorities*, n. 18, p. 147.

the science of school-divinity, as being uncertain and so unapt to beget a science... Much less is Scripture wordishly interpreted apt to build faith on; the unwaveringness of which kind of assent must be grounded and secure in the principles which beget it, and not merely actually such as it were by accident; whereas interpretations thus made (faith's principles in this case) are liable to possible if not probable mistake.[16]

The problem of Tradition need not be raised in relation to the homiletic use of Scripture for illustration of the faith. For culling images, facts, parables and teachings from Scripture commits to nothing further than the doctrine thus illustrated, which draws its immediate origin in the preacher's own faith rather than in his scriptural references. Tradition comes in when Scripture is read as Word of God, delivering the mind of Christ with absolute certainty. Yet Tradition, as we are now going to see, implies more than reading Scripture.

As qualified by John Sergeant at the beginning of his Fifth Discourse, Tradition is called "oral or practical": "By which we mean a delivery down from hand to hand (by words, and a constant course of frequent and visible actions conformable to those words) of the sense and faith of our forefathers".[17] Sergeant distrusts a purely oral or verbal conception of the transmission of faith. Like Serenus Cressy and others, he does not view tradition as a formal teaching of doctrines delivered in class-room fashion through explanations given by an instructor. The transmission he envisages may be implicit in acts as well as explicit in words, since deeds witness to the principles and ideas that have inspired them. This is clearly borne out by Sergeant's explanation of the natural way of tradition, or of tradition as a natural phenomenon universally observed in the educational process. If we look at the way children learn, he tells us, "we shall observe that they first gleaned notions of these several objects either merely through impressions on their senses by the thing itself alone, or by the help of having them pointed at, or something practised about them at the same time they were named; and afterwards learnt to repeat the same words after others, more and more intelligently by degrees, and to practise the same actions".[18] This is, with some elaboration, the transmission "from father to son" already

---

[16] l.c., p. 148.
[17] l.c., *Fifth Discourse*, n. 1, p. 41.
[18] l.c., n. 2., p. 42.

outlined by Thomas White. Since this process joins generation to generation and ensures the preservation of knowledge through the ages, it occupies a central place in all human life. Transported into the Church, it corresponds exactly to Christian Tradition:

> We want nothing now but to apply this self-same method to spiritual or ecclesiastical affairs, and to reflect how it brings down faith by doctrine couched in words and expressed in conformable practices; and then we shall have gained a complete and proper notion of Faith-Tradition, which is the Tradition we speak of.[19]

There follows a long description of the process of learning Christianity, as children see, hear, learn to do, to think and to pray like their parents and teachers, "according as the young brood of eaglets, made to see the sun in its full glory, grow up to a capacity of having their tender eyes acquainted first with the dawning, afterwards with the common daylight of Christian doctrine".[20] Sergeant sums it up in suggestive formulas:

> Tradition being the open conveyance down of practical doctrine by our best senses of discipline, that is, our eyes and ears, and this by sounds daily heard and actions daily seen and even felt, it is easily appliable to all sorts, or evident to them as to its existence, as it is to see and hear: so that it can be insinuated into or affect not only the rudest vulgar and little children, but in some degree even very babes.[21]

And again:

> Reflecting then on the nature of Tradition as before explicated, we shall observe that it has for its basis the best nature in the universe, that is, man's, the flower and end of all the rest; and this, not according to his moral part, defectible by reason of original corruption; nor yet his intellectuals, darkly groping in the pursuit of science by reflected thoughts or speculations amidst the misty vapours exhaled by his passions predominant over his rational will; but according to those faculties in him perfectly and necessarily subject to the operations and strokes of nature, that is, his eyes, ears, handling, and the direct impressions of knowledge, as naturally and necessarily issuing from the affecting those senses as it is to feel heat, cold, pain, pleasure or any other material quality.[22]

These passages point to two fundamental directions of Sergeant's theology. In the first place, when he refers to Tradition, he always

---

[19] l.c., n. 3, p. 43.
[20] l.c., n. 4, p. 45.
[21] l.c., n.7, p. 47.
[22] l.c., n. 12, p. 53.

considers the process rather than the contents, the active (to use expressions he was not familiar with) rather than the passive aspect, transmission rather than transmitted beliefs. Sergeant was aware of the difference between these points of view and he even complained that some Protestant disputants, confusing problems,

> take so wrong an aim that they dispute against *res traditae*, or the things delivered, instead of Tradition itself, and therefore accuse us for holding human Traditions, or things invented by men for faith. Whereas, when we speak of the Rule of Faith, we mean by the word Tradition only the method of publicly delivering and conveying down tenets held to have come from Christ in the manner before declared.[23]

In the second place, this channel of Christian beliefs is purely natural, in the sense that exactly the same process is universally used in education, whether we have in mind the transmission of purely natural knowledge, or that of the tenets of all religions. This universal phenomenon accounts, for instance, for the Moslems' knowledge of Mohammed and, in Protestantism, for the transmission of doctrines and the education of children and disciples.[24]

Yet if Sergeant underlies the universal process of Tradition, its natural self-evidence and indefectibility, which are due to the immediacy of contact between father and son, to the convergence of the same testimony given by all the fathers to all their children and to the practical impossibility of a gap in the transmission of knowledge between generations, he preserves a careful distinction between the common structure of all Tradition and the supernatural elements that are proper to Christian Tradition and reinforce its certainty. The natural factors of Tradition and the motives, "connatural to our souls",[25] which impel man to spread and legate what he knows, are "affected supernaturally" by "those motives supervening to mere nature, which we rightly call assistances of the Holy Ghost, in regard they are built on perfections of will in the faithful, or on virtues, the effects properly attributed to that divine person".[26] Since "grace is to perfect nature in whatever is good in it",[27] the Christian heart is more faithful to the truth of revelation than the natural one to the truth of nature; supernatural motives of love and hope are infinitely more

[23] l.c., n. 6, pp. 46-47.
[24] See l.c., *Ninth Discourse*, n. 2-3, pp. 82-84; *Third Discourse*, n. 5, p. 30; *Seventh Discourse*, n. 3, pp. 69-70.
[25] l.c., *Ninth Discourse*, n. 1, p. 81.
[26] l.c., p. 82.
[27] l.c., n. 6, p. 86.

compelling than natural motives of loyalty. Whatever certainty the natural phenomenon of tradition already enjoys is increased a thousandfold in Christian Tradition: "The advantage then with which Christian doctrine in the mind of each, and the Holy Ghost in the hearts of most of the faithful, rivet and confirm this natural care of credit to the preserving Tradition inviolable, is incomparable and in a manner infinite".[28]

Sergeant ends on an amazing page which I will quote in spite of its length: it shows that besides the strength of its natural certainty and the added force of its supernatural elements, Tradition enjoys the support of most sciences. It then becomes the epitome of all the human soul's achievements and privileges:

> It would require a large volume to unfold particularly how each virtue contributes to show the inerrable Indeficiency of Tradition, and how the Principles of almost each Science are concerned in demonstrating its Certainty: Arithmetic lends her Numbering and Multiplying Faculty to scan the vast number of Testifiers; Geometry her Proportions to show a kind of Infinite Strength of Certitude in Christian Tradition above those Attestations which breed Certainty in Human affairs; Logic her skill to frame and make us see the Connections it has with the Principles of our Understanding; Nature her Laws of Motion and Action; Morality, her first Principle that nothing is done gratis by a Cognoscitive Nature, and that the body of Traditionary Doctrine is most conformable to Practical Reason; Historical Prudence clears the Impossibility of an undiscernible revolt from points so descended and held so Sacred; Politics show this to be the best way imaginable to convey down such a Law as it concerns every man to be skillful in; Metaphysics engage the Essence of Things, and the very notion of Being which fixes every Truth, so establishing the scientific Knowledges which spring from each particular nature by their first Causes or Reasons exempt from change or motion; Divinity demonstrates it most worthy God and most conducive to bring Mankind to Bliss. Lastly, Controversy evidences the total Uncertainty of anything concerning Faith if this can be uncertain, and makes use of all the rest to establish the Certainty of this first Principle, and, which settled, secures Scripture as far as is requisite, and all things else that can mainly concern Salvation.[29]

The main section of *Sure-footing in Christianity* is followed by forty-one rather polemical corollaries which draw logical conclusions, relevant to the controversies of Sergeant's time, concerning the scope and absolute certainty of Tradition. Each of these takes the

---

[28] l.c., n. 13, pp. 92-93.
[29] l.c., n 14, pp. 93-94.

form of a brief thesis that is succinctly explained and justified. The first eleven theses rule those who are not "traditionally Christians" out of the number of the faithful. Theses 12 to 23 state that it is not possible to argue demonstratively against Tradition out of Scripture, reason, history or Tradition itself, thus leading to the conclusion that "there is no possibility of arguing against Tradition rightly understood, or the living voice of the Catholic Church, with any show of reason".[30] Theses 24 to 32 spell out the authority of Tradition in the Church and its consequences for the certainty of doctrine held by the whole body of the faithful and taught by Councils and by the Roman See. Nonetheless, according to corollaries 33 to 39, "erroneous opinions and (their proper effects) absurd practices may creep into the Church and spread there for a while"[31] (Cor. 33), although they cannot last very long and they may not be attributed to the Church herself. The last two corollaries underline the importance of "the knowledge of Tradition's certainty" as "the first principle in controversial divinity".[32]

In *A Letter of Thanks from the author of Sure-footing to his answerer J.T.* (Tillotson) (Paris, 1666), Sergeant confesses that, having shown his manuscript to some friend, he was advised to protect himself and his doctrine by quoting authorities, especially from the Fathers, in support of his own views, for fear less scholarly or more prejudiced readers would think his conception of Tradition a new one, invented as a polemical weapon to silence all non-traditionary divines. Following his friend's advice, Sergeant added a long esaay entitled "Consent of authority to the substance of the foregoing discourses". This is a systematic, if unavoidably incomplete garnering of testimonies from Scripture (p. 126-128), the early Councils (p. 129-130), the Fathers (p. 131-141), the Council of Trent (p. 141-149), followed by a few concluding pages.

In his citations from and comments on the Fathers, Sergeant adds some reflections, remarking that "though some Fathers and Councils speak highly of Scripture, as that it contains all faith, etc., it is first to be marked whether they speak of Scripture sensed, or as yet to be sensed; and if the latter, by whom, or whether any Father says that Scripture wrought upon by private interpretation and human wit is apt to ascertain faith (or be the rule of faith), which is the true point

---

[30] l.c., *Corollary 23*, p. 114.
[31] l.c., *Corollary 33*, p. 118.
[32] l.c., *Corollary 40*, p. 123.

between the renouncers of Tradition and us".[33] The Fathers also never suffer "to bend Tradition to the outward show the Scripture's letter seems to bear as interpreted by human skills, or to say universal Tradition is insufficient or uncertain unless the Scripture's letter thus interpreted came to clear or assist it".[34]

The most important passage refers to the Council of Trent, or rather to what the Church's "own living voice pronounced in her late famous representative, the Council of Trent".[35] Sergeant shows that "in every session definitive of faith it professes to follow Tradition, either in most express or equivalent terms",[36] and he quotes relevant texts from Sessions 4, 5, 6, 7, 13, 14, 21, 22, 23, 24, 25, in which the Council professes to follow the past in its uninterrupted transmission of faith, and "makes the suggestion of the Holy Ghost, or sanctity in the hearts of the faithful, efficacious to perpetuate the delivery of received doctrine",[37] thus pointing out the very heart of Tradition. The Council seldom mentions Scripture together with Tradition, "and when it does so, it only expressed that faith is contained in them, but when it brings places of Scriptures to ground definitions upon, it perpetually professes to interpret them by Tradition". The Council thus sees a great difference between Scripture "wordishly interpreted" [38]—which the *Letter of Thanks* calls "the airy gingling of words" [39] or even, "the critical method"—and "the practical way of interpreting Christ's sense, or Tradition, to the interpreting Scripture used by the Catholic Church": [40]

> In a word, Tradition gives us Christ's sense, that is, the life of the letter ascertained to our hands, which therefore must needs move the letter, its body, naturally; the other way takes the dead letter, and endeavours to move it artificially to counterfeit that life which it truly wants.

Once this sense is known and Scripture comes alive, the Catholic faith gives it primacy over all other documents, and "honours Scripture-testimony so as to put it before Tradition or the delivery

---

[33] l.c., *Consent of Authority*, n. 15, p. 140.
[34] l.c., n. 15, pp. 140-141.
[35] l.c., n. 16, p. 141.
[36] l.c., n. 16, pp. 141-142.
[37] l.c., n. 17, p. 145.
[38] l.c., n. 18, p. 43.
[39] *A Letter of Thanks*, p. 33.
[40] *Sure-footing . . .*, *Consent of Authority*, n. 18, p. 149.

of Christ's doctrine from hand to hand: Scripture, thus alleged and secured, having the same force as if the Apostle or Evangelist himself should sit in the Council and by way of living voice declared his own sense in the matter".[41]

In this painstaking study of Tradition, Sergeant does not breathe a word about the possibility of development, which, as we know, was a moot question with many Catholic controversalists of his time. It would even seem excluded by Corollary 31: "Tradidion established, nothing can be received by the Church as held from the first or ever, unless ever held", a thesis which is commented upon briefly: "Tradition is self-evidently a certain method of conveying down matters of fact as they were found; it follows that, Tradition established, points not ever held must be conveyed down such as they were found, that is, as not held ever, and consequently not as held from the first or ever".[42] However, one may still wonder if Tradition cannot convey doctrines known not to have been explicitly held from the beginning, and yet taught now by the living voice of the Church as implicitly included in Revelation. Yet that Sergeant would think along such lines remains doubtful in view of the fact that the following Corollaries mention only "erroneous opinions" as likely to "creep into the Church" in the course of time.

A point of view which at first sight appears complementary, is given some place in *A Letter of Thanks from the author of Sure-footing*, a book written, according to confidences made in the *Sixth Catholic Letter* [43] (1688), during a serious illness shortly after the publication of *Sure-footing*. In answer to objections proposed by Tillotson, John Sergeant distinguished "between the substance of Tradition (that is the infallibility of the living voice and practise of the Church essential in conveying down uninterruptedly Christ's doctrine), and the explication of it".[44] The former commits the Church; the second engages only individual Churchmen. What a man says or does "as a believer or Christian", is not the same as what he writes "as a divine", relying "on his own human skill in explicating faith or its grounds, and his talent in deducing right consequences". Nobody should then be surprised if the authorities in the Church often look askance at theological explications. For whereas speculation may

---

[41] l.c., n. 19, pp. 149-150.
[42] l.c., *Corollary 31*, p. 118.
[43] *Sixth Catholic Letter*, p. 23.
[44] *A Letter of Thanks*, p. 20.

open new avenues of thought, the Church feels a natural reluctance to newness:

> Those explications of divinity looking new to them, and it being the natural genius of the followers of Tradition to be jealous of anything that is new, and this not only in faith but also in explications of faith, in regard these pretend a coherence and connection with faith itself, it seems to me to sound a laudable zeal both in them and others to be suspicious of and less a friend at first to what is new, till it be farther looked into and appear innocent.[45]

Sergeant does not say what part theological explication may play in the successive transmission of Christian teaching. Yet, although doctrine must be handed down just as it was received in the beginning, he certainly envisages some progresses in the course of this transmission and at least the apparent mutation which is at times occasioned by heresy. Thus Sergeant warns that he is going to "amuse" Tillotson with "another paradox", "namely that the deserting Tradition strengthens it; I mean that Tradition, when a heresy arises, gains more of intensiveness and vigor than it loses in its extensiveness; nay, that the intensiveness that accrues to it by that means is the way to make it branch out afterwards into a far greater extent".[46] The intensiveness in question results mainly from the subjective reaction of those who, refusing to follow the heretics, strengthen their own faith thereby. It is also the effect of the stricter discipline which authority, alerted by revolt, imposes in order to reform Church-life. "The faithful not only grow more virtuous by the reformation of Church-discipline, but even by the calumnies of their adversaries; again the learned party in the Church are excited to far greater industry and consequently knowledge. . .".[47]

The course of the Church's reaction to heresy is traced by Sergeant, who sees it passing through several steps: promotion of "worthy officers"; renewed recommendation of "the points of faith to the *Ecclesia credens*, as the *depositum* preserved uninterruptedly in the Church from Christ and his apostles";[48] making "these more intelligible and rational by explicating them more at large"; defining and declaring them "in language more properly suiting to the sense writ in the hearts of the faithful"; lastly, excommunication of heretics.

---

[45] l.c., pp. 21-22.
[46] l.c., p. 99.
[47] l.c., pp. 102-103.
[48] l.c., p. 102.

All in all, the Church arises from such crises on the bright side, for "by occasion of a heresy (which purifies the Church of all her ill humors, and rectifies and makes sound what remains) Tradition renews as it were its youth and recovers its vigor",[49] the outcome being a greater incentive to the geographic expansion of the message.

Whatever development takes place affects the depths of our commitments, the adequacy of our explanations, our missionary activity; but no objective enlargement of the deposit is envisioned.

Sure-footing was published in 1665. 1666 was the fatal year of the Great Fire of London. According to his reminiscences in the *Sixth Catholic Letter*, John Sergeant was barely recovering from the serious illness during which he had been persuaded to write his ironic *Letter of Thanks* to Tillotson, whom he thanked for refuting him so ineptly that his own cause had been strengthened by criticism! In the enemy camp however, two and two were being put together, and some connection was suspected between the fiery writings of Sergeant and the Great Fire of the City. Accused of helping to spread the fire by "a friend of Tillotson", Sergeant was warned in time and fled to safety in the Netherlands where he remained four months. Returning to his country after the hysteria spread by the Fire had quieted down, he resumed his polemical writing career, successively producing *Faith Vindicated* (1667), *Reason against Raillery* (1672), *Error Nonplust, or Dr. Stillingfleet shown to be the man of no principles, with an Essay how discourses concerning Catholic grounds bear the highest evidence* (1673), *Method to arrive at satisfaction in religion* (1674).

The major themes of *Sure-footing* are taken up and explained, chiefly in *Error Nonplust*, although in a more polemical vein than formerly, with frequent digs at Stillingfleet, who "though he have a very good wit, yet by reason of his sole application to verbal divinity which never reaches the ground or bottom of anything it talks of, is very ignorant of what is meant by Christian life and its opposite, vice or sin".[50] Whereas he praises Herbert Thorndike for his understanding of the ground of faith, Sergeant does not think much of Stillingfleet's principles, and intends "to discover their oppositeness to all logic, true learning and common rationality, and that there is nothing at all in him of what was pretended, neither principles,

---

[49] l.c., p. 103.
[50] *Error Nonplust*, p. 191.

consequences, connection, conclusion, reduction, influence nor end".[51]

Sergeant's own stance has not wavered since the time of *Sure-footing in Christianity*. Tradition is still "the way of open attestation of a world of immediate Christian fathers to a world of children by living voice and constant practise of what they had learned by their daily sensations";[52] it is "no more but delivery of faith by daily teaching and practise of immediate forefathers to their respective children; and it is not possible that men should be ignorant of that to which they were educated, of that which they daily saw, and heard, and did".[53] But Sergeant has been accused by Protestants of differing from other Catholics on this matter of the Rule of Faith, and his arguments have now taken an occasionally apologetical tone. There is a new edge to his voice, in which one may feel the concern of one who is suspected, though it be by Protestants, of not being totally Catholic. That his language may be at variance with that of other theologians, Sergeant does not deny. But the problem is always—our author is still fundamentally interested in method—to sift the things meant from the words used. Alas, it would be easy to reach purely verbal agreement, against which Sergeant gives this timely warning:

> And I much doubt should any Catholic divine out of a charitable intention of union (which I shall ever commend and heartily approve) trusting to the equivocalness of the word, say that Scripture is the Rule or a Rule, I much doubt (I say) that, when the thing comes to be examined to the bottom, it will scarce tend to any good; for however words may bend, yet the true grounds of Catholic faith are inflexible; and we must take heed that, while we yield them the word, they expect not (as they may justly, having such an occasion) that we should grant the thing properly signified by that word; which if they do, we must either recede or else forgo Catholic grounds.[54]

Between himself and some other Catholics, Sergeant grants, there may be a discrepancy in words, though not in things;[55] between Catholics and Protestants there is disharmony in things even when words are common. Differences in vocabulary concerning the Rule of Faith arise from the fact that this expression is metaphorical when used to mean "a spiritual or intellectual direction". If the metaphor is used properly, to indicate which principles send us to the right

---

[51] l.c., *Preface to the learned of this nation*.
[52] l.c., p. 39.
[53] l.c., p. 248.
[54] l.c., pp. 49-50.
[55] l.c., p. 44.

direction, all agree that it then denotes the living voice or Tradition of the Church; yet some authors take it improperly, in the sense of a "container of Christ's doctrine".[56] Only in this improper meaning can it be applied to Scripture.

This distinction of two meanings, proper and improper, of Rule of Faith, is, as Sergeant explains, basic to the Council of Trent, for which the Rule of Faith is always the Tradition. Of Scripture the Tridentine Fathers say "only that it contains faith, as also Tradition does; but whether it contains it in such a manner that all those who are to have faith by relying on it, may by so doing be absolutely secured from erring, which is requisite over and above to make it in true speech deserve the name of a rule, the Council says nothing".[57]

Where then do Catholic authors differ? Sergeant, who has hitherto paid scant attention to the dualistic theology, now alludes to it:

> I am sure the distinction now given shows my sentiment consistent, if not perfectly agreeing, with that common opinion of our divines, that Scripture is a partial rule, or that Scripture and Tradition integrate one complete rule. For they clearly mean by those words that faith is partly contained in Scripture, partly in the Tradition of the Church. So that what they had an eye to in so doing was not the evidence requisite to a rule, but only the degree of extent of Scripture to the matter contained in it; whence it is evident they meant only that Scripture contained some part of faith, which I perfectly allow to it, and perhaps more.[58]

"Perhaps more": Sergeant does not feel quite happy with the theory of partial containers of faith. As usual, his main interest lies in the formal rather than the material aspect of Tradition. Revelation and Tradition may designate an act or a thing, a way of delivery or a thing delivered, an action or its effect, a showing or the thing shown. The context ought to show the true significance of the term used. And Sergeant notes that it ordinarily refers to the "thing revealed or delivered"[59] when the article is used: "a divine revelation, or a tradition", or, in the plural, "divine revelations or traditions". His preference, however, is to refer consistently to the act of delivery. As for the contents thus transmitted, it remains doubtful whether man's limited capacity of grasping the fulness of God's message may be transferred to the message itself. Therefore, "perhaps more":

---

[56] l.c., p. 46.
[57] l.c., p. 47.
[58] l.c., p. 49.
[59] l.c., p. 25.

perhaps there is more in Scripture than meets the eye. To contain is also a metaphor: it really means to signify; and the significance of an event cannot always be materially restricted to the visible boundaries of it. Thus John Sergeant is led to admit the full extent of Scripture as conceived by Stillingfleet:

> I grant those Holy Books contain all he pretends, some way or other, either implicitly or explicitly; either in express words or by necessary consequence.

The following proviso does not limit the contents of the Books, but the manner in which we know them:

> But that those Books contain, or signify (for they are the same) all that is to be believed and practised so evidently that all persons who sincerely endeavor to know their meaning, and this for all future ages, may thence alone (as his discourse aims to evince), that is, without the Church's interpretation, arrive to know what is necessary for their salvation with such a certainty as is requisite for the nature and ends of faith and the obligation annexed to it, I absolutely deny.[60]

This tallies with the doctrine of Vincent of Lerins, for whom the Canon of Scripture is "perfect and sufficient for all things", yet "it is not said simply: It suffices for all things; but: *Sufficit sibi ad omnia*: it is sufficient to itself for all things, which can only mean that it has all the perfection due to its own nature".[61] Sergeant concludes: "Since then I allow Scripture all sufficiency and perfection but this of being sufficiently clear to private understanding so as to build their faith on their own interpretation of it, I allow it all this learned Father or the ancient Church ever did".[62] Still commenting on Vincent of Lerins, Sergeant agrees that the reason why a private spirit cannot fathom Scripture does not lie in any fault of man, but in "the depth or deep sense of the Scriptures", for there is a "disproportion of the Scripture to private understandings in dogmatical points of Christianity, as I constantly maintain".[63] Understanding Scripture needs "the sense of the Catholic Church", which is ultimately the rule of faith. This sense, for Vincent, "is intimated to be antecedent to all interpretation of Scripture, and therefore the Church must have had this sense or knowledge of faith by Tradition, there being no other way becoming God's ordinary providence but these two". Finally,

---

[60] l.c., p. 86.
[61] l.c., p. 269.
[62] l.c., pp. 269-270.
[63] l.c., p. 270.

Vincent of Lerins' position is far removed from a simply dualistic view of Scripture and Tradition as two distinct containers of faith: "It is most evident", Sergeant believes, "that when in the former chapter he mentioned the authority of the divine Law (meaning the Scripture) and the Tradition of the Catholic Church, he meant them jointly". It is equally distant from the Protestant contention that faith is found through the Scriptures. The purpose of the joint action of Scripture and the Church in Christian life is not to bring men to faith, but to preserve faith in those who already believe:

> And since he attributes in this chapter convictiveness of what is faith only to the Church's sense, it is manifest all that remains to be attributed to Scripture is agreeableness of its letter (if a good pastor expound it) to the present faith of the Church, to see which exceedingly comforts faith in the hearts of the already faithful, who must needs have a high reverence for the Holy Scriptures' authority.[64]

While he was still parrying blows from Protestants, John Sergeant found himself suddenly attacked from another side. In 1675 a certain Lominus, who was widely rumored to be Peter Talbot, archbishop of Dublin (1620-1680), published at Ghent *Blackloanae Haeresis Confutatio*,[65] in which White's conception of Tradition was branded as being pelagian and naturalistic. The links between White and Sergeant were clear. "I account Rushworth's *Dialogues* my best friend",[66] had Sergeant stated in *A Letter of Thanks*, where he also admitted not having read Henry Holden's *Analysis Divinae Fidei* for the simple reason that he had been assured Holden went the way of Rushworth's *Dialogues*.[67] Little surprise then that the *Fifth Catholic Letter* presents *Haeresis Blackloana* as designedly written against Sergeant, although he was then satisfied that Lominus was not Peter Talbot and that the Archbishop of Dublin could be quoted as supporting his doctrine.[68] However, this may be, Sergeant's teaching was examined by judges selected by the Archbishop of Paris. The judges found his doctrine orthodox.[69]

Soon, the problem moved to Rome, where Sergeant was denounced to the Inquisition and five of his books accused of containing hetero-

---

[64] l.c., p. 271.
[65] A second book was published at Lyon in 1678, with the following title: *Scutum Inexpugnabile Fidei adversus haeresim blackloanam*.
[66] *A Letter of Thanks*, p. 62.
[67] l.c., p. 30.
[68] *Fifth Catholic Letter*, pp. 26-27.
[69] l.c., pp. 18-22.

dox opinions. In the event, Sergeant was again cleared of heterodoxy, although a certain ambiguity was found in his way of speaking and he received an admonition to make his meaning clearer. The following passage, as quoted by Sergeant himself, is indicative of the concerns of the Holy Office:

Si D. Sergeantius existimat unum ex potioribus mediis convincendi hereticos protestantes et trahendi ad catholicam fidem esse traditionem dogmatum quae perpetuo fuit in Catholica Ecclesia ideoque eos teneri ad ea recipienda, et hanc traditionem ipse appellat Regulam Fidei, clarius debet id exponere, et docere quod non loquitur de requisitis intrinsecis ad credendum, sed de extrinsecis praecedentibus actum credendi et disponentibus hereticos, ut profertur, ad credendum.[70]

The Roman censors exhibited their interest in both the conversion of Protestants and the purity of the Catholic faith in regard to the supernatural structure of the act of faith. Sergeant's primary concern had not been the conversion of heretics, but the investigation of truth; and his inquiry had not been focused on the intrinsic nature of the act of faith, but on the phenomenon of the transmission of faith over the ages by human means. Sergeant had no difficulty clearing himself of all suspicions and, as far as Rome was concerned, the matter went no further. In 1677, he published *Clypeus Septemplex*, which directly answered the *monitio* he had received and was addressed to his judges at the Holy Office. He clarified his position as to the meaning of the expression Rule of Faith, and certified that the Rule of Faith, as envisioned by himself, is antecedent and exterior to the act of faith: "I did not speak of what is intrinsically necessary to believe, but of external factors which precede the act of faith and prepare heretics to believe".[71] In the matter of Tradition, Sergeant had not meant "the things transmitted, in which sense this word is frequently used by the authors insofar as it is distinguished from the written dogmas; but the very transmission or translation of the dogmas which, handed down by hand, are found in the Catholic Church either in Holy Scripture or in the Traditions".[72] Tradition in this dynamic sense he called the Rule of Faith.

This little exchange with Roman authorities, annoying as it must have been, helped Sergeant to focus his own thought. For another apology written during that period introduces an important distinc-

---

[70] *Clypeus Septemplex*, p. 22.
[71] l.c., p. 23.
[72] l.c., p. 24.

tion between two aspects of Tradition. In *Vindiciae Joannis Sergeantii* (1678), Sergeant replies to Lominus rather than to the Holy Office. "The entire controversy", he explains, "lies in whether one can prove, independently of the supernatural infallibility of the Church (which they—that is, Protestants—deny) that the faith now confessed by the Catholic Roman Church has been transmitted by Christ and the Apostles".[73] Having renounced the supernatural Tradition, Protestants are unable to conclude to the apostolicity of the Catholic faith. But such a position is logical only if there is no purely natural means of ascertaining that Catholic doctrine has indeed been transmitted from the beginning. The main point of Sergeant's theology is precisely to insist that there is such a means, "the human witness of the Catholic Roman Church".[74] It is this purely human testimony that Sergeant's works often call "principle of faith, foundation of faith, premise, motive or means to prove faith, rule of faith, justification for faith".[75] In such a context the supernatural infallibility of the Church does not come into question. The only point is that the Church, as a human society, gives a reliable testimony to the transmission of its doctrine in the past and from the past to the present. She enjoys a "natural infallibility",[76] so that there are in reality two rules of faith, natural and supernatural, with two distinct scopes. "The natural is a rule that proves faith to the heterodox precisely as being Christian, that is, transmitted by Christ; the supernatural is a rule that proves to the faithful that it is also divine". The latter belongs intrinsically to the act of faith, which trusts in God revealing himself; the former is preliminary to faith, implying only a historical judgement on the continuous transmission of belief from the beginning. "Therefore, by 'evident motive', I did not envisage some means which would be interior to the article (of faith), but rather the natural principles that are fundamental to the certainty of Tradition or of the Church's human testimony".[77]

The ambition of *theologia controversialis* is precisely to demonstrate the rule of faith "in relation to us", namely as the human witness of father to son down the centuries.[78] The supernatural aspect of the rule of faith cannot be forgotten. The process of transmission (is

---

[73] l.c., pp. 8-9.
[74] l.c., p. 9.
[75] l.c., p. 10.
[76] l.c., p. 11.
[77] l.c., p. 31.
[78] l.c., p. 103.

guided by the Spirit. Yet historical study cannot assess this dimension and must restrict its attention to observable facts. As transmission of doctrine, Tradition is empirically knowable; as channel of Revelation, it belongs to the realm of faith. What Sergeant claims to prove beyond doubt is that Tradition does hand down the Apostles' message; what he then presents to faith is that this message is Revelation. Thus the separate domains of the intrinsic structure of the act of faith and of the legitimate independence of human sense-experience are respected.

Another ten years, and Sergeant's controversy with Stillingfleet over the Rule of Faith flared up again, this time in the form of a series of long "letters" published in 1687-1688. Sergeant's contribution is called *Five Catholic Letters concerning the means of knowing with absolute certainty what faith now held was taught by Christ, upon occasion of a conference between Dr. Stillingfleet and Mr. Peter Gooden* (London, 1688). There were in reality six letters, the first five appearing openly in London with royal license under James II, the sixth being clandestinely published after the revolution that expelled the Catholic king and brought William and Mary from the Netherlands. The letters are interesting for their autobiographical contents, for they—mainly the last two—tell the story of Sergeant's previous controversies and the difficulties aroused by Lominus. Doctrinally, Sergeant follows the line already drawn in *Sure-footing*. Tradition is still described as "a testimony for doctrine received",[79] "a delivery of a practical doctrine, publicly preached to great multitudes at first, practised by them, and held and recommended as divine and the way to salvation".[80] Sergeant still wonders why Protestants hesitate to recognize such a phenomenon: "I cannot for my heart discern what great difficulty there can be to remember all along their yesterday's faith, or to be willing to be guided and instructed by their yesterday's fathers, teachers and pastors, especially the sense of the points (to omit many other means) being determined by open and daily practise".[81]

Again we find the insistence, which became stronger after the Holy Office's intervention, on the two aspects, human and divine, of Tradition, namely the observable phenomenon of transmission by

---

[79] *Third Catholic Letter*, n. 16, p. 34.
[80] l.c., n. 29, p. 56.
[81] l.c., n. 22, p. 23.

human means, from hand to hand, from mouth to ear, and the invisible guidance of the Spirit over this historical process. As a visible series of witnesses and of acts of witnessing, Tradition engenders what Sergeant now calls—rather unfortunately—a "human faith" in the transmission of Christ's authentic doctrine, which is propedeutic to divine faith in its revealed truth:

> The immediate effect then of our Tradition is human faith; the remote effect is to give us knowledge of a doctrine of faith which is divine, not proved to be such by Tradition, but acknowledged to be so by our mutual concession. . . Human faith is the way or means to know divine faith.[82]

The pelagianism of which Sergeant has been accused by "but one unknown nameless author Lominus" [83] is still carefully eschewed, the formal cause of faith being entirely distinct from the historical means of conveying doctrine. Yet the rationality of the act of faith requires something else besides supernatural assent: it demands a reasonable satisfaction that the doctrine taught by the Church is indeed that of Christ and his Apostles. "No authority", Sergeant states, "deserves any assent farther than reason gives it to deserve".[84] Thus he has pinpointed the function of Tradition in relation to faith; it is to manifest the historical reliability of the Church's proposal of the Christian message. Yet Sergeant would not be put out, were one to retort that the reconstruction of Tradition, as done by historical science, provides no apodictic proof of the Church's fidelity to the original kerygma. For the sort of proof that reason demands in this order does not belong to that of quantitative demonstration. The "judgement of discretion" must be qualitative, tending to "find out a certain light to walk by in those sublime passages in which the light of our own reason is very dim".[85] And one may say of it what Sergeant suggests of the belief in infallibility: it "does not so much need proof as reflection".[86]

That Tradition or the Rule of Faith are not robots that work automatically, but invite sincere on-lookers to pass judgement on them, makes it possible for mistakes to be made and misunderstandings to be entertained. This is, in Sergeant's opinion, the sad

---

[82] *Fifth Catholic Letter*, n. 78, p. 148.
[83] l.c., n. 55, p. 93.
[84] *Second Catholic Letter*, n. 5, p. 6.
[85] *Fifth Catholic Letter*, n. 53, p. 87.
[86] *Second Catholic Letter*, n. 33, p. 39.

situation of the Anglicans, who themselves claim to stand by Tradition while they actually distort it. When Anglicans plead Tradition, "it is but finding some expressions in an ancient writer, not couched with prophetical foresight enough to avoid being understood as some will desire it should, and it will serve turn to pretend to antiquity, and bear the name of Tradition".[87]

On one point the *Catholic Letters* mark a definite advance on Sergeant's previous work. We have seen him timidly broaching the matter of development in *A Letter of Thanks*. Now he looks at the problem squarely and deeply. The *Second Catholic Letter* briefly answers the objection that "blind zeal, ignorant devotion, superstitions, rigour and vain credulity" can add false doctrines to the original deposit. This he denies, as contrary to the very notion of Tradition as the daily transmission of what was believed yesterday. Yet he continues:

> Though perhaps some points involved in the main body of faith, yet so particularly or universally known, might, on emergent occasions, be singled out, defined, and more specially recommended than formerly, without detriment to the faith received, but rather to the advantage and further explication of it.[88]

Sergeant thus looks toward a flowering of the deposit of faith as it were from inside, which does not nullify his basic observation that "Innovation and Tradition being formerly and diametrically opposite, what proves she could not innovate proves also that she could not leave Tradition, for this were to innovate".[89] Again, the *Fifth Letter* alludes to this, asking Stillingfleet why he does not attempt to answer "that most concerning point proved against him, that the Church has power to declare diverse propositions to be of faith, not held distinctly before, without any prejudice at all to Tradition".[90]

It is, however, in the *Third Letter* that Sergeant endeavors to treat the question thoroughly. The process of what he calls "unfolding" is illustrated with the help of two related analogies, the progress of thought in every human being, and the literary phenomenon of the development of a theme, here the topic of a sermon. The first analogy is well depicted by Sergeant, who, in this, largely anticipates New-

---

[87] *First Catholic Letter*, n. 17, p. 18.
[88] *Second Catholic Letter*, n. 48, p. 62.
[89] l.c., n. 49, p. 63.
[90] *Fifth Catholic Letter*, n. 91, p. 165.

man's future considerations on development of dogma as the unfolding of an idea:

> You may please to reflect on what you already know by experience, that, let any man advance a single tenet, and afterwards, upon occasion, set himself to explicate at large the sense of that proposition, it is plain, there will be found in that large explication many particular propositions, not adequately the same, but in part different from that which he went about thus elaborately and distinctly to explain; of which perhaps even himself was not aware while he did not reflect, not being yet invited to make it clearer or to dilate on it. And yet he held, even at first, the sense (and not only the words), nay the whole sense of that main tenet or sentences; though he saw not distinctly every single proposition contained in it, till he became obliged to scan and study his own, undistinguished, but true, thoughts concerning it.[91]

The two horns of the dilemma of doctrinal development come to light in this analogy. The "tenet" is the same before and after its explanation; there is not more in the fully explained congeries of particular ideas than in the first pregnant though single general idea. Yet the final result of reflection is at least partly different from the original form of what was later investigated, reflected upon, explained and elaborated.

The scope of Sergeant's conception becomes clearer as his second analogy unfolds. By selecting the case of a preacher who makes a number of doctrinal and moral reflections about a scriptural passage taken as the "text" of his sermon, Sergeant actually suggests a multiple analogy. The orator's comments are, from one point of view, drawn from the verses of Scripture that inspired them; from another, they originate in the preacher's own mind and are added by him to the text he has borrowed. Here the psychological and intellectual process of advancing thought, the scriptural phenomenon of layers of authentic spiritual meaning under one letter, the traditional emergence of posterior explanation without which the anterior writing would not be understood by many: all these factors tend to create a singularly complex convergence in thought which may be equally well described as an increase of thought being brought to bear on the original Scripture, or as the text itself unveiling its meaning into the reflection it occasions:

> The same may be said of every sermon and its text, supposing it be rigorously held to, and no more be attended to but to explain its

---

[91] *Third Catholic Letter*, n. 6, p. 16.

intrinsic and full meaning. In which case, the preacher sticks not to assure his auditory that what he has preached to them all the while is God's Word, and to press them to regard it as such, as far as his small authority over them can reach. And had he more, in case he did verily judge his explication of that text was genuine and, consequently, Christ's true sense, he would questionless esteem himself bound to make use of that authority to his utmost, to edify them with the explicit belief of each particular contained in so excellent a truth.[92]

Sergeant nicely ties this up, in the hypothesis of a preacher who has "more authority", with the Church's development of her faith and the implied possibility of defining further doctrine:

This being so, why should not the same privilege be granted to the Church and her pastors, to explicate, upon due occasion, the sense of Christ's faith, in many particular propositions involved in the main tenet (even though we should suppose them to be not heard of, perhaps not distinctly thought of, before), which is allowed to every private man and any ordinary preacher? [93]

Here again, what is thus defined is, from one point of view, "newly singled out", and from another, "included" in accepted points of faith. In which case, it is not for the sake of novelty that new insights into the datum are defined, but "out of their duty and zeal to preserve Christ's faith entire". The proper way of conserving the faith may pass through further definitions. It is, as we may paraphrase it, not only through the past that the present should be understood; it is also through our anticipation of the future that we may understand the past.

John Sergeant takes very seriously the basic objection that this is no longer Tradition, but addition. Yet he falls back upon the related concept of infolding and unfolding. "I distinguish", he says:

These propositions were held ever and descended ever as they were involved in the entire point; in the bowels of which the sense of those others were found. But as singled out in such and such particularizing manners of expression, they were (perhaps) not held ever, I say, not held ever formerly, at least not universally. Which is the true reason why some private writers, nay possibly some great men, might (out of a dutiful fear not to add to faith) have doubted of them, perhaps opposed them; till the collective Church, or some great body of them, who are able to look more intelligently into those points, declared and unfolded the sense of the main article, in which they were hitherto enwrapped.[94]

---

[92] l.c., n. 6, pp. 16-17.
[93] l.c., n. 6, p. 17.
[94] l.c., n. 7, pp. 17-18.

Truly, such an unwrapping may take many forms in different places and times, so that various points may have been at times "more particularly explicated in some parts of the body of the Church than in others".[95] But whatever the special history of each Christian dogma, it remains that, when the process Sergeant has described has taken place, a point "included in the total sense" has been "disclosed by a full explication of it". In other words, it has come "to be discovered to be a part of it, that is, in part it".

"A part of it, that is, in part it": this cryptic expression well sums up Sergeant's theology of development. What reflection discovers in the faith is already the faith, and therefore was it all along. Yet without reflection, this would never have been perceived. And the reflection in question, intellectual and rational as it must be, belongs also to other orders of reality. According to what light, Sergeant asks himself, does the Church "come by this knowledge of making implicit points explicit?" He answers:

> By Tradition, giving her the sense of Christ's whole law and each entire point of it; and by the light of nature purified by supernatural knowledges antecedently; as also by her application, when occasion required, to reflect upon and penetrate deeply into that sense; which enables her to explicate her own thoughts (or the points of faith) more clearly now; which she has indeed before, but did not so distinctly look into them or set herself to explain them.[96]

With John Sergeant, English Catholic theology reaches a peak that it will never climb again until Newman, a century and a half later. Admittedly, Sergeant's thought should not be separated from that of his predecessors and contemporaries. The entire century was concerned with problems in the theology of Tradition; and Sergeant's trail had been blazed by some of his more perceptive forerunners. There were few negligible authors among the Recusants of the 17th century, and several attained to genuine theological stature. Matthew Kellison, Thomas Worthington, William Bishop, Edward Maihew, Lawrence Anderson, Serenus Cressy, Vincent Canes, were controversialists of real value. Christopher Davenport, Thomas White and Henry Holden undoubtedly rank in a higher category, where John Sergeant belongs too. Sergeant harvested where his predecessors had sown the seed and watered the ground.

---

[95] l.c., p. 18.
[96] l.c., n. 33, p. 63.

CHAPTER ELEVEN

THE RECUSANTS AND LATER THEOLOGY

The preceding chapters have shown us the English Recusants as a highly articulate and diversified group of churchmen and authors who, in the unfavorable circumstances of exile or of the penal legislation in England, produced an imposing literature of theological controversy. They polemicized extensively against Anglicans and Protestants and, no less bitterly, among themselves. But they also did better than polemicize. They attempted to deal responsibly with some of the major problems inherited from the later Middle Ages and the sixteenth century. The present volume has examined their positions on four related topics, Scripture, Tradition or the traditions, the nature of faith, the development of doctrine. In at least two other areas, the spiritual life and sacramental theology, their contributions are well worth studying.[1] What A. C. Southern wrote of the sixteenth century Recusants can be applied, *mutatis mutandis*, to their successors in the seventeenth century: ". . .even the theological treatises of the Recusants had a much wider vogue than has generally been supposed, and we would maintain. . . that we cannot neglect these treatises if we are to gain a right perspective of Elizabethan literature and life".[2] Replace Elizabethan by Stuart, and this quotation is valid for the seventeenth century. The Recusants contributed to the English religious literature of the period. And their contribution, which has its own value in the context of Catholic theology, can also help to understand the Anglican development, at least in relation to Chillingworth and to Stillingfleet.

Admittedly, the Recusants' theological problems and positions do not make so engrossing a story as those of seventeenth century Anglicanism, during the preparation, the happening, and the sequel of what Herbert Thorndike called "the tragedy of the Church of England",[3] namely the Puritan Commonwealth. Caroline divine,

---

[1] Horton Davies's *Worship and Theology in England. From Andrewes to Baxter and Fox, 1603-1690*, Princeton, 1975, is a recent example of a valuable study which would have gained from a better knowledge of Recusant literature.

[2] A. C. Southern, *Elizabethan Recusant Prose, 1559-1582*, London, 1950, p. 43.

[3] Herbert Thorndike, *Epilogue to the Tragedy of the Church of England*, 1659; see *The Quest for Catholicity*, ch. 4.

Puritan, Covenanter, Highchurchman, Cambridge Platonist move on the broad canvass of English history at the very moment when, partly under the impact of religious struggles at home, this is branching out into American history. In comparison, the quarrels among the small group of the Recusants—between secular and regular, between Blackloist and Jesuit, between the English College at Douai and Thomas White—may well seem to be tempests in a tea cup. Yet at least Christopher Davenport, Thomas White and John Sergeant deserve to be ranked among the important theologians of England at the time, along with many of the Anglicans and with Richard Baxter among the Puritans. In the Catholicism of the Counter-Reformation, the Recusants are not of the calibre of the great systematicians of Spain or Italy, like Bellarmine or Suarez. They do not have the leisure to write the kind of historical theological synthesis that is being produced in France by Petau and Thomassin. They do not have the biblical scholarship of Richard Simon. Yet, as theologians, they easily support comparison with the most famous of their French contemporaries, such as Bossuet or Fénelon.[4]

As has already been noted, on several points the English Recusants anticipated the theology of more recent years. Davenport stands out on several counts. His interest in the Thirty-nine Articles makes him remarkably ecumenical, eager to dialogue rather than to polemicize. Whatever the singularities of his interpretation of the Articles, his endeavor to formulate a Catholic theology of fundamentals also throws ecumenical light on his thinking, since the distinction between fundamentals and non-fundamentals is basic to the theology of the Caroline divines. Further, his approach to the meaning of the Tridentine decree on Scripture and the apostolic traditions underlines his modernity. He anticipates questions that were asked shortly before Vatican Council II. And his interpretation of the decree is not far from that which was proposed by Josef Geiselmann.[5] If, as Geiselmann indicates, the Anglican William Palmer, of Worcester College, an Oxford man who participated in the Tractarian movement, interpreted *and*, in the Tridentine expression, "Scripture and the apostolic traditions" as a non-distributive and simply connective conjunction,

---

[4] On these aspects of seventeenth-century France, see *La Tradition au XVIIe siècle*.

[5] Josef Geiselmann, *Das Konzil von Trient über das Verhältnis der Heiligen Schrift und der nicht geschriebenen Traditionen* (Michael Schmaus, ed., *Die mündliche Überlieferung*, Munich, 1956, pp. 123-206).

this was already Davenport's understanding. Whether or not Davenport was a source of Palmer, his explanation of the Council of Trent breaks the supposed unanimity of the Counter-Reformation's reading of a two-source theory of Scripture and Tradition in the Tridentine decree.

Be that as it may, it is in reference to the problem of doctrinal development that the contribution of the Recusants is the most startling, given the subsequent history of the problem in England. A more detailed study of this history will provide a test case of the intrinsic importance of the theology of the Recusants.

Already in the sixteenth century, some of the Catholic polemicists and theologians showed awareness of the problem. Johannes Driedo or Johannes Faber denied any development (without however using this expression). Yet Alonso de Castro and Albert Pighius affirmed that a progressive understanding of the apostolic faith takes place. But this growth in wisdom, this "very great progress" remains, for Pighius, in line with the Vincentian canon of apostolicity, unanimity, universality. For a few authors, this progress in understanding is coupled with the reception of new revelations in the Church, when from time to time the Holy Spirit inspires a Council or even a theologian. By and large, however, what Jacobus Latomus calls the "life and growth" which God gives to the Church are not a matter of new revelations; they are a progressive understanding of the "Gospel in the heart", which is understood more thoroughly as the Church grows older and wiser. Similar positions and expressions are found among the Elizabethan Recusants, notably Thomas Harding.[6]

All in all, however, the sixteenth century did not develop theories of development. The problem was posited by the Reformers with remarkable lucidity if also with some degree of acrimony: What was the nature of the medieval accretions to faith, worship and ceremonies? Were these additions necessary, legitimate, permissible, regrettable, intolerable? Were they the result of divine guidance over the Church or of human idolatrous arrogance? By insisting on the twofold standard of Scripture and of justification by faith, the Reformers sought to guarantee the purity of Christian faith and life through the conjunction of a material and a formal principle of judgment. This did not make development impossible. But it placed most lawful develop-

---

[6] See *Holy Writ or Holy Church*, ch. 8-11.

ments in the category of *adiaphora*, of non-obligatory ceremonies or opinions.

Because their primary concern was to preserve what had hitherto been developed, the Catholics had a more difficult problem on their hands. In the sixteenth century, the most alert among them showed awareness of this problem, and a few stated some basic principles regarding it. But they themselves did not yet find the categories in which some sort of satisfactory solution could be couched. Candido Pozo's study of the Spanish scholastics of the period shows that the theologians of Salamanca contributed to the solution of the problem chiefly through their concept of tradition as the very life of the Church.[7] This allowed them to break out of the narrow problematic of the central question which they, like the other late scholastics, faced: Are theological conclusions definable as dogmas of faith? As Marín-Sola had already shown, the Counter-Reformation's discussion of the definability of theological conclusions dealt with the problem of doctrinal development.[8] While they could not meet the Reformers' concern for authenticity in the formulation of faith, these debates gave rise to "logical" theories according to which rational deduction from scriptural or traditional premises is the proper means of the development of doctrine. In this case, development appears as the unfolding of the logical implications of Revelation. It evidently presupposes that Revelation is available to us in propositional form: only propositions embody ideas in such a way that deductions can be made.

In contrast with this logical-rational approach, Jan Walgrave describes two other types of conceptions as emerging in the seventeenth and eighteenth centuries.[9] "Transformistic" theories of development are associated with Latitudinarianism, to be later adopted and transformed by the Liberal Protestantism of the nineteenth century under the influence of Hegel and other German philosophers. The properly "theological" theory of development emerges later: it is a product of the nineteenth century, where it appears in Germany with the School of Tübingen, especially in the writings of Johann Adam Möhler, and in England with John Henry Newman.

Whereas Pozo's study was intentionally limited to Spain, Jan

---

[7] Candido Pozo, l.c., pp. 253-263.

[8] Marín-Sola, *La Evolución Homogenea del Dogma Católico*, Madrid, 1952.

[9] Jan Walgrave, *Unfolding Revelation*, Philadelphia, 1972; see Richard Boeckler, *Der Moderne Römisch-Katholische Traditionsbegriff*, Göttingen, 1966.

Walgrave's attempted to outline the entire history of the problem of
development of doctrine. Yet one group of authors has been missed,
the English Recusants of the seventeenth century. As we have seen,
Paulinus Cressy, Thomas Bailey, Vincent Canes, Edward Worsley,
Henry Holden, Abraham Woodhead, John Sergeant spoke about the
development of doctrine. The question was raised explicitly by the
Stillingfleet controversy. The Recusants did not limit their view to a
purely logical, deductive unfolding of a conclusion out of clearly
stated premises. By and large, it was the Gospel written in the heart
which provided the clue of their conception: the Spirit guides the
Church and its members toward a fuller understanding of what has
been imprinted in the heart by faith. But such insight does not reach
greater depth only, or even chiefly, by way of syllogistic reasoning.
Of paramount importance is docility to the Spirit. The unanimity of
the Church's teaching at a synchronic moment becomes a better
warrant of doctrine than logical deduction from an original deposit.
By affirming the Church's infallibility, Woodhead located the development of doctrine in the Spirit's guidance over the Church and its
bishops rather than in the deductive capacities of theologians. Sergeant
used two analogies to throw light on the process: the growth of an
idea, and the literary development of a theme. Since the literary
development of a theme is itself one application of the general structure of the growth of ideas, Sergeant was actually seeking to express,
in different ways, the correspondence he had perceived between the
growth of an idea and the development of doctrine. And this will be
at the heart of John Henry Newman's researches.

While these advances were being made in England, some Catholic
authors in France were also facing the question. In *La Tradition au
XVIIe siècle*, I drew attention especially to two men. The Great
Arnauld among the prominent Jansenists insists on the "perpetuity
of faith", which constitutes his major apologetical argument in
defense of Eucharistic doctrine. Even more than Bossuet, Arnauld
wants to see the Christian doctrine given, at the beginning, already
in its final form. But Arnauld opens another avenue when he asserts the
importance of an "interior revelation", of an interior feeling, of
"purity of heart" while we read the Scriptures, for then we are able
to perceive many truths which otherwise would remain hidden,
and, which is still more important, we are able to love and practice
these truths. On this basis Arnauld fought for the right of the laity and
especially of women to read the Scriptures: women, he believed, are

particularly apt to understand the Scriptures. Yet Arnauld also maintained the principle that the true meaning of Scripture is found only in its agreement with the universal tradition of the Church.[10]

In *From Bossuet to Newman*, Owen Chadwick presented the great court preacher Bossuet, as a symbol of the principle of immutability of doctrine. Bossuet indeed defended this principle, and used it apologetically against what he called "the variations of Protestantism". Bossuet "knew that he stood in the immobile, unvarying tradition of a continuous system of doctrines". Progress he identified with the spread of the faith in extension throughout the world, not with "a deeper *understanding* of the word once delivered".[11] Admittedly, there is some truth in such a description of Bossuet, who coined the astonishing proposition: "Catholic truth, having come from God, has its perfection at the beginning".[12] Yet there are also other aspects of Bossuet. Bossuet's belief in the immutability of Christian doctrine is compensated and somewhat corrected by other perspectives. Like other great preachers of the century of Louis XIV, Bossuet held to a realistic conception of the word of God, with which he identified the word proclaimed from the pulpit. Secondly, Bossuet did not reject the possibility of a creative exegesis which would attempt to discover the meaning of obscure texts of the Scriptures. The Book of Revelation is, in his eyes, especially open to new insights. Thirdly, Bossuet maintained the classical view that theology has the task of pursuing the intellection of faith. The problem that Bossuet posits to his interpreters concerns the possibility of harmonizing these perspectives with his contention that doctrine is given already in a state of perfection. But Bossuet never felt this as a problem. In any case, the standard image of Bossuet as the advocate of a totally immutable Christian doctrine needs to be touched up considerably.

Whatever the exact positions of the Catholics of sixteenth century France on questions relating to doctrinal development, the eighteenth century in England brought the problem nearer to a solution.

Jan Walgrave's survey of the matter shows the Latitudinarians among the initiators of the transformistic theory. Briefly, this is the theory that, since Revelation is essentially non-propositional, the propositions in which the Revelation is expressed can, in the course

---

[10] *La Tradition au XVIIe siècle*, ch. 3.
[11] Owen Chadwick, l.c., p. 17.
[12] *La Tradition au XVIIe siècle*, p. 169.

of time, change to the point of being transformed into their opposite. This need not affect the truth of Revelation, which is not of the rational order. The transformation of doctrine then becomes basically a cultural phenomenon. Christianity gives itself the form demanded by the human culture in which it thrives. Such a view would originate in German Pietism, in Dutch Arminianism, in English Latitudinarianism. It would reach its height in the Liberal theology inherited from Schleiermacher and in Catholic Modernism at the beginning of the present century. In our own time, it would flourish in a number of authors, notably in Paul Tillich's systematic theology.[13]

This overview calls for some remarks. For if indeed the seeds of a transformistic theory may be found in the English theology of the eighteenth century, other trends of the same period, in the same line as the Recusants' concerns, anticipate the Oxford movement and what Walgrave calls the "theological theory" of development.

Already Richard Hooker and the Caroline divines stressed the part of the human reason in what became the traditional Anglican balance of Scripture, tradition and reason. After the Restoration the Cambridge Platonists spread the conception that there is a profound abiding harmony between reason and revelation. The world of nature was deemed to be religiously transparent to the enquiring mind in quest of the traces of God in nature. Christian mysticism and nature mysticism hinted at two complementary aspects of God's creation.

The eighteenth century was too deeply rent asunder by the growing polarization between science and faith to preserve such a harmonious balance. Yet the new apologetics which saw the light toward the middle of the century appealed to similar basic assumptions. Joseph Butler published *The Analogy of Religion, Natural and Revealed, to the Constitution and Course of Nature*, in 1736. This book argued against the deistic conceptions that were being promoted both without and within the Church of England. Butler did not deal explicitly with the problem of development. Yet he found in the processes of nature a model to understand the Church and its beliefs. An analogy between creation and revelation was already suggested by the philosopher Berkeley.[14] But Butler's systematic use of the idea resulted in the argument that the organic structure and the development of nature

---

[13] Jan Walgrave, l.c., pp. 179-277.
[14] George Berkeley, *Alciphron*, in A. A. Luce - T. E. Jessop, *The Works of George Berkeley, Bishop of Clogher*, London, 1963, vol. IV.

are divinely intended to provide insights into God's dealings with humankind both in the natural and in the supernatural order. Even if one instance of this harmony does not by itself carry conviction, there is enough convergence of a multitude of such instances to make the Christian position rationally unimpeachable. Butler's presentation of the evidence for faith and its later use by William Paley directly influenced Newman's analysis of assent.[15]

But there is more to Butler's contribution to a theory of doctrinal development. Chadwick already drew attention to a remarkable passage of the *Analogy*, to which Newman himself referred. Here, Butler finds an analogy between the Church's progressive discovery of the truths contained in Scripture, and the progress of human knowledge. Not all of Scripture is understood yet. If it "ever comes to be understood. . . it must be in the same way as natural knowledge is come at: by the continuance and progress of learning and of liberty; and by particular persons attending to, comparing and pursuing, intimations scattered up and down it. . . . For this is the way in which all improvements are made; by thoughtful men's tracing on obscure hints, as it were, dropped by nature accidentally or which seem to come into our minds by chance. . .".[16]

Admittedly, the prime analogate here lies in the scholarly research into nature which gives occasion to new knowledge. Butler underlines reason as the interpreter of Scripture. But he also pays attention to what our age likes to call "the signs of the times". For he adds: "And possibly it might be intended that events, as they come to pass, shall open and ascertain the meaning of the several parts of Scripture". The meaning of events, and their relevance to the interpreta tion of Scripture, are matters of insight, not of deductive reason. Thus Butler opens the way to the conception embodied in Newman's third note of a genuine development of an idea, "its power of assimilation".[17]

One could have expected the study of the Trinitarian controversies of the patristic age to provide a starting point for a theology of doctrinal development, especially in Anglican circles, where great attention was paid to the consensus of the first few centuries. In

---

[15] William Paley, *Views of the Evidences of Christianity*, 1794. Some differences between Newman and Paley are indicated by Newman in *The Grammar of Assent*, New York, 1955, pp. 329-333.

[16] Joseph Butler, *The Analogy of Religion* (W. E. Gladstone, ed., *The Works of Joseph Butler*, vol. I, New York, 1896, p. 235).

[17] *Essay on the Development*, New York, 1960, pp. 189-192.

seventeenth century France Petau's ascription of subordinatianism to
the ante-Nicene Fathers made the Council of Nicaea, with its decision
concerning the term *homoousios*, the very type of legitimate and
necessary development of doctrine. But French theology did not
exploit this insight of a French historian. In seventeenth century
England, however, the works of George Bull (1634-1710), bishop
of St David's, in defense of the Nicaean Council, tended to eliminate
the problem. For Bull concluded, against Petau, that there was no
subordinatianism among the early Fathers; the doctrine of Nicaea
had been taught from the beginning. "I have shown", Bull maintained, "by many and clear testimonies, the consent of primitive
antiquity with the fathers of the council of Nice".[18] This argumentation paralleled Antoine Arnauld's apologetics, based on the alleged
perpetuity of faith.

But Trinitarian controversies, momentarily stilled by George
Bull, erupted again in the eighteenth century. Samuel Clarke, in
1712, expressed the opinion that the doctrine of Nicaca was unreasonable; he himself preferred a kind of moderate semi-Arianism.
Some strayed still further from classical orthodoxy, notably Robert
Clayton, bishop of Clogher in Ireland, with his *Essay on Spirit* (1751).
Among those who defended Nicaean doctrine against the rationalism
of Clarke or Clayton, one finds the little known group of authors who
were called, and who called themselves, the Hutchinsonians.[19]

Followers of John Hutchinson (1674-1737), whose interest in
theology lay chiefly in the spiritual exegesis of the Hebrew Bible,
the Hutchinsonians claimed to find in the Old Testament intimations
of the major Christian doctrines. This was not entirely new; similar
opinions were already shared by the Christian cabbalists of the
Renaissance, who read the doctrine of the Trinity in various parts of
the Talmud. The Hutchinsonians gave further scope to the method:
with some of them at least, the principle that Christian dogmas are
implied in the very language of the Old Covenant turned into a
principle of the development of doctrine.

Some of the Hutchinsonians, like James Hervey (1714-1758) and
William Romaine (1714-1795) became prominent pioneers of the

---

[18] George Bull, *A Defense of the Nicene Creed* (*Library of Anglo-Catholic Theology*,
vol. 32. Oxford, 1852, p. 655). On Petau, see *La Tradition au XVIIe siècle*, ch. 2.

[19] There are few studies of the Hutchinsonians. See *The Quest for Catholicity*,
pp. 124-131; William Carroll, *Hutchinsonisme: une Vue de la Nature comme Théophanie
au cours du dix-huitième siècle*, 1968 (unpublished thesis for the University of Stras-
bourg).

Evangelical movement in the Church of England. Yet most were decided highchurchmen. In *The Quest for Catholicity* I identified these as forming a major link in the transmission of highchurchmanship in a century dominated by Latitudinarianism. On matters relating to the development of doctrine these highchurch Hutchinsonians left an important milestone between the tentative views of the Recusants and the theory proposed by Newman in the nineteenth century.

It is not in their refutation of Samuel Clarke's anti-Trinitarianism that one can find intimations of a theory of doctrinal development. William Jones of Nayland (1726-1800) defended "the Catholic doctrine of a Trinity" by professing to find the doctrine in the names of God used in the Scriptures, including the Old Testament. Indeed, Jones' conclusion is the opposite of what a developmental understanding of doctrine would imply: "The Bible we know to be the infallible word of God; the rule of our faith and obedience. I find this doctrine revealed in it; therefore I firmly believe and submit to it".[20] Where Jones deserves to be counted among the thinkers who contributed to the formation of the Tractarian theory of development lies in his understanding of the process of belief. Like the Traditionalists in nineteenth century France, the Hutchinsonians tend toward fideism: "All that can be known of the true God, is to be known by *revelation*".[21] Yet, in their judgement, acceptance of the Revelation is not obedience to a heteronomous law. It requires a preparation of the heart, a welcome by the whole person:

> Behold then the true source of our religious differences; they proceed from the blindness and corruption of the human heart, increased and cherished by some false principle that suits with its appetites: and all the prudence and learning the world can boast will exempt no child of Adam from this miserable weakness: nothing but the grace of God can possible remove it. Where that is suffered to enter, and the heart, instead of persisting in its own will, is surrendered to the will of God, the whole gospel is sufficiently clear, because no text of it is any longer offensive.[22]

Acceptance rests upon a previous process of unveiling: "The evidence that before was dark and unconclusive, became on a sudden clear and irresistible". This does not exempt anyone from the necessity to research and critique what is proposed to faith: "You judge of

---

[20] William Jones, *The Catholic Doctrine of a Trinity*, New York, 1813, p. 149.
[21] l.c., p. 20.
[22] l.c., pp. 30-31.

truth by its proper evidence".[23] But only those who are morally prepared can arrive at the correct judgement: "Their opinion was altered", Jones says of the Apostles, "because their affections were cleansed from this world".[24]

In a *Course of Lectures on the Figurative Language of the Holy Scripture*, which he delivered at his parish church of Nayland in 1786, Jones argues in favor of the mystical interpretation on the ground that Scripture uses a type of language which is symbolic at two levels:

> Of all the objects of sense we have ideas, and our minds and memories are stored with them. But of invisible things we have no ideas till they are pointed out to us by revelation: and as we cannot know them immediately, such as they are in themselves, after the manner in which we know sensible objects, they must be communicated to us by the mediation of such things as we already comprehend. For this reason, the scripture is found to have a language of its own, which does not consist of words, but of signs or figures taken from visible things. . . Words are the arbitrary signs of natural things; but the language of revelation goes a step farther, and uses some things as the signs of other things; in consequence of which, the world which we now see becomes a sort of commentary on the mind of God, and explains the world in which we believe.[25]

Jones therefore suggests, not only that revelation uses a new kind of language, but also that a new faculty of knowledge is necessary to grasp it, which is commensurate to the language that needs to be deciphered. Thus he says:

> . . .when God speaks of things which are above nature, his meaning must be received by a faculty which is not the gift of nature, but superadded to nature by the gift of God himself. For spiritual truth there must be a spiritual sense; and the scripture calls this sense by the name of *faith*: which word sometimes signifies the act of believing; sometimes the matter which is believed; but in many passages it is used for that sense or capacity of the intellect, by which the invisible things of the spirit of God are admitted and approved.[26]

As this text suggests, William Jones simply gives the name of faith to a faculty which is not unlike what John Henry Newman will call the illative sense, and in which Newman will see the instrument of religious knowledge, at work especially in the process of the

---

[23] l.c., p. 162.
[24] l.c., p. 31.
[25] *A Course of Lectures on the Figurative Language of the Holy Scripture*, in *The Theological and Miscellaneous Works of William Jones*, vol. 3, London, 1810, p. 5-6.
[26] l.c., p. 10.

development of doctrine. On the one hand, the Hutchinsonians' conviction that the very language of the Old Testament conveys Christian truths militates against the notion of a true, objective development. On the other, the faculty which they see at work in the knowledge of faith will eventually favor the notion of doctrinal development, when Newman will build upon it a full theory of religious knowledge. Also like Newman, William Jones sees the whole of nature, when read in the right way, as revelatory: "To those who understand it, all nature speaks the same language with revelation: what the one teaches with words, the other confirms by signs; insomuch that we may truly say, the world is a riddle, and Christianity the interpretation".[27] And again: "Nature itself is Christian, and the world itself a daily miracle; the heavens speak to us, and the earth and all things therein join in the same testimony".[28] Such accents are germane to those of many sermons of Newman. Beyond the apologetical use of nature by Joseph Butler or William Paley, they already point to its epiphanic use by the author of the poem, "Lead, kindly light".

To my knowledge, Newman never acknowledged any special debt to the Hutchinsonians; nor do the classical accounts of the Tractarian movement trace some of his ideas to this little and eccentric group of highchurchmen. Yet to the historian of ideas the Hutchinsonians present themselves as some of the few witnesses to the growth of highchurchmanship during the eighteenth century. They anticipated some of the major conceptions of John Henry Newman's epistemology.

This brings our survey to the birth of the Oxford movement. It is on purpose that I speak of the movement itself, and not only of John Henry Newman. Newman indeed overshadowed the other Tractarians, both by the impact of his own history upon his friends and by the wider scope of his theological thought. But in reality his predominance was not as total as it may seem. Historians of the idea of doctrinal development have commonly neglected the contributions of the other Tractarians to Newman's theory. Yet Newman himself acknowledged his debt to Hurrell Froude. Through Froude, he was indebted to the artisans of the Gothic or medieval revival which affected English romanticism and which may be gauged by the

---

[27] l.c., p. 174.
[28] l.c., p. 175.

Gothic novels of Walter Scot, by the vogue of Gothic esthetics with Ruskin, by the paintings of the pre-Raphaelites. Through a somewhat fanciful image of the Middle Ages, some of the Tractarians saw the medieval religious synthesis as the high point of a remarkable growth, as the crowning touch of an impressive edifice to which a whole civilization contributed. This at least was the perspective of Hurrell Froude and of William Ward. Froude's conceptions were embodied in the posthumous writings collected by Newman and Keble under the title, *Remains* (1839). Ward's views were expressed in his volume, *The Ideal of a Christian Church* (1844). Although Ward could assert that Catholicism is "in doctrine, ever one and the same", yet he could also see it as resulting from "consistency of progress", as "the majestic and wonderful development of a real idea".[29]

Yet it is more particularly to John Keble that attention should be drawn. Even before Newman began to write the *Essay*, Keble had tilled and watered the ground where Newman's idea would grow. His authorship of Tract 89 places him at the forefront of a search for a theory of development based on the older practice of the spiritual interpretation of the Scriptures. This Tract is devoted to an explanation and an eloquent advocacy of the theory of the "mystical sense" of the Scriptures as practiced by the Fathers of the Church. Though Keble was not primarily a historian, he used his not inconsiderable patristic expertise to illustrate the mystical hermeneutics of the Fathers. And the depth of his religious conviction served him well in his appeal to a return to what had been the standard hermeneutical method before the sixteenth century.

In Keble's perspective, the symbolical sense of Scripture is related to a broader epistemology, according to which the proper medium for apprehending the meaning of nature is the poetic imagination. The human mind thinks in images. The poetic communion with the world of nature leads to a moral interpretation which—following Butler's *Analogy*—finds in nature the paradigm of moral behavior and judgement. This in turn, by purifying the heart, prepares for the mystical interpretation, which pertains properly to the theological imagination. These three stages, poetic, moral, mystical, are not unlike the three stages of Kierkegaard, the esthetic, the ethical, the religious, although Keble sees a much greater continuity between the last two than Kierkegaard. Applying this analogy to the life of the

---

[29] See *The Quest for Catholicity*, pp. 167-168.

Christian community, Keble is able to claim that Jesus Christ formulated "a Poetry of His own, a set of holy and divine associations and meanings", which are recorded in "of course, Holy Scripture and the consent of ecclesiastical writers".[30] Here, the canon of Vincent of Lerins ceases to be a norm from the past, as it chiefly was for the Caroline divines. It has become an all-encompassing principle of the continuity of Church life and thought. In a remarkable passage Keble joins together the life of the Church and the light from Christ in a dynamic way to show that all of humankind shares to some degree the manifestation of the divine light:

> The secret Presence of the Word and His communication of Himself has been the principle of Life to all that have lived, so, whatever real Light the children of men have at any time enjoyed, or in any measure, it has been wholly due to this same divine Presence: —a spark as it were of the vital fire mysteriously abiding within them, struck out by His providential working according to the counsel of His own will. The Light of mankind has been, is, and ever will be, the Manifestation of the Life within them of the Living and Life-giving Word.[31]

Yet, whatever the religious depth of his vision, Keble was unable or perhaps unwilling to work out, either historically or philosophically, the implications of this broad conception for a theory of development. His forte lay in pastorally accenting the participation of the faithful in the light and the life of Christ through the sacraments. The implications of the Light of Christ for the nature of faith and for the historical expression of the divine mystery required a more thorough investigation. But Keble felt an instinctive distrust for the "school whose leading principle is, that theology, like other sciences, improves by time".[32] Indeed, Keble does not consider it outrageous to think that modern theology may be wrong:

> Unless we are prepared to say positively. . . that theology is, like other sciences, really advancing, of course, as the world grows older; we cannot but in candor allow it at least possible, before examination, that the ancients may have been in the right, and we in the wrong.[33]

The problem of development, as Newman handled it, lay precisely in assessing how there could be a real development from the past to

---

[30] *On the Mysticism attributed to the Early Fathers of the Church, being n. LXXXIX of Tracts for the Times*, Oxford, 1868, p. 144.

[31] Quoted in W. J. A. M. Beek, *John Keble's Literary and Religious Contribution to the Oxford Movement*, Nijmegen, 1959, p. 117.

[32] *On the Mysticism . . .*, p. 7.

[33] l.c., p. 10.

the present. Newman brought his considerable talents to bear on this in a historical perspective with his *Essay on the Development of Christian Doctrine* (1845), and in a speculative direction with his *Essay in Aid of a Grammar of Assent* (1870). More than Hurrell Froude, Ward or Keble, Newman thought with categories and methodologies that can be called "organicist". In this he caught the *Zeitgeist* of his period better than the other Tractarians. Organicist thinking prevailed at about the same moment in biology with Darwin, and in economics and politics with Karl Marx after having triumphed in philosophy with Hegel. Like these other geniuses of the nineteenth century, Newman followed a thought-pattern in which one can easily recognize the unfolding of a basic idea. His basic idea is not physical life as for Darwin, societal relationships as for Marx, God as for Hegel; it is Christianity.

Whether we look for Newman's conceptions in his sermons or in his major essays on development and on assent, we encounter the notion of Christianity as an idea, a basic idea, which, given once for all at the beginning, grows through the centuries, progressively unfolding its implications. Like all ideas, it passes from an implicit to an explicit state. Its beginnings are rich in potentialities, but vague in the actual expression of the faith. And only gradually does the Christian mind, looking reflexively at itself, reach awareness of its contents. Thus, Newman's sermon on "Implicit and explicit reason" (June 29, 1840) describes faith as "the simple uplifting of the mind to the Unseen God, without conscious reasoning or formal argument".[34] These two aspects stand to each other like faith and reason: when we believe, we have faith; when we know that we believe, we have reason which takes faith as the object of its attention. It is faith which gives value to life. And there is a human and Christian duty to go as far as possible toward the full explicitation of the wealth of faith:

> We are not only to "sanctify the Lord God in our hearts", not only to prepare a shrine within us in which our Savior Christ may dwell, and where we may worship Him; but we are so to understand that we do, so to master our thoughts and feelings, so to recognize what we believe, and how we believe, so to trace out our ideas and impressions, and to contemplate the issue of them, that we may be "ready *always* to give an answer to *every* man that asketh us an account of the hope that is in us".[35]

---

[34] *Oxford University Sermons*, n. XIII, New York, 1872, p. 253.
[35] l.c., p. 252-253.

Reasoning, in Newman's sense of the term, is "a living spontaneous energy within us, not an art".[36] That is, all people reason, "not by rule, but by an inward faculty". Only philosophers and like-minded intellectuals are able so to observe their reasoning that they can break it down into rules and follow its successive steps in their own mind. Then we have "the words, science, method, development, analysis, criticism, proof, system, principles, rules, laws, and others of a like nature".[37] Mere reasoning Newman calls implicit reason; its scientific analysis he calls explicit reason.

Now it is a characteristic of Newman's method that he easily transfers to the individual Christian what his historical studies have found to have been the collective Christian experience of the past. Vice versa, he applies to the Church as a moral body what he has found to be true of the individual in his own experience. Thus, faith, implicit reason and explicit reason become types or symbols of the great trajectory which passes from the Scriptures, where faith is at its simplest, to the Creeds, which emerge from time to time according to need as products of the spontaneous implicit reasoning of Christians at a given time and place, to "Evidences", that is, to investigations of "the means whereby, and the grounds whereon, and the subjects wherein, the mind is bound to believe and acquiesce, in matters of religion".[38] In other words, there is a passage, both in the believer who is fully aware of the contents, implications and grounds of his faith, and in the Church at large as it evolves through history, from faith to belief to theology, from Scripture to Creeds to theological research.

One point here is not a little puzzling. Newman thus anticipated the theory of doctrinal development recently proposed by Bernard Lonergan: doctrine develops by passing from the *quoad nos* of its early stages to the *quoad se* that can be arrived at only through reflexive reasoning upon the sources of faith and the formulations of doctrines.[39] Yet Newman's own theory of development, starting from the above broad conception, was elaborated in a different direction. The central point both of his sermon on *The Theory of Developments in Religious Doctrine* (February 2, 1843) [40] and of the *Essay on the Development of Christian Doctrine* is that the development of doctrine is analogi-

---

[36] l.c., p. 257.

[37] l.c., p. 259.

[38] l.c., p. 255.

[39] On Lonergan's theory, see Robert L. Richard, *Contribution to a Theory of Doctrinal Development* (*Continuum*, II/3, Autumn, 1964, pp. 502-527).

[40] *Oxford University Sermons*, n. XV.

cal with the development of an idea in the mind. But ideas do not always develop from phenomenology to ontology, from *quoad nos* to *quoad se*. As described by Newman, the development is not only centripetal, tending to greater and more accurate perception of the inside of the idea. It is also centrifugal, tending to greater influence and radiation outside, and being nurtured by the encounter with the world. Of the five kinds of development of doctrine envisaged by the *Essay*, only the last is "metaphysical": this is the development of Trinitarian doctrine as exemplified in the Athanasian Creed.[41] The other types are called "political" (the development of the episcopate as a structure of the Church), "logical" (the belief about the *Theotokos*, which logically grows out of Christology), "historical" (the computation leading to the fixation of a date for the birth of Jesus), and "ethical" (the sacramental developments, which Newman focuses on the Eucharist). Of these five types and of the examples used to illustrate them, only the Trinitarian development may be said to have been from *quoad nos* (the cosmological Trinity of the ante-Nicene Fathers) to *quoad se* (the immanent Trinity of the Councils, culminating in the declaration of the Second Council of Constantinople, in 553, about the "consubstantial Trinity"). Generally speaking, the development of ideas is from inside to outside; it follows of necessity on the fact that a basic idea has so taken hold of a person that it shapes the growth of that person and that, in turn, it is given successive and more explicit formulations as the person learns to draw out the implications of the idea.

There is no need, for our purpose, to analyze the details of Newman's investigations. His *Essay on the Development of Christian Doctrine* chiefly proposed a list of tests by which one may recognize a true from a false development; and it illustrated this proposal with historical examples. His *Essay in Aid of a Grammar of Assent* completed the work by making explicit the epistemology which undergirded Newman's understanding of the growth of an idea and its application to the growth of Christian doctrine as a basic idea passing progressively to the state of explicit reason in the Creeds. The heart of this epistemology is the conception of the "illative sense": this is the faculty which arrives at a conclusion and reaches certitude out of a convergence of evidences, none of which, taken by itself, would be able to bring about a reasonable conclusion and a certitude. "It is

---

[41] *Essay on Development*, New York, 1960, pp. 63-75.

the mind that reasons, and that controls its own reasoning, not any technical apparatus of words and propositions. This power of judging and concluding, when in its perfection, I call the Illative Sense".[42] It determines "the start, the course and the issue of an inquiry".[43] The illative sense is the mind itself at work in the process of arriving at the judgement by which it takes cognizance of, and it assents to, an insight.

Jan Walgrave sums up one aspect of Newman's theory in these words: ". . .the only guarantee of true development is supralogical. It is the guidance of the Holy Spirit who is present in the Church and works in it as a supernatural 'illative sense' ".[44] That is, the notion of illative sense is extended to the whole Church. Or, the theory of doctrinal development, worked out before Newman explicitly discovered the illative sense, rests implicitly on the assumption that something like an illative sense functions in the Church as the moral or collective body of the faithful. The complementary aspect has already been touched upon: Newman does provide seven notes for judging the authenticity of doctrinal development. In so doing, he assumes that one's illative sense, working retrospectively on the doctrinal developments that have already taken place, will attune itself to the Church's illative sense. The tests will show if such a convergence of the collective and the individual does take place. When it does not, one may assume, provided it is really the illative sense that one follows, and not some human logic or some human desire, that in fact the illative sense of the Church was not at work in the instance under study. There would have been a false development. Newman did insist on the infallibility of the Church, notably in *Apologia pro vita sua* and in *Difficulties of Anglicans*. In his Roman Catholic period, he often professed to submit his judgement to that of the Church. Yet he also indicated that authentic development of doctrine falls within the scope of legitimate critique. It is in the power of the human mind, functioning as Christian mind, to judge of the genuineness of a development. His essay, *On Consulting the Faithful in matters of Doctrine* (1859), indicates even that the consensus of the people of God is a major factor in the development of doctrine, thus stressing a point that is not emphasized in the *Essay* of 1845.

---

[42] *Grammar of Assent*, New York, 1955, pp. 276.
[43] l.c., p. 283.
[44] Walgrave, l.c., p. 308.

I do not wish to claim too much for the Recusants of the seventeenth century. Newman's theory of doctrinal development was
more systematic and more historically grounded than their brief
suggestions could be. Newman answered their questions with more
thoroughness than they did. He envisioned the problem of development as the center of the problem of Tradition.[45] Doctrinal development is the test of any theory of Tradition, since it is at the point of
its development that the Christian tradition's relation to the norm of
Scripture is to be challenged. Newman certainly went further and
deeper than the Recusants in the study of doctrinal development.
Yet several points of his theory were already indicated by them.
Holden's investigation of the structure of faith anticipated his own.[46]
Worsley envisioned a growth of faith proceeding by way of explicitation. Woodhead tied together the notion of doctrinal development
and that of infallibility. Sergeant held that one can test the authenticity of a tradition and of a doctrinal development, and that development of doctrine is a process taking place within faith itself, that is
comparable to the progress of thought in the human mind. This last
point contained already the very seeds of Newman's analogy between
the development of an idea and the development of doctrine. To my
knowledge, Newman gives no indication of being acquainted with
Recusant literature, with the exception of Holden. Yet whatever the
direct sources of his thought, he follows the Recusants, as it were,
naturally, carrying to their logical end many ideas which they had
disseminated.

The history of the problem of doctrinal development since Newman
belongs to the broader history of the problem of Tradition. The
school of Traditionalism which flourished mainly in France in the
early nineteenth century, did not last. But the so-called Roman school

---

[45] On Newman's understanding of Tradition, see Heinrich Fries, *J. H. New-
mans Beitrag zum Verständnis der Tradition* (Michael Schmaus, ed., *Die Mündliche
Überlieferung*, Munich, 1956, pp. 63-122); Günter Biemer, *Newman on Tradition*,
Pittsburgh, 1967. (This is a shortened version of *Überlieferung und Offenbarung. Die
Lehre von der Tradition nach John Henry Newman*, Freiburg, 1961.) Jean Stern,
Bible et Tradition chez Newman. Aux origines de la théorie du développement, Paris, 1967.
[46] Holden's conception of scriptural inspiration presents analogies with that
of Newman. According to Robert Murray, Newman possessed a copy of Holden's
Analysis divinae fidei, which he probably read in 1846. See J. Derek Holmes and
Robert Murray, ed., *On the Inspiration of Scripture. John Henry Newman*, Washing-
ton, 1967, pp. 68-69; Jaak Synaeve, *Cardinal Newman's Doctrine on Holy Scripture*,
Louvain, 1953.

dominated neo-scholasticism and eventually inspired the schema *De fontibus revelationis* presented to Vatican Council II by the Preparatory Theological Commission. The school of Tübingen had a lasting impact through its conception of tradition as living: this conception was incorporated in chapters I and II of the conciliar constitution *Dei Verbum*.[47]

Newman's insights into the complex process of the development of doctrine did not go unchallenged by followers of the Roman school. But, early in this century, Maurice Blondel's philosophy, which stressed the primacy of action, tended to see the doctrinal tradition as implied in the acts of Christian piety and ethics, thus supporting the view that development is not primarily a matter of logic.[48] Yet, it was only after the First World War that another major study of doctrinal development was published, with Marín-Sola's *La Evolución Homogenea del Dogma Catolico* (1923). Marín-Sola, however, who shared neither Newman's problematic nor Blondel's approach, reduced legitimate development to logical unfolding. He was of course unacquainted with the English Recusants. Although the question of doctrinal development was raised again in the debates around the so-called "new theology" in 1946 and after, no major new study appeared. Yet, somewhat surprisingly, the schema *De deposito fidei pure custodiendo*, prepared by the Preparatory Theological Commission of Vatican II, but never examined by the Council, contained a remarkable chapter V, *De progressu doctrinae*. While this chapter maintained that progress is not in the "deposit of revelation" but in the human knowledge of it, it also attributed the development of doctrine to something more than merely logical unfolding. It is this chapter which is summed up in the following passage of the Constitution *Dei Verbum*:

> The Tradition that issues from the apostles progresses in the Church under the assistance of the Holy Spirit. Insight into the realities and the words transmitted grows: this results from contemplation and study by the faithful who ponder over them in their heart, from their experience of a profound understanding of spiritual realities, from the preaching of those who, with the episcopal succession, received

---

[47] There are no general studies of Traditionalism. On the Roman School, see J. P. Mackey, *The Modern Theology of Tradition*, New York, 1962; Walter Kasper, *Die Lehre von der Tradition in der Römischen Schule*, Freiburg, 1962. On the School of Tübingen, see Josef Geiselmann, *Die lebendige Überlieferung als Norm des Christlichen Glaubens*, Freiburg, 1958; *Die Heilige Schrift und die Tradition*, Freiburg, 1962.
[48] Maurice Blondel, *L'Action. 1893*, Paris, 1950; *Histoire et Dogme, 1903* (in *Les Premiers Ecrits de Maurice Blondel*, Paris, 1956, pp. 149-254).

the unfailing charism of the truth. Through the centuries the Church always strives after the fullness of divine truth, until the ultimate fulfillment of God's words in itself.[49]

As this already shows, some of the problems with which the Recusants struggled emerged again around the time of Vatican Council II. The pre-conciliar discussion on the Tridentine doctrine concerning Scripture and the traditions, new though it appeared to be at the time, was not really new: Christopher Davenport had raised similar points in his exegesis of the decree of the fourth session of the Council of Trent. Had the seventeenth century literature been better known, the partisans of the two-source theory would not have been able to claim that they spoke in the name of the entire Counter-Reformation theology, and the supporters of a one-source theory would not have looked like innovators. But in this case, the schema *De fontibus revelationis* would have been less assertive in assuming that only a two-source theory is compatible with the Catholic tradition. Then, the conciliar debates of November 14, 1962, would have been less sensational; and there would have been less acrimony in the accompanying and following discussions outside the plenary sessions of the Council. By the same token, there would have been less triumphalism among the partisans of a one-source theory when the preparatory schema was replaced by the Constitution *Dei Verbum*; and the appeal to Scripture of more recent theologies would be less one-sided. The post-conciliar commentaries might not have forgotten that the Council did not intend its text to put an end to any discussion, but published a Constitution which could be compatible with both a two-source and a one-source theory.

On a broader scale, Vatican Council II would not have looked so revolutionary as it has appeared to be; for it would not have given the impression of totally repudiating the theology of the Counter-Reformation. Instead, it would have brought back some aspects of the Counter-Reformation which were not commonly known. The contemporary discussions would have continued controversies which were already taking place in the seventeenth century. Since the contemporary "traditionalists" would not be opposing revolutionary theologies, the polarization in the Catholic Church would not be so tense as it is.

These remarks are of course highly speculative. Yet it is not

---

[49] George H. Tavard, ed., *Dogmatic Constitution on Divine Revelation of Vatican Council II*, New York, 1966, pp. 65-66.

forbidden to dream of what might have been, if history had been better known. At any rate we can learn the lesson that theological questions that remain unsettled are likely to reappear later—and perhaps in circumstances that are less favorable to a lasting solution.

Be that as it may, the progress of the linguistic and semiotic sciences in our century is now placing the problems of Scripture, tradition and doctrinal development in a new context. Post-Vatican II theology must approach these questions in ways that were unsuspected in the past. If Vatican II, or Newman, or the Recusants, can indeed contribute to the on-going debate, we can no longer rest where they arrived.[50]

---

[50] See my recent volume, *La Théologie parmi les Sciences Humaines*, Paris, 1975, esp. pp. 108-143.

INDICES

NAMES

TOPICS